Robert Rainy

Delivery and development of Christian doctrine

The 5th series of the Cunningham lectures

Robert Rainy

Delivery and development of Christian doctrine
The 5th series of the Cunningham lectures

ISBN/EAN: 9783337262006

Printed in Europe, USA, Canada, Australia, Japan

Cover: Foto ©Lupo / pixelio.de

More available books at **www.hansebooks.com**

DELIVERY AND DEVELOPMENT

OF

CHRISTIAN DOCTRINE.

PRINTED BY MURRAY AND GIBB

FOR

T. & T. CLARK, EDINBURGH.

LONDON, ... HAMILTON, ADAMS, AND CO.
DUBLIN, ... JOHN ROBERTSON AND CO.
NEW YORK, . . . SCRIBNER, WELFORD, AND ARMSTRONG.

EXTRACT DECLARATION OF TRUST.

MARCH 1, 1862.

I, WILLIAM BINNY WEBSTER, late Surgeon in the H.E.I.C.S., presently residing in Edinburgh,—Considering that I feel deeply interested in the success of the Free Church College, Edinburgh, and am desirous of advancing the Theological Literature of Scotland, and for this end to establish a Lectureship similar to those of a like kind connected with the Church of England and the Congregational body in England, and that I have made over to the General Trustees of the Free Church of Scotland the sum of £2000 sterling, in trust, for the purpose of founding a Lectureship in memory of the late Reverend William Cunningham, D.D., Principal of the Free Church College, Edinburgh, and Professor of Divinity and Church History therein, and under the following conditions, namely,—*First*, The Lectureship shall bear the name, and be called, 'The Cunningham Lectureship.' *Second*, The Lecturer shall be a Minister or Professor of the Free Church of Scotland, and shall hold the appointment for not less than two years, nor more than three years, and be entitled for the period of his holding the appointment to the income of the endowment as declared by the General Trustees, it being understood that the Council after referred to may occasionally appoint a minister or professor from other denominations, provided this be approved of by not fewer than Eight Members of the Council, and it being further understood that the Council are to regulate the terms of payment of the lecturer. *Third*, The lecturer shall be at liberty to choose his own subject within the range of Apologetical, Doctrinal, Controversial, Exegetical, Pastoral, or Historical Theology, including what bears on missions, home and foreign, subject to the consent of the Council. *Fourth*, The lecturer shall be bound to deliver publicly at Edinburgh a course of lectures on the subjects thus chosen at some time immediately preceding the expiry of his appointment, and during the Session of the New College, Edinburgh ; the lectures to be not fewer than six in number, and to be delivered in presence of the professors and students under such arrangements as the Council may appoint ; the lecturer shall be bound also to print and publish, at his own risk, not fewer than 750 copies of the lectures within a year after their delivery, and to deposit three copies of the same in the Library of the New College ; the form of the publication shall be regulated by the Council. *Fifth*, A Council shall be constituted, consisting of (first) Two Members of their own body, to be chosen annually in the month of March, by the Senatus of the New College, other than the Principal ; (second) Five Members to be chosen annually by the General Assembly, in addition to the Moderator of the said Free Church of Scotland ; together with (third) the Principal of the said New College for the time being, the Moderator of the said General Assembly for the time being, the procurator or law adviser of the Church, and myself the said William Binny Webster, or such person as I may nominate to be my successor : the Principal of the said College to be Convener of the Council, and any Five Members duly convened to be entitled to act notwithstanding the non-election of others. *Sixth*, The duties of the Council shall be the following :—(first), To appoint the lecturer and determine the period of his holding the appointment, the appointment to be made before the close of the Session of College immediately preceding the termination of the previous lecturer's engagement ; (second), To arrange details as to the delivery of the lectures, and to take charge of any additional income and expenditure of an incidental kind that may be connected therewith, it being understood that the obligation upon the lecturer is simply to deliver the course of lectures free of expense to himself. *Seventh*, The Council shall be at liberty, on the expiry of five years, to make any alteration that experience may suggest as desirable in the details of this plan, provided such alterations shall be approved of by not fewer than Eight Members of the Council.

DELIVERY AND DEVELOPMENT

OF

CHRISTIAN DOCTRINE.

The Fifth Series of the Cunningham Lectures.

By ROBERT RAINY, D.D.,

PROFESSOR OF DIVINITY AND CHURCH HISTORY, NEW COLLEGE, EDINBURGH.

EDINBURGH:
T. & T. CLARK, 38 GEORGE STREET.
MDCCCLXXIV.

PREFACE.

THE Cunningham Lecture for 1873 was originally allotted to a minister, distinguished alike as a student and as a preacher, whom circumstances unfortunately prevented from executing the task. Called to fill the vacant place, on his resignation, I was led to fix on the subject of this volume, not without a hope of ultimately giving to it a more complete treatment than a fixed number of oral lectures can easily admit. Under the influence of the same hope I have too long delayed the publication; but have discovered, as I might have foreseen, that to recast a performance like this with a view to another kind of treatment, is an enterprise too unpromising and too irksome to be carried through. As the Lectures now stand, they are not much altered, and very probably they are not at all improved.

I fear that the title may lead some reader to expect an attempt to exhibit, in historical detail, how the actual Christian Doctrines, collectively and separately, have been delivered and developed. Nothing could be more interesting, if successfully performed; but certainly no undertaking could be more preposterous, when six Lectures, or a single octavo, is the space allotted for the performance. My task is a more humble one. Such explanations as the nature of it requires will be found in the close of the first Lecture, and in Note M subjoined to it.

CONTENTS.

LECTURE I.

PRELIMINARY.

	PAGE
Occupancy of Christian Mind with Doctrine,	1
Debates,	2
Organization of Doctrine as Science,	3
History of Doctrine,	4
Doubts regarding it,	5
Theories of Doctrinal Method drawn from History,	6
Successive Forms—Fathers,	7
Schoolmen,	9
Reformation,	11
Conceptions of History of Doctrine—Romish and Reformed,	13
Common Ground,	15
Variation of Romish Theory—Development,	16
Dr. Newman,	17
Protestant Orthodoxies,	21
Modern Criticism,	21
Method,	23
Conception of Genesis of Doctrine,	25
Application to Question of its Worth,	27
Question of Competency of Dogmatic,	29
Effort of Unbelievers to appropriate the Bible,	30
Topics of the Course,	31
Formal, not Material,	33

LECTURE II.

DELIVERY OF DOCTRINE IN OLD TESTAMENT.

Historical Method, Successive Lessons,	35
Concrete,	36

	PAGE
Manifestation of God entering into History,	37
The Supernatural and Miraculous,	40
Method adapted to Man, Fallen or Unfallen,	40
Our Information, how far Complete,	42
Great Themes: Character of God,	43
Evil of Sin,	43
Hope of Deliverance,	44
Elements of this World—the Means of Impression,	45
But related to Conscience, and filled with Presence of God,	46
Revelation of Gospel to Early World,	47
Abrahamic Covenant—Land and Seed,	48
How the Discipline was vitalized,	49
Variety and Fulness of Training made good,	53
Expectant Attitude of Church,	53
Mosaic Legislation—Law,	55
Stringency of Rules,	56
The Kingdom—Righteousness and Peace,	60
Prophetic Ministry,	62
Messianic Prophecy,	63
Psalms,	64
Doctrinal Developments from these Materials.	64
But more distinct to us than to them,	65
Results,	66
Christ in Old Testament,	67
Summary,	69
Identity of Faith with Diversities of Knowledge,	71
Fulness of God's Thought, and Poverty of Man's,	72
Old Testament implies and requires Doctrinal Revelation following,	72
Combination of the Apprehensible and the Profound,	73

LECTURE III.

DELIVERY OF DOCTRINE IN NEW TESTAMENT.

Variety of Elements besides the Doctrinal,	75
Contrasts between Old Testament and New Testament—Old Testament Church looking forward to what New Testament Church has received,	76
Progressive Revelation in contrast with Completed,	77
Implicit Teaching in contrast with Explicit,	78

CONTENTS.

	PAGE
Historical Method in both,	80
Especial Elements which enter into New Testament History,	80
Relation of History to Doctrine,	81
Gospels,	84
Early Apostolic Teaching,	85
Epistles,	86
Regulation of Thought by Principles of Truth a Leading Object in the Epistles,	87
Church to be trained in Doctrine as never before,	89
Doctrine not delivered in School Methods,	89
Method of Discussion,	91
Illustration of Adaptation of New Testament Teaching.	93
All Human Capacities addressed,	96
Freedom in Use of Language,	97
Hence Clearness of Scripture,	98
Occasional Character of Epistles,	99
Conclusion: New Testament Administration of Truth determined by Relation of its Doctrines to Facts of Divine History,	100
And to Christian Practice,	102
Not Statical, but Dynamical,	104

LECTURE IV.

FUNCTION OF CHRISTIAN MIND WITH REFERENCE TO DOCTRINE.

Doctrine as professed by Believer, and as delivered in Scripture,	106
Right of former,	108
Case of Single Mind,	109
Passive and Active Functions: Elements dealt with,	110
Appropriation of Teaching, what it implies,	112
Proportion between Meaning and Terms,	112
Disciple's Meaning—how expressed,	114
Doctrine as uttered by the Believer is formally human,	117
Worth of this Distinction,	118
Objection,	121
Answer,	122
Teaching received to be reproduced,	125
Obligation to use Care in verifying and defining Doctrinal Statements,	127

	PAGE
Various Ends or Uses of them,	127
Conditions which affect the Doctrinal Process: Historical Method of Scripture,	129
Relation to Practice,	131
Effects of these Conditions,	132
Church—Bearing of her Calling and Office on Doctrine,	133
What said of Believer applicable to Church,	133
Distribution of Parts,	134
Office of Church as instituted Society,	135
Influence of the Community on the Individual,	136
Church trains the Individual,	137
Influence communicated to gifted Members of the Church, and to Bearers of Office,	138
Further Influence of Church as Teaching Institute,	140
And as Disciplinary Institute,	141
Care of Doctrine part of Church's Life,	142
Ultimate Tribunal,	143

PART II.

Difficulty as to Measure within which Dogmatic Activity should be confined,	145
Argument against Dogma,	146
Two Main Lines,	147
First, from Nature of Source in Scripture: Scripture Statements Analogical only,	148
The Analogical Teaching also Experimental,	150
Analogical Knowledge, Worth in other Departments,	151
Limits of Knowledge,	153
Second, from Limits of our Faculties: Knowledge relative,	155
Scripture professes to deliver Reliable Knowledge,	155
Mediation of this Knowledge,	156
Pattern or Specimen Articles,	157
Analogy of Knowledge of Children,	157
Limits to be acknowledged,	160
Question as to Inferential Reasoning,	161
Cannot be excluded,	162
Limits depend on the Ends the Revealer had in view,	164
And on the Relation of our Terms to Scripture Thoughts,	164
Lessons from Experience in other Fields,	165
Summary,	169

CONTENTS.

	PAGE
Doctrine—the Obedience of our Thoughts to the Scriptures,	170
Doctrine of the Trinity,	171
Consciousness of Ignorance,	173

LECTURE V.

DEVELOPMENT OF DOCTRINE.

Development in Scripture, .	175
Development subsequently a Distinct Question, .	175
Development asserted by Rationalists,	176
And by Romanists—Dr. Newman,	177
Not the Old Romish View,	178
Old Protestant Position,	178
Fluctuations,	180
Opponents of Dr. Newman—Concessions,	180
Considerations which suggest Development,	182
Development asserted,	183
Starting-point of Development,	183
Illustration from Case of Individual,	185
Differences of the Case of Early Church, .	187
State of Church, how to be conceived,	189
Defect of Doctrinal Views : Existing in different Ways—Simple Elementariness,	190
Result of Human Blindness and Indocility,	192
Aim of the Development from Starting-point thus assigned,	195
Errors in estimating Starting-point,	195
Amount of Doctrinal Knowledge always present in Church,	196
Sense of Resource, .	198
Virtual hold of Truths not yet explicitly brought out,	198
Progress from this Starting-point rendered possible by the Structure of the Christian Revelation,	201
And by the Structure of the Christian Church,	202
Objection from View implied of State of Early Church, .	204
Objection from Difficulty of conceiving Questions not yet raised,	206
Objection on Ground of Unity of the Faith,	207
Development might be conceived to proceed simply by successive Existence of Generations of Christians,	207
Other Sources of Impulse, in Point of Fact : Collision of Faith with pre-existent Opinions,	208
Collision of Faith with Heresies, .	211

Arianism, ... 212
Systematic Influence, not powerful in Early Days, . 213
Questions rise successively, and cannot be anticipated, . 215
Permanent Effect which follows, ... 215
Guiding Rule, ... 217
Possibility of False Development, . . . 217
Sources of it, ... 219
No Ideal Programme of History of Church, 221
Reformation a Doctrinal Development, . . 222
Summary, ... 223
Successive Attainments, ... 225
Development not always the Present Work, . . 227
Progress of Church's Thoughts regarding the Old Testament, 229
Attitude to be maintained towards the Past, . . 231

LECTURE VI.

CREEDS.

Diversities of Judgment regarding Doctrine, and Primary Duties in connection with them, ... 235
Whether they may be borne with, ... 236
Action of the Church : Disciplinary Decisions, . . . 238
Respect due to them—Romish and Protestant Views, . . 239
Use of Creeds for Instruction, especially with reference to Doctrinal Antagonism, ... 241
Apostles' Creed : Nicene, ... 243
Reformation Confessions, Double Object, ... 245
Application to Members and to Office-bearers, . . . 247
Argument in behalf of Creeds, ... 248
Objections, ... 249
Admitted that Churches have dispensed with Formal Creeds as Foundation for Discipline, ... 250
Replies to Objections, ... 252
Liberty of the Church, ... 252
Distinction between Members and Office-bearers, . . 253
Admission as to Tendency of Creeds, ... 255
Right of Church to use Creeds argued from Case of Heresy, . 256
Duty of Church in that case, ... 258
Creeds in relation to this Process, ... 259
Further Argument from Open Questions, . . . 261

	PAGE
Secondary Elements in Creeds and Confessions,	261
Grounds on which introduced,	264
Operation of Creeds for Protection of Ordinary Members—Introduction of Secondary Elements in this Connection,	267
Secondary Elements, as justified from consideration of Existence of other Churches,	270
Question regarding Creeds as inherited from the Past,	271
Defence on this Point,	272
Readiness to undertake Revision essential on Protestant Principles,	274
Difficulties of Revision,	275
Ought not to be allowed to shut out the Duty,	276
Extent of Confessions in relation to Liability to Revision,	278
In relation to different Classes of Office-bearers,	282
Dangers in this relation, illustrated by Experience of the Church,	284

NOTES, . . 291

LECTURE I.

PRELIMINARY.

THIS Lecture shall be devoted to explain the ground over which I mean to travel, and to indicate the views which have suggested the selection of it for treatment in the present course.

One of the great objects which occupy and exercise the minds of Christians and of Churches, is doctrine. Articles, claiming to be articles of belief or knowledge, drawn from the Christian Revelation, are entertained, advocated, and applied over the whole field of Christian profession. They refer to what God is, and has done, and is doing, and is yet to do: they refer to the relations in which man was originally placed to God, in which he now stands, which he may attain or realize, and to the ultimate issues in either case. The centre of them all is Jesus Christ—come, dead, risen, and ascended. These doctrines, these articles of belief or knowledge, are identified, they are brought to our own memory, or to the knowledge of others, in forms of words which men have selected for the purpose of briefly and clearly expressing them. Or if Scripture words or sentences are employed, it is in some determinate sense, which has been fixed in disquisitions and discussions that are later than the close of Revelation. About doctrines, then, there has notoriously been much disagreement among Christians. Most of them have been vigorously debated; rival statements contest with one another the palm of legitimately representing what God would teach; also, where one party asserts that solid footing can be found, another maintains that nothing can be said except by trespassing wildly beyond the limits of the revealed.

Now the debates hence arising must occupy themselves primarily with the evidence supposed to be available in behalf of, or against, the tenets in dispute. But not unfrequently the debate goes down, or back, into more fundamental points. Pleas and arguments are introduced which depend on such questions as these: What the conditions are under which, and the limits within which, the human mind may be warranted in laying down doctrines; and how far it is reasonable to think that the Bible or the inspired teachers designed to furnish us with materials to be used in that way, to be fused and reproduced in those definite and invariable forms. Especially are such considerations raised when doctrines are in dispute, of which one side affirms that they travel into matter outside the sphere of intelligent and intelligible thought, and outside the sphere of unambiguous revelation.

But if considerations of this kind are suggested in connection with questions of doctrine, still more inevitably do they arise in connection with the exciting question of creeds. Creeds are statements of doctrine adopted by Churches, for the purpose of holding forth to the world what they profess, and fixing the standard of their constant and invariable teaching. Here, therefore, doctrine is pressed with a greater weight of authority; and the convictions of individuals on the one hand, and of societies of long duration and wide extent on the other, have to be adjusted, or else come into collision. But is it fit that any doctrine should be placed in this position? and, if any, how much of doctrine? and how should the Church conceive itself to be related to the creed—how the Church, and how the individual? All these questions turn on the true nature and reason of this form of thought and speech which we call doctrine, on the warrants for the function performed by the believer and the Church in the field of doctrine, on the length to which it is legitimate to carry it, and the uses to which it may legitimately be put.

There is still another way in which the same considerations are forced into notice. Christian doctrine assumes the character of a science; it has been treated in that character by many schools, and thrown into many forms. The systematic tendencies thus set in motion have often reacted strongly on the doctrines themselves, sometimes on the very form of them, often on the associations with which they are invested, and the kind of influence which they exert. But here two parties, at least, hint a doubt, and more than hesitate dislike: on the one side, those who may be called Bible Christians, starting from their impressions of the way in which Bible teaching was meant to operate on the mind; on the other side, those who, without imputing so much authority to the Bible, regard the whole subject of religion as lying beyond the horizon of precise statements and logical arguments. Both of these parties (each from its own ground) question the right of Christian doctrine to assume the character of science. And both, therefore, recur to the question: By what right Christian doctrine exists, and what its nature, warrants, and legitimate uses may be thought to be.

Further, Christian doctrine not only has a being, it has a history; a very large, various, and interesting history it is, not soon mastered, not easily judged. In this department an immense amount of effort has been put forth. The work has exercised the minds of men profoundly. The record of it extends into great masses of literature. The fruits of it have exerted a great and widespread influence, whether the influence in the separate cases, or on the whole, may have been for evil or for good. Those fruits have formed an element, not the least powerful and significant, in the movement of our race down the track of history.

Moreover, the work has not gone on harmoniously —far otherwise. The pages that record it are scarred with controversies, full of discomfort and anxiety for those whose hearts trembled for the ark of God. Not that these trials were without their compensation. It is very doubtful whether vigilant converse with revealed truth, and progressive insight into it, are to be had in this world on any other terms. Yet the trials are so great, that all along men have been questioning uneasily, whether the work to be done in this department could not be better done, and some wiser mode of view found, that should escape these evils. For still the safety and refreshment of the Church lay in passing back out of all debates into the field of Scripture, there to find a wonderful rest, and fulness, and freshness. But could not this benefit be enjoyed without the necessity of passing out of it into that hard toil, and passing through the toil back into the green fields again? Men questioned uneasily—questioning more often than getting an answer. For the controversies proved inevitable; and when questions were once raised, it was never possible to make as if they had not been raised, and forget them again.

Partly in connection with the controversies, partly in connection with the mere eager interest in their work cherished by dogmatic men and dogmatic periods, there have come warnings and doubts, from an early date, concerning the danger of mistaking the road. The apprehension is again and again expressed that a foreign element—a mixed speech—is intruding into this part of the Church's work. Speculative men proved prone to take the great thoughts of Revelation, and weave them into one web with their philosophies. Thus subtle transmutation passed upon the truth. In the new connection it seemed to be the same as before, but it was not really so. And keen, critical men subjected the living words of Scripture to a cold, curious dissection and cross-questioning, with the effect of bringing the truth into captivity to the methods of unbelief, or compelling the faith of Christians to measure itself by a standard not its own. 'Non complacuit Deo in dialectica salvum facere populum suum,'[1] is a warning uttered in many forms. It raises still the question, What kind of work are we really called to here, and how should it be done? It is to be noticed that these warnings and reclamations did not come only from one quarter or one side. Heretics are as eloquent as orthodox, and orthodox as heretics, in favour of Biblical simplicity, and against school terms. Often enough, a heresy, infected with thorough rationalism at the outset, turned round and became Biblical, or *quasi* Biblical, at a certain point. As soon as a counter statement, adapted to expose its own sinuosities, began to gain ground, an outcry was raised that this was going beyond the words and thoughts of Scripture.[2]

Nor is this the only way in which, during its long history, men have been led to dwell on the conditions under which doctrine exists. For they have been led to dwell on the conditions under which it passes down from one age to another. The process has gone on so long, that morals have been gathered from the mere survey of how it has gone on. This began almost as soon as it was possible it should; men drawing on the past history of doctrine for arguments to settle what the present doctrine should be. The same thing continues to this hour: only now the history of doctrine is rather drawn upon for arguments to settle whether doctrine has any right to be at all; or, at any rate, whether it can claim to be more, in any of its forms, than so much changeable human opinion.

A brief survey will show how these various interests

[1] Ambros. *De Fide*, i. 5.   [2] Note A.

have attached themselves to the progress of doctrinal discussions.

In the earliest ages of the Church, the teaching was, no doubt, extremely simple, and drawn in grand Scripture outlines. Soon, however, it became the occasion of controversies, the most important of which had respect to the Trinity and the person of Christ. In the West, the effects of the fall, and the effects of the grace which saves, came subsequently into discussion in addition. Now the questions arising, as one alternative after another was put prominently forward, were mainly debated and decided on the ground of the testimony of prophets and apostles, as recorded in the Scriptures. But yet very soon another kind of plea made its appearance in the field. It was an application of historical considerations. In substance it came to this: when a doctrine or mode of view presented itself as claiming to pass for Christian truth, it was controverted by saying, 'It makes its appearance too late. If it had been authorized, it would have been heard of before. If it were part of the faith once delivered to the saints, it would not have been so late in putting in an appearance to claim its right.' The allegation was made good by proving that, since the time when revelation ceased, the doctrine in question had not been heard of in the Churches,—for instance, in the great representative Churches, which might serve for specimens of the whole Church. Commonly enough, this consideration came in after much of the argument on either side, bearing precisely on the disputed point, had been pleaded. In its own nature, however, it was a prejudicial plea. It raised a prior issue on the mere facts of history, antecedent to going to issue on the merits of the evidence. It proposed to establish a prescription which should wrest from the article alleged all right to be heard on the merits, or should at least disable it from pleading them to any effectual purpose.

In application to some of the questions raised in those days, this line of argument had real and great force. It lay open, indeed, to such dangerous amplifications, that one would think an intelligent man could hardly use it without feeling the necessity of urging it with caution. There may be newness of expression when the thing expressed is old. There may be newness of application, which only contributes unlooked-for fertility to an old principle, doing it no wrong, doing only right to it. And there may be a new development, which only draws from the divine revelation unexpected elucidations and confirmations, adding light, harmony, and fulness to what was received before. At any rate, with such reasonable qualifications or without, the line of argument we speak of was felt to be attractive. It was early presented and forcibly pressed in Christian discussion. It is pleaded by Irenæus; it forms the burden of a whole treatise of Tertullian; it became a commonplace of succeeding controversialists; and it contributes to the famous rule of Vincentius of Lerins (*quod semper quod ubique quod ab omnibus*)—vague, treacherous, and worthless as it is—any measure of plausibility it possesses. In its earlier days it was urged only on behalf of fundamental truths. Further applications of it were not yet in view.[1]

---

[1] Note B.

In the patristic discussions which have now been referred to, definite theological tendencies appear conspicuously; and different schools of thought, animated by different tendencies, bring out characteristic types of doctrine, conceived and stated according to the tendency that prevailed in each school. But as yet, nothing very rounded or detailed in the way of complete treatment and arrangement had been attempted. The summaries of Christian teaching which were then given forth do not suggest the idea of a great ambition in the direction of system-building.

It was otherwise when the schoolmen arose. For them, it was a settled thing that the prevailing traditions of the Fathers, as well as the solemn determinations of the Church, were to be taken as of conclusive authority. But, along with this submission, the most audacious efforts of the reason went hand in hand. What the schoolmen undertook was to represent truth from the point of view of faith; so that the whole world of mind, the whole body of principles, natural and revealed, which determine the life of man, and regulate the world of which he is a part, should fall into a blessed order, and shine out with their own intrinsic evidence. Reason, entering at the door of faith, was to find open pathways in all directions, and to take conscious possession of the inner reason and meaning of the spiritual world. It was, in a manner, an attempt to scale heaven, and to think the thoughts of God; only it was confessed that our thoughts must be explicated into ordered series, linked and deduced the one from the other, while His thoughts have the unity proper to His simple and eternal nature. It was a strange mixture of materials; and in the treatment of them there was a strange variety of strength and weakness, all alike being submitted to the same dexterous logic, and obliged to take rank as that might dictate. With the contents of these systems—the measure of truth and of falsehood in them—we do not meddle here. We note only that systematic completeness was the object aimed at, and a defensible systematic harmony was a condition always in view in the treatment of each point. In this view no alternative was to be left unsifted, no question allowed to slumber unexamined.

Hardly were the first beginnings made, when uneasiness and alarm at this method of theologizing were expressed by some of those who represented the point of view of the practical Christian mind.[1] But all efforts to arrest it were thoroughly vain. It would have been as easy to stop the crusades. The impulse went on, learning, as it did so, to reconcile more skilfully the ready submission to authority with the dialectic audacity. If there were some who exposed themselves to suspicion, or fell utterly into discredit in point of orthodoxy, there were others who became the champions of the faith, and established their method as the true defence against its enemies, and the appropriate discipline for those who desired to penetrate the mysteries of Christian wisdom. Warning and doubting voices still sounded, not greatly heeded. It was from internal causes rather than from external admonition, that scholasticism became haunted with a doubt, and visited with a slow decay. The wonderful edifice that

[1] Note C.

had been in building so long, was still to be kept, and swept, and builded higher. But it was somewhat in the spirit of men who knew not well whether all they builded might not be such stuff as dreams are made of.[1] The enthusiastic confidence of the early schoolmen was annulled; and, long before the Reformation, the decay of scholasticism was adding its contribution to the other kinds of decay which made the temple of God a ruinous heap.

When the Reformation came, with its awakening of the conscience, its direct appeal to Scripture teaching, and its frank dealing with the necessities of human souls, it brought with it a strong recoil, not only from the scholastic doctrine, but from the scholastic method. The form in which this was usually expressed, was to denounce the mixture of philosophy which had been combined with the teaching of the schoolmen, and their substitution of the wisdom of men for the wisdom of God. Almost all the great Reformers spent much of their time in the work of expounding the word of God, and it was a leading conception of the new administration of the truth that it was to be *Biblical.* The early arrangements for theological instruction in several churches of the Reformation bore the stamp of a time when direct converse with the Scriptures was held to be the main, almost the exclusive, discipline in which a theologian should be trained.[2]

However, the Protestant teaching had to be gathered up into heads and articles. Moreover, it retained of course so much of the earlier doctrine as it judged to be agreeable to God's word. The form and cast of

---

[1] F. C. Baur, *Christl. Dogmengeschichte,* ii. 235.   [2] Note D.

the doctrine thus retained bore the stamp, in many articles, of the work spent upon them by the keen scrutinizing labourers of the schools. Still further, the conception of an ordered system consistent with itself, superior in its origin to the whole system of truth that is naturally discoverable, yet, when rightly conceived, harmonious with it, was still cherished. It was a legacy from the scholastic age that abode with strength in thinking minds. Soon, therefore, men were eagerly employed in setting forth, in careful organic delineation, the whole doctrinal result and achievement of the Reformation, settling the adjustments of doctrine with doctrine, evolving what was implied, supplementing what seemed defective. The task was sure to be attempted in any case; but the great examples which the schools had left suggested it the more strongly. It was urged on, too, by the necessities of controversy, which refused to be shut out from any corner of the theological field when an apparent inconsistency could be challenged, or a plausible distinction improved. The confessions had to be expounded, compared, defended, attacked; so there rose over against one another the systems of the Protestant and the Catholic Churches, both based professedly on apostolic teaching—the first finding it in the Scriptures, the latter in the Scriptures and tradition, guarded and expounded by the infallible Church. Then the Protestant systems diverged from one another, according to the peculiarities of the Churches; and the Catholic schools diverged also, though a strong hand held them circling endlessly round fixed and allotted points.

In the conflict between the Protestants and the

Church of Rome, arguments soon began to be employed which turned on the conception that ought to be formed of the history of doctrine, and the conditions under which it must unfold itself. These arguments may be said to have prepared the way for the modern criticism of Christian doctrine. The critical schools of the eighteenth and nineteenth centuries have, of course, contemplated doctrine from a point of view very different from that which the controversialists of the seventeenth century occupied. Yet their debates prepared abundant material and also abundant suggestions for the later critics, and there is a real connection between the two.

The Church of Rome maintained that the Reformation teaching in all its main peculiarities was an innovation on the faith of the early Church, and of the Church of all ages. It could not be the true faith, for it was new. The Reformers, on their side, brought a corresponding accusation against Rome. Her doctrine, they said, in a hundred different articles, was to be classed as recent corruption. This accusation was by far the more dangerous of the two, because Rome professed to rely so much on the continual witness of the Church in her favour. The Reformers laid their finger on doctrines and practices which had grown up gradually in late ages. These being as unknown to the early Church as to the Scriptures, were as much to be rejected on the principles of Rome herself, as on the principles of the Protestants. It was an obvious argument on both sides, perhaps, and could hardly fail to be adduced. The worst of it was, that it led into an immense field, and assumed a bulk wholly disproportioned to its intrinsic importance. Moreover, it involved the adduction and discussion of an immense amount of citation, the meaning of which was doubtful, and the relevancy disputable. Nor did either side escape uninjured from the temptation to twist and torture patristic testimonies, to adduce them in a sense which was far from the author's meaning, and to force meanings on them in cases in which the author perhaps had written without much meaning of any kind. For each party undertook to acquire for itself explicit testimony and sanction of the early Church in behalf of the main things it taught, and to disprove as much for its opponent.

On the Protestant side, for instance, the assumption and assertion made were, that the main truths taught by Protestants and rejected by Romanists, were not only taught in Scripture, but were also the faith of the early Church. It was not so material to the Protestant cause to maintain the latter assertion, for the Scripture constituted the Protestant rule of faith. Still, *ex abundanti*, the Protestants were willing to maintain that the facts of early ecclesiastical history corroborated their exposition of Scripture teaching; and, confident in the goodness of their cause, they very frankly claimed to be as ready to face an issue on this ground as on any other. Therefore they held that, bating phrases and modes of explaining, the early Church had and held the full evangelical doctrine which the Protestants now held forth from the Scriptures. So, on the other side, they argued that if the teaching of Romanism were true, it must be found first, of course, in Scripture, but also secondly in the early Church. They undertook, therefore, to show that Romanism included a mass of novelties unknown to the Church for many ages.

The Romanists, again, were the more obliged to labour in this field, because, according to them, tradition formed part of the rule of faith. Therefore, while they assailed Protestant peculiarities as novelties, they had to maintain that the faith of Rome had been held in the Church of Christ from first to last. This burdened them with very serious argumentative responsibilities, but such as could hardly be declined. In the earlier stages of the controversy, before criticism had done its work in thoroughly sifting the patristic writings, the means of getting up a plausible case were more plentiful than they were afterwards. When explicit passages could not be produced to sustain Romish teaching, it remained to assign reasons for thinking that it might have been held and taught in those ages, though not expressly delivered in the remaining writings. The lamentable loss of early literature, the corruptions of heretics, and the *disciplina arcani*, did duty for this purpose. Passages positively adverse could be explained away.

On each side, therefore, the tendency was to ascribe to the early Church an explicit maintenance of all truths agreed on by Protestants and Romanists, and also what each party, as distinguished from the other, held to be sound teaching. Neither side, of course, was disposed to doubt that phrases and modes of statement might vary from age to age, as circumstances might suggest, and especially as the necessities of controversy and the subtlety of heretics might dictate.

But this applied to the form of expression or explanation, not to the articles held and taught, believed and applied to practice. Meanwhile, these controversial motives urged on a survey and scrutiny of the whole history of doctrine, which was not always impartial, but was certainly keen and sifting.

Now, although the issue, as I have stated it, was the issue commonly taken between the controversialists, yet there were circumstances on the Romish side that were fitted to suggest another view of the facts. First, there was great controversial difficulty in maintaining that the whole breadth of Romish doctrine was current in the Church during ages in which it had palpably not yet been contrived. But, secondly, there was the habit of looking to Rome to decide emergent questions as they turned up. When Rome spoke, the view in favour of which she decided became a 'faith,' although before it was but a disputable opinion, and although it referred to a matter which, but a stage or two further back, was not discussed at all. With every theological decision the 'faith' grows. This was fitted to suggest the idea that a good part of the Roman 'faith' might probably have originated in the same way. Thirdly, there has, no doubt, been considerable variety from age to age in the amount of doctrinal teaching prevailing in the Church, and authorized by her collective Christian voice; and as research went on, the impression due to this fact grew. Altogether, there was much to suggest to studious men this idea as a convenient solution of difficulties,—viz., that the Church not only fixes traditions, but also developes doctrines, or completes the doctrinal system, by educing and expressing deliverances on matters on which the primitive teaching had nothing direct or certain to say.

Instances of some reference or allusion to such an idea may be gleaned from various periods. One, which created a good deal of attention both in the Church of Rome and among Protestants, had no reference to the Reformation controversy, but to the course of opinion on the doctrine of our Lord's divine nature. Petavius, in his great work, gave a statement of facts as to alleged changes of opinion, and an explanation of them, which amounted pretty nearly to a doctrine of development. It was not well received, however, even in his own communion, and he found it expedient to qualify his statements.[1] The champions of Rome continued, on the whole, to assert a thorough unity of doctrine from first to last, and to face, as best they could, the difficulties imposed on them by the conditions of their argument. Still, in particular emergencies, they resorted to explanations, which really came to this, that the recent teaching of Rome must be admitted to be in some sense new, but that it had been legitimately delivered, and was now authoritative.

Latterly, however, the tendency to form explanations, such as those now referred to, into a general theory, has begun to prevail in the management of the debate. Defenders of the infallibility of the Church, whose circumstances have led them to survey history in a comparatively free and speculative way,

[1] Note E.

have felt the necessity of recasting the argument, and representing the history of doctrine as a grand progressive development. Möhler[1] may be referred to as inaugurating this mode of representing the case; but it is Dr. Newman who is chiefly to be kept in view. Others have occasionally resorted to explanations which virtually involved the notion of development, or have advanced the idea in a brief and passing manner. But it is he who has set it forth as a general theory, underlying and explaining the whole succession of facts in the history of doctrine. The theory is this: that a great part of Christian doctrine existed at first, but as mere germs or points of commencement; fruitful ideas capable of various growth were barely deposited in the Church's mind; so that nothing in the Scriptures, or anywhere else, could at that time furnish ground for a conjecture as to the full-blown dogmatic development which has since ensued. But these germs were to be unfolded. They were sufficient to set agoing tendencies of the Church's spirit, movements of her affections, aspirations of her faith, religious longings and yearnings. These give rise, as time goes on, to various pious opinions in the minds of men, and devout observances in their worship. Opposition is made, perhaps, at first to the new forms of speech and practice, but they gradually grow and gain ground. Here comes in the infallible authority of the Church. There is in the Church a power to sift the results of this development. Some of the results approve themselves to the infallible tribunal, and it communicates to them

[1] Note F.

—such of them as it finds to be sound and valid—a divine sanction. Thenceforth men are bound to receive them with a divine faith. The theory is made to apply not merely to points in dispute between Romanists and Protestants, but to many others. It is maintained that the whole history of doctrine establishes this theory, and requires it. It is also maintained that a just conception of doctrine itself, and of the function of human minds in connection with doctrine, leads necessarily to the same conclusion.[1] Since the publication of Dr. Newman's book, which was written and published just at the time of his joining the Church of Rome, his views have gained ground with many Romanists and Anglicans; and in the former communion, even those who do not adopt them unreservedly, show a disposition to speak of them approvingly, as supplying a useful alternative for the explanation of historical difficulties.[2] The theory is, at the same time, curiously acceptable to his Protestant opponents, who entirely agree with him that the system of Rome *was* developed very much as he says, and only differ with him as to the infallibility of the Church in sanctioning its development.

So much for the use made of considerations drawn from the history of doctrine, in the well-debated controversy between the Reformation and Rome. It is time now to advert to the use made of the same topics in a quite different quarter,—by those, namely, who do not place confidence in doctrinal systems, nor care to rank themselves among the adherents

[1] Note G. [2] Note H.

of either side in controversies between churches. To them, indeed, both Möhler and Newman owed the hints on which they worked. Newman's weapon had been wielded in a very different cause from his, before he took it, new forged it, and baptized it for the purposes of Rome.

Revert for a moment to the point at which we stood some pages back—the epoch of the separation of the Roman Catholic and Protestant conceptions of the Christian faith. From that time, and during a couple of centuries which followed, the theology of the churches of the Reformation was taking and maintaining its systematic form. As I have said, it claimed, eminently, to be Biblical; and therefore the Biblical type was everywhere impressed on the dogmatic work. The appeal was always made to the direct authority of Scripture; the study of the text of Scripture was everywhere pursued. Besides, another grand corrective and guarantee existed in the fact that the doctrine was continually preached to the people from the open Bible; it was therefore brought to trial before the tribunal of the popular understanding, and tested against the conscience and the heart of the body of believers. Yet the theological enterprise betrayed its liability to the well-known dangers. It offered the opportunity, it supplied the temptation, to handle the materials with a confident dogmatism alien to the simplicity and the obedience of faith. Warnings on the subject of undue speculative licence, warnings indeed against the mere danger of too great absorption in doctrinal discussion, even where the matter of it might be sound and defensible, abound in the seventeenth century. They proceed not unfrequently from men who were themselves noted for their power both in doctrinal exposition and doctrinal debate.[1] For all that, the interest, for the present, went into the field of dogmatics too strongly to be repressed. Most abundant labour in that field has left its monuments behind. The two great Protestant orthodoxies, the Lutheran and the Reformed, rose over against the repaired and renovated system of Rome; while the Socinian and Arminian systems seemed rather to protest that other alternatives might be tried, than to dispute the ground effectually with those great antagonists. I have no wish to confound under one category all this various labour, in which many men, of various minds, took part. Some were men of great intellectual power, and of great moral qualities. Others were short-sighted, arrogant, and rash. It is enough to say that, human nature being what it is, we need not wonder if many writings and many controversies of that time went far beyond the line of wise or profitable doctrinal statement.[2]

But a great change was in preparation. It came partly as a recoil from the temper which had prevailed so thoroughly; in part it was due to other causes, which we cannot stay to specify. The seventeenth century saw the change beginning. Ere the eighteenth century had advanced far, the tide was plainly leaving the channel in which it had run so strongly. An indifference to doctrine spread abroad which was soon to be followed by hostility. This temper applied itself to a cool critical survey of the

[1] Note I.   [2] Note J.

whole mass of doctrinal effort which the past had left on record. The history of the process began to be traced, and very pregnant morals were deduced from it. A succession of movements, down to our own day, have proceeded from this general tendency. One school after another has revised and modified the way of putting the case, and the way of stating the conclusion.[1] But the tendency itself has worked without interruption; and in our own day, various influences combine to give intensity to the feeling which inspires it, and precision to the conclusions which it draws.

Those whom I have now in view are not to be referred to one class. They do not occupy the same position. Some have no dogmatic prepossession; some are prepossessed against all doctrine; some retain Christian beliefs, but reject most of the formal doctrines as commonly laid down by Christian churches. Some of them regard Christianity as a mistake; some accept the teaching of Jesus, but not that of any of His followers; some desire to abide by the Bible, but renounce the theologians and the systems; some raise no dispute with the teaching of their church, but feel a stronger interest in the philosophy of history than in the polemical merits of debated questions. Men of all these types take up Christian doctrine simply as one chapter, a large chapter, in the history of the human mind. It is a great subject, great at least in its mass, great in the part it has played in human affairs. Here is this activity which men have plied so sedulously, so resolutely, often so

[1] Note K.

fiercely, for hundreds and hundreds of years. Here are the results of it, in a large and various teaching, —drawing into itself the deepest thoughts and words, and hopes and fears of man. Here it stands in each of its competing forms, so concatenated, rising like a great spiritual form on the eye, moving all together if it move at all. Here is the place which doctrine claims, the place it occupies,—challenging the attention of every mind, sitting in the front of every church, pervading and giving shape to the mass of Christian literature, entering the mind in youth, moulding it to old age. Here are the definite inevitable antagonisms which its mere existence creates, the sharp alternatives which it makes inevitable, the yes and the no which it forces out as its pressure tells on men and things. What now shall we think of it? what judgment shall we pass on it? in what methods shall we approach and appreciate it? Well, it has had a history. Men have been at it now for many hundred years. The mere process of the past, duly looked at, will yield us lessons for the future; it will furnish a commentary, both on the enterprise, whether it be legitimate, and on the efforts, whether they have been fruitful. The history, duly examined, will show us what is to be expected in this department, what not. It will suggest to us the conditions under which the human mind has been working. It will shed light on the question, whether this practice of deriving and expounding doctrine is at all valid; if valid, how it should be gone about; in any case, what kind of weight may be wisely laid on the results. Such are the method and the spirit in which doctrine is considered. The tendency to approach the matter on this side has become deliberate and resolute in our day, in conformity with well-known tendencies of the age. It means, you see, that, instead of approaching the questions raised in the department of doctrine on the apparent proper ground of testimony and argument, we should apply a critical and experimental method. This is to furnish us with impressions of what, on the whole, may be expected from these materials, and what, on the whole, may be expected of our tools in working with these materials. 'You dogmatists have drawn on the history of your own department, in order to furnish materials of debate between yourselves on questions that belong to it. Let us now draw on it for material towards a more fundamental question, viz. what is to be thought of this whole field of labour, and what principles should be applied in estimating both the work and the fruit. We scrutinize the history, and mark the road by which existing positions have been reached. Criticism shall comment on the merits of the process thus disclosed, on the validity of the methods, on the likelihood of truth being reached along the line which has been followed.'

Now, in working on these principles and from this point of view, two assertions have been made, or rather, two kinds of assertion, which deserve our attention. One has respect to the history of the process, or to matter of fact; the other has respect to the starting-point of the process, or the right it had ever to begin at all.

As to the first, it was exceedingly natural that, contemplating the subject more or less in the spirit I have indicated, men should arrive at the conclusion that, in the main, in all its various lines of orthodoxy and heterodoxy, doctrine has been a matter of development—it has grown and become by virtue of processes and tendencies of human minds. Accordingly, the idea of development, as a general formula for the history of doctrine, had been suggested and applied long before Newman took it up. And this, as I say, was natural : First, because there is a great deal in the facts to suggest it. Secondly, because the tendency of criticism is to mark differences. As criticism passes from period to period, it notes and makes much of changes; it strives to bring those changes under a law—and so it gets development. Thirdly, because the philosophical theories about man and mind prevailing of late years seemed to require that Christian doctrine should have come into being by a process of development, and therefore furnished a motive for discovering that it had been doing so. Now what interests us here is the application of the theory. For while, with some, it remained a mere way of explaining and linking the facts of history, by others it has been brought into play, more or less sweepingly, as an implement for subverting theological positions. The argument is framed in this way : Every statement of Christian doctrine now advanced by a Christian community, professes to be a statement of revealed truth. Only in that character does it lay claim to the peculiar attention and respect which are asserted for Christian verities. If it were set forth as a speculation of the reason only, it would fall to be canvassed, like other human opinions, on principles applicable equally to them all. But if it professes to be a statement of revealed truth, then it is a statement of what has been revealed truth ever since Revelation was completed. And if it is proposed as important and fundamental, then it has been important and fundamental in Christian religion ever since the same period. Well, then, it is asserted concerning a given doctrine, that it was developed at some known date subsequent to the apostolic age; or if not developed at a known date, then formed gradually by processes hardly admitting of definite chronology, but at all events later than the close of the canon. It may be all very well, then, it is said, for you to imagine that you have found out arguments for this doctrine in the Scripture; but if it originated so late, you *must* be deceiving yourselves, and it becomes unnecessary to examine those alleged arguments. Thus, for instance, it has been said that the doctrine of a vicarious atonement, proposed by all the great historical churches, was developed somewhere about the twelfth century, and cannot therefore claim, at best, any respect beyond what may be due to a human speculation.[1]

Such is the way in which the principle may be applied in the hands of men who wish only to subvert some form of opinion which they think they can convict of comparative novelty. But the principle can lend itself to much wider operations, designed to bring down all the Christian doctrines and all the Christian churches in one common ruin. For it may

[1] Note L.

be said: You all profess to be teaching revealed truth. Yet all of you alike have reached your present position by a progress which can be pointed out. You have none of you been standing fast in the primitive truth, if there were such a thing. You have all moved. Your type of doctrine has become what it is by development. The forces of history, of human society, of the human mind, have mastered you, and moved you, from age to age. Now, looking back on the long process, we can see that you have accomplished no small distance from the starting-point. What does this prove? Not only that none of you can claim to be holders forth of what was held forth at the beginning, but that nothing ever was held forth that could continue to be held forth for many generations together. Men's thoughts broke out of it, whether they would or no. If, as all the churches (however they differ) teach, a sure doctrine, constant and equal to itself, is needful to Christianity, then the Bible, the Christian Revelation, is historically proved not to have furnished it. For such a purpose it has failed. That, it will be said, is proved. And the suggestion follows, that the Bible itself is a development, the remarkable birth of its own age, due to the forces and tendencies which were working in the world during the ages which produced it. The same development, with its mixed results, has been going on ever since; only hampered and marred by the idea that men were bound to adhere to an unchanging doctrine, which in fact they have never done, which in fact they never can do.

So much for this apprehension of the history of

doctrine as exhibiting a process of development. You see it may be taken in different ways. Dr. Newman says, Unquestionably Christian doctrine has been gradually developed; that was intended, and a proper authority was appointed to ensure that what is so developed should be divine truth. Another says: Yes, Christian doctrine has been developed; it is a fruit of the exercise of reason; exercised well in some cases, ill in others. We were meant to guide ourselves by our own reason; and so far as reason has worked well in this department, let us walk by it. Another says: Yes, Christian doctrine, so called, is a development; set aside a few simple articles that are rather facts than doctrines, and all the rest is an unwarrantable parasitic growth. Let us reject all that. Another says: Yes, Christian doctrine turns out to be a human development, while it has all along held itself to be revealed truth; this lets us see what a delusion the whole system is, in all its forms.

So the various schools speak, suggesting the question: How far *is* there development of Christian doctrine? and do the facts of its history really involve anything inconsistent with what we hold of the authority, completeness, and sufficiency of the word of God?

But I said that the same line of contemplation gave rise to another kind of assertion, having respect to the starting-point of the process, and bearing on the question of the right it had ever to begin at all.

For the survey of the history brings too clearly before our eyes the infirmities that have attended men in this work, and the extravagances, excesses, and aberrations of which they have been guilty. There is quite enough of this to make it a plausible thing to say: The whole labour has been a mistake from the beginning. Men were never intended, and they never had a warrant, to begin to deduce any doctrines at all such as make up these systems of yours. Men have gone wrong, because in this field there was no going right. Such is the argument; and an influence working in a deeper region tends to dispose men towards the same conclusion. Doctrine is just that department of the Christian's life and work in which is most emphatically and clearly brought into view an element of Christianity to which a great repugnance is cherished in many minds: I mean, the element of authoritative information regarding things unseen, and our relations to them—information for which we are dependent solely on testimony. Doctrine, with its precise affirmations, brings this into view, not always wisely,—for divines are not always wise,—but always strongly. And in many minds a recoil follows. Men justify themselves in rejecting this element, on this account, that it seems to remove religion from the firm ground of experience, of known moral relations verified by the understanding and the conscience, and to bring it into a region where it becomes arbitrary and artificial. So a stand is made against doctrine, but in degrees, and from motives, as we have already seen, that are distinctly different. Sometimes we have the Christian man recoiling from what he thinks (justly, very likely) the over-subtle, over-dialectical, over-confident manipulation of the dogmatist. He gets tired of watching him, and discussing questions of more and less with him,—all the more, because, as he discusses, he feels that he is getting—cannot but get—dogmatical himself. Therefore he falls back on a more general position. I will take the truth, he says, as it lies in the Bible; but I do not believe that the Bible was intended to furnish material for any such definition, connection, elaboration, as make up your systems. Sometimes we have the opponent of every peculiarly Christian belief taking up the very same ground. The idea that any such positions and trains of teaching as the churches set forth can be validly got out of the Bible is, he says, a mere blunder of the divines—an equal blunder in all the schools, Protestant, Popish, Socinian.

And the view of the Bible which is relied on in support of the position is this: Its language, it is said, in those passages where it seems to lend countenance to your doctrines, is not proper, but analogical—it was never meant to be strictly taken. No exact quantum of meaning was ever meant to be got out of it. You only kill the sense of it when you turn it into strict assertions, and link it into lengthened arguments. You ought never to have begun that work.

Indeed, it is a very singular thing to mark how the progress of men's minds is influencing this department of men's thoughts. All thinking men have been growing, of late, in the perception of the power for good which the religion of the Bible has exercised in the world, and of the decisive influence which the appearance and testimony of Jesus Christ has exerted on the race. Unhappily this has not been attended, in many cases, by a disposition to receive Scripture teaching with a docile mind. But it has led many thoughtful men to make the effort, with great earnestness and pains, to wrest the Bible, as it were, out of the hands of the believing Church,—*i.e.*, to represent matters so as to enable them to say : It is not yours, but ours ; we understand it ; we have the key to the meaning of it ; we will show you how to use it. And one form in which this is done, is to undertake to show that, in drawing definite faiths from it, still more in drawing systems of faiths, the Christians have been only misusing and misconstruing it, so that it is time at last to show the bewildered Church how truly good the Bible is, and what it is truly good for.

Finally, all these doubts regarding the general method of doctrine, regarding the success of the Church in setting forth what can be maintained, regarding her right to have set forth anything at all, are brought to bear, of course, on the question of creeds.

I do not propose to involve myself and you, in a course of half a dozen lectures, in the historical and controversial details which enter into the discussions on which I have touched. But there is a topic suggested by them all which it may be useful to single out and dwell upon : How ought we to conceive the place and use of doctrine, considered as a function and a fruit of the Christian mind ? In what relation does it stand to the calling of the believer and of the Church ? How should the handling of it be conceived to arise out of the Christian calling? And what uses and applications of it are suggested by the place we thus assign to it? All the various arguments drawn from the history of doctrine, and all the conclusions indicated as to the competency of dogma, in any of its degrees or all its degrees, must be referred at last to some conception, either of the way in which doctrine ought to pertain to the believer and the Church, or else of the place that should be claimed for it as pertaining to them. Possibly, if we could fix a clear and sound perception upon these points, some of the applications made of the history of doctrine would vanish of themselves, and others would come into a form in which they can be more readily weighed and appreciated. What I propose to do in this matter, is not so much to construct an argument, as to offer a statement, in the hope that it may be such as will prove credible and useful.

I propose to treat mainly of three points: first, of the utterance of doctrine as a function of the believing mind; second, of development of doctrine; thirdly, of creeds. But in order to treat of these, a prior topic must first come under consideration; for the way in which doctrine ought to be drawn forth and used, depends on the manner in which it has been delivered by God. I shall therefore preface what I have to say on the three points named, by offering some considerations on the manner in which doctrine has been delivered, first in the Old Testament, and secondly in the New Testament. These will occupy the next two Lectures; and the three topics which I just now named will follow in the fourth, fifth, and sixth.

The discussions thus suggested have reference not to the matter, or the material merits, but to the form and formal qualities of doctrine. However, in treating them, I speak from the position of a disciple of the Reformed theology, and I will frankly make the assumptions which that position implies, whenever I have occasion. This is not only expedient with a view to avoid circumlocution; it is necessary in order to avoid a disguise which would be disingenuous. The views which I am to present on the somewhat abstract and formal topics I have specified, are presented as views which might approve themselves to those who share my own position with reference to the material questions of theology. They appear to me to be coherent and credible, viewed from that position, and to supply a reasonable solution for questions which men in that position have to answer. If, in addition, they are able to commend themselves to any of those who occupy other positions, so much the better.[1]

[1] Note M.

LECTURE II

DELIVERY OF DOCTRINE IN OLD TESTAMENT.

THE attempt to represent the method in which doctrine is delivered, in one great section of the Scriptures, is apt to expose to a charge of presumption which I would not willingly incur. It is in the line of our duty to seek to gather from Revelation whatever it contains; but in proposing to represent its method, one may seem to take the presumptuous attitude of standing above the Scriptures, to survey and assign the manner of their teaching. And this all the more, when it is not a single book that is in view,—in which case one might deal with the manner and working of the human mind employed in its production,—not this, but the whole Old Testament, where the common method, if it exists, is to be ascribed to the one Spirit, in whose wisdom holy men spoke and wrote. We do well to remember, then, that we are but gazing upward from below. Yet for this part of our task we have the advantage of a New Testament position from which to look.[1]

We read the Old Testament with the aid of New Testament light. Now, all that in this light becomes evident to us was not evident in the same manner to those to whom the Old Testament revelations were

[1] Note A.

primarily made. Our present task is to consider how the Church was dealt with by its Lord during the times of the Old Testament, and how the communication of truth to believing minds was then measured and administered. Considering this, we are also at the same time to mark how the communications then made were fitted to become more luminous and significant to us in these latter days. In which connection I make this remark, viz. that we may be able in a good degree to determine the respects in which our Old Testament predecessors fell short of us in point of privilege, especially in this matter of knowledge. But we may not so well be able to estimate, or even at all to conceive, compensations made out to them in the practical course of God's dealings with them, by which, on some other side of their case, they were brought up again to a nearer and fuller participation of evangelical grace, than we can construe for them by any scheme that we can now lay down. Some part of their experience is our concern as well as theirs; but their full experience and its full result was their own concern, and that of their covenant Lord, who took care of it. The impression of this is to be kept alive upon our minds throughout the present inquiry.

Now the broad fact which first of all strikes us is, that God was pleased to make Himself known to His Church, not by a body of teaching delivered all at once, but progressively, by lessons which follow one upon another, evolved in due succession, as the times arrived at which they might be fitly given. There is obvious progress, multiplication of principles, increased complexity and fulness in the scheme, as we advance from the patriarchal to the Mosaic dispensation, and, under the latter, as we descend to the period of the later prophets. It is all of a piece, indeed, the same key-note throughout, some great lessons sounding only louder and louder as time passes on. Yet at successive critical periods clear additions come, fresh and new as compared with anything given before; and then these are rehearsed, set in new lights, sent home with new impression, by the teachings and the providences of the periods which follow.[1]

Moreover, when we speak of progressive lessons, a distinction should be made. There might be a process of teaching by successive lessons, so delivered that each lesson should be abstract and general,—'doctrinal,' as we say,—coming as a maxim that shall be always applicable to that case as long as human knowledge subsists under its earthly conditions. It might conceivably have been so; but such was not the divine method. From the first, God has dealt with men *in the concrete*. He has dealt with them about facts; He has taught them through events, —those facts and events being the centre and the hinge of His teachings. This method was suited to the end in view. For He was to reveal Himself, not merely as a God of magnificent attributes capable of abstract determination, and not merely as a God related to us according to general principles, capable of being measured and assigned, but as one in contact with us, as one with whom we become acquainted by experience, as one who makes Himself personally known. He has come forth in a long

[1] Note B.

succession of *dealings* with men. These have always, indeed, been prefaced or accompanied by His enlightening word; and they have been intrinsically consistent in their principle with a great and harmonious scheme of divine procedure. Yet for the most part, the revelation in each case has been designed to guide men aright with respect to the dealing presently in hand. So God has manifested Himself as the Living One; as having a mind and a will, a purpose and a course, about those facts, those details, concerning which we also can have a mind or will, can form a purpose or take a course. As He unfolds His mind over against man's, and His will, and His purpose, and His course, men come into actual and definite contact with Him on every side of their being.

It is of the greatest importance to mark this. For here is what should be recognised as fundamental in the Biblical exhibition of truth concerning God. The Bible recognises and dwells on the manifestation of God in nature: its ordered and stable forces, with their wonderful effects, are all referred to Him, for all are His servants. The Bible recognises and dwells on the manifestation of God in conscience; it turns a vivid light on the handwriting there, that intensifies every line and every character. It makes us feel how unchangeably God is the God of moral distinctions, the righteous Lord who loveth righteousness. However, the way which it takes to bring us acquainted with the certainty and the glory of God's being, in both these forms of manifestation, is to add another. When I have nothing but the abiding forces and principles of nature operating in their stedfast order, it is hard for me to be assured or persuaded that there is anything here but an eternal system, of which I must make the best I can. It has a meaning, but not necessarily any meaning that aims at me; it may have quite other aims stretching far away. I may have a meaning, viz. to make the best I can of it; but I am left in doubt whether this meaning and aim of mine is anything more than my solitary and private plan, which I am allowed to carry out as long as the great plan does not involve the crushing of mine. Again, when I realize the law of conscience, I advance to a higher region; and yet here also it is hard for me to be assured that I have to do with anything more than some mysterious principle that makes righteousness a source of strength and peace, and unrighteousness a source of disquiet and ill. It is another great and very inward element coming into the plan and reckoning of my life, imposing on me a new constraint, and opening to me a new kind of good. I do not say that this is a small thing; I do not think it is. But I say it may be hard for me to be assured and stedfastly persuaded that conscience implies anything more. There is an immediate suggestion, indeed, that there is something more: there is a craving in the soul that stretches out its hands and lifts up its heart for more; a persuasion thrills through me that there must be more; I name the great name of God. But this—God—how much is He more than the principle of a stedfast order, than the maintainer of an influence that establishes right? How far is there, in all this, any meaning that takes account of me, and of my meaning, and effort, and result? How far any voice to speak, any ear to hear?

The Biblical answer is not merely to reveal permanent principles concerning the relation of God to His works, and to His moral creatures. It does reveal such. But it establishes and prepares that conviction by exhibiting God, from the first, in another attitude. This God of the stedfast order of nature, this God of the persistent and inextinguishable admonition of conscience, is seen with His mind in motion, Himself in motion towards me, in a manner that betokens a meaning, a purpose, a counsel bearing on me. The meaning need not be clear at first, certainly not in all its scope. The great thing is, that some particular meaning and purpose, here, now, at this place, at this time, comes into manifestation—embodied in fact, event, transaction. Instantly the whole aspect of the heavens is transformed. God is one entering into communion with me, into transactions in which He has part and I am to have part, tending to a result, to which, and in which, His meaning and my meaning shall go hand in hand. Instantly nature and conscience become luminous with a faith. The great world *has* far-stretching meanings, and bearings which I cannot estimate; but there is a meaning for me,—a divine presence and intention with which I am to have fellowship, not merely a set of commandments of which I must make what I can. And this persuasion is continually recruited and reinforced as I recognise Him who is in nature and in conscience, coming forth in acts and deeds that are more than the order of nature, and more than the monition of conscience;

that involve the utterance of a purpose and meaning circumstantiated to the case of a man who is moving through his experiences, and seeks a heart to rest on, and an arm to cling to.

This is the Biblical foundation, or implication, of God's personality. And this it is that draws after it the whole idea and exhibition of the supernatural. The whole question of miracle, so idly debated, runs up to this. And the question is, first, whether man is a being who, besides being adapted to deal with nature and to live by conscience, has in him that which is fitted for a further experience, and is unsatisfied without it—something that craves for communion with one above him; and secondly, whether there is anything in the divine nature that makes it impossible or unfit that God should draw into historical communion with man, by dealings that determine a meaning on his part additional to that which nature and conscience disclose. If, then, history viewed in its ordinary aspects, the common history of men and nations, be, as it is, a revelation of man, into this history has been entwined another, along which is evolved the Revelation of God.[1]

God, then, has been pleased to reveal Himself in a historical way, so that we see succession and growth in the Revelation, as it is achieved along a line of transactions and events. Now, what we possess in point of fact is mainly the Revelation of God to a fallen race, connected with His carrying on a great work of redemption. The circumstances of a fallen race suggest some special justification for the adoption

[1] Note C.

with respect to them of a method so progressive, and made to turn on successive events. But we have no right to assume that the method is exclusively adapted to this state of things, or that it could not be suitably applied to another. We know, indeed, very little of the unfallen state. Beyond the fact that man *was* then unfallen, in God's image, what we gather about it is mainly collected by way of inference from the representations given us both of the effect of the fall, and also of the method and aim of man's recovery. Divines have been often tempted to overpress these inferences to a too confident particularity of determination. Man, standing in the image of God, certainly had (according to the Scripture indications) in his intelligent nature, his unperverted affections, his unpolluted conscience, the germs of, and the preparation for, glorious attainments in knowledge, as he should walk with God, and as he should survey the world in which God's goodness placed him. But what he had attained in knowledge is quite another question. This we gather, that he was forthwith called to enter on a practical history, a life of earthly works. These were to constitute the body, of which his spiritual life was to be the soul. The special revelation made to him concerned one of the created things near him, and called for obedience to a plain outward injunction. That was the suitable way of beginning. This may suggest to us what is in itself credible on all accounts, that to be taught and trained after this historical fashion is proper to our race, not merely as sinful, but as human.[1]

[1] Note D.

However this may be, and whatever might have been the course of training suitable for a race of men preserved from sin, in point of fact, things took another course. And so began the evolution of law and grace over against sin,—that long strange story of the ways of man and of the ways of God, of which we are ourselves a part.

In this history various elements may be traced, each proceeding in its own distinguishable line, while each combines with all the others.[1] That which principally concerns us is the course of divine revelations, whether by divine words or by divine transactions. With respect to this, we are entitled, I think, to regard the information contained in the Scriptures as practically complete. We should not, indeed, be warranted in assuming that no word of God visited the earth, except those which have found a record in the Scriptures. We might not be justified in asserting that no divine communication reached Adam, or Enoch, or Noah, except those which are there set down. But it seems agreeable to all we know of Scripture, and of the principles on which it has been constructed, to believe, that if there were any such, they corresponded, at each stage, to those which have been recorded, and were of the same character. They were in their nature subordinate and accessory; and if they had been recorded, they would not have revolutionized the impression of the divine order and method of revealing which we receive from the Scriptures as they stand.[2]

It appears to me that there were three great themes

[1] Note E.   [2] Note F.

which from the first were very vividly presented, and which continued to be made matter of teaching throughout the Old Testament; viz. the character of God, the malignity of sin, the hope of coming good and deliverance.

As regards the manifestation of God, we may distinguish, on the one hand, the revelation of that absolute love of right, and upholding of it, which He unites with His eternal power. The sense of this stedfast character of God was to grow into that burning consciousness of the divine rectitude, which glows so magnificently in the Prophets and the Psalms. On the other hand, growing principally out of the instances in which definite transactions bring Him near to men, we have the assertion of His majesty, as having absolute right to be obeyed; and we have the disclosure of His interest in men and in their history,—that wonderful interest which sin does not extinguish, which is big with purposes of kindness, and which binds itself to effect them. These last are the attributes which grow into the great names of mercy, faithfulness, and truth. Although the teaching is nowhere dogmatic in form, yet these views of God are so clearly involved in the manifestations made, that we may well say, so much doctrine concerning God began to be unfolded and conveyed into the minds of men; confirmed, so far as the light of nature might have suggested then; delivered, so far as nature fell short of such suggestion. It would be finical to say that so much was not doctrinally held.[1]

These disclosures and impressions concerning God

[1] Note G.

were very specially implicated with what appeared upon the other two points which I have mentioned. First, the malignity of sin, brought out on the one hand by the experience of the doom which it entailed, and the peculiar manner in which men had to deal with God and approach God about it; brought out, on the other, by making it evident with what extraordinary power and dominion it laid hold of the race, and pervaded it. Here is the beginning of the peculiar Biblical view of the condition of man as fallen and depraved; and a consciousness of it is preserved, one way or other, in all the succeeding stages. This may be marked as an article of doctrine too: not that there was detailed teaching on the intrinsic nature and precise effects of man's depravity; but that the impression conveyed to teachable minds was sufficiently direct and distinct to secure a conviction we may well call doctrinal, of the actual dominion of sin in the race of man.[1]

With respect to the hope of good and deliverance, that started from the promise of the woman's seed, and was upheld by the manifestations of God as dealing with man and men, moving on (as time moved) to dealings not yet exhausted, bringing blessings not yet disclosed. What the goodness of God meant by the promise of the woman's seed, we know by the event. That seed was Christ. How much the promise was fitted or able to convey to the minds of men situated as those were who lived in early days, is not so easily settled.[2] I do not know that the conviction was at first necessarily more than this, that

[1] Note H.   [2] Note I.

in the line of the woman's seed God was to bring them a kind of deliverance and success such as they needed, such as it became Him in His greatness and His goodness to confer. But this, like other divine beginnings, was to have its great contents unfolded by many a following revelation.

These seem to be the fundamental notes, so to say, in the harmony of doctrine as it began to be delivered. These points are exhibited with sufficient distinctness to warrant us in speaking of them as doctrines taught; but the effect produced would be more fully described by saying that a certain kind of impression, in these different departments, was produced upon believing and docile minds, capable of being indefinitely intensified, widened, and deepened as time went on.

Now observe how earthly experience is made to build up the history, and to furnish the material of the impressions which are to be produced. Thus, the instances by means of which the evil and the doom of sin are made palpable to the sinning race, stand in elements of this world. Sorrow and death—sorrow which mars, and death which ends, the 'goodness of the Lord in the land of the living,'—these are the expressions of the tendency of sin, and of the displeasure of God against it. So also the hope of redemption is brought out in a manner which fixes the expectation upon the earthly scene, and the succession of earthly events. It is the woman's seed in whom victory and deliverance are to be made good. The eye is directed along the succession of human generations, and taught to look for victory and deliverance emerging palpably in the earthly history.

At the same time, let us remember that it is the human conscience, with its capacities of shame, dismay, remorse, that is confronted and dealt with through these instances. And let us especially remember, that that with which human conscience is confronted, is God Himself, the living one. For, in truth, the more we mark how elements of this world are the things on which the attention of those early scholars was fixed, the more must we remember that the central and vitalizing element of these early revelations, as of all revelations, is God in them, manifested; God's definite interposition, dealing with men to fixed and known effects,—doing so in the competency of an absolute authority and a supreme will,—doing so also in the consistency of that holy character, according to which He loves righteousness and hates evil, yet is long-suffering and of great compassion. This is the essential element, which gives life and meaning, which gives height and depth, to everything else. This is what vitalizes and calls into play those capacities in man which place him in relation to God as made in God's 'image;' and this makes the suggestions derived from these earthly instances so momentous, so far-reaching, so profitable. Meanwhile, the cast of the transactions in which this God calls men to meet with Him, furnishes new types by which to conceive their relation to Him (*i.e.* types such as nature could not indicate), and directs to new issues towards which their dealings with Him should go forward. The principles on which He proceeds are not explained, and they are such as men were quite unable to measure or assign beforehand; but as those dealings go on, a growing assurance might arise that they are worthy of God, and harmonious with all that conscience sanctions as fit to be ascribed to God's majesty.

It is a question on which men have been very much divided, how much perception of evangelical relations, or of the provisions of an evangelical scheme, ought to be ascribed to men in these earliest periods of religious history. But anxiety in reference to exact determinations on this point may be reasonably quieted, if full effect be given in our minds to the position of a believer in those days, in relation to the sources of impression which have been referred to already. Conceive a man under the vivid impression of God as the God of nature, ruling everywhere, the God of right, upholding right within him and without, and as God dealing with him, or with his representatives, in particular, historical, progressive transactions. Conceive him aware of and impressed with the malignity of sin, as it involves the race and has involved himself, and yet conscious of being led to desire and seek God as the righteous one, to desire to be drawn back into that element again. Conceive him looking forward to the issues of a process of·dealing, in which God's goodwill is leading him and his fellows onward to some deliverance that is to be worthy of God, and is to be real deliverance, in God's goodness, from sin and death,—and you have surely all the elements of an evangelical attitude and an evangelical experience. The God with whom such a man deals *is* God in Christ. The voice that sounds in his ears, is of one saying, Lo, I come.

It is this chiefly, I think, which prepares us to

appreciate the further course which things now take, when the next great step comes round in the call of Abraham, and the cluster of revelations connected with it. A good deal may be made, unquestionably, of this, that men move forward to it under the influence of all the previous lessons, which it is reasonable to think were within their knowledge, as they are within ours; such as the lesson involved in the history of the fall—the lesson of God watching and judging the developments of sin—of God's goodness, not only in the constant supply of common blessings, but in His cherishing and carrying forward far-reaching purposes of mercy towards the world. But here surely lies the very spring of life in the Abrahamic revelations and experiences, viz. God, the God of nature, the God of conscience, the God of all previous dealings with the wayward race! God, calling Abraham out from country and kindred, undertook to be a God to him, his God—to make him and his a seed of blessing in the earth; to be his friend, in a word, in an alliance offensive and defensive.[1] Here, no doubt, was immense and wonderful good, to be entertained with wonder and gladness. Here was sure resource, to be confided in and reposed upon with perfect trust. But what was it to mean in particular? What kind of births and fruits were indicated as like to spring of it, on which the mind was to fasten, in them to realize more particularly the goodwill on which it had so sure a hold? It was explicated into two promises—the promise of the land, the promise of the seed: a land in which Abraham was to sojourn

[1] Note J.

under God's care, but which was to come into actual possession long after his day; and a seed which, after long waiting, came at last in one precious son, but which was to be multitudinous as the stars of heaven, and was to involve and comprehend the blessing for all nations.

Of this land, we know that faith, disciplined through many an experience about it, was to find it in the end to be nothing worse than the better country, that is, the heavenly. And of this seed, we know that faith was to find it to be nothing less than the very Word incarnate, born to the hope and the travail of many a waiting and longing soul. To discern and show how this 'whole of good' was expressed and made out to those who in early days lived by faith, in what sense they saw it and tasted it, has been a recurrent problem in New Testament times. The faith of Old Testament believers, no doubt, clung to the very words of God, and to the immediate thoughts which those words inevitably suggested, not to inferences at all subtle or remote. In order to establish the identity of the faith of God's children in all ages, and the persistent sameness of their life in God, the attempt has been made to construct, as it were, for the Old Testament believers a perspective, along which they should be conceived to look, and discern the very end, remote but clear, to which those things reached that presently were near them. I should rather think that the result was reached by turning back, by reverting to the foundation promise, 'A God to thee.' The fulness of that promise overflowed into each of the particular instances, and set it in its proper light. A land was given—an actual land, with hills and valleys, corn and wine,—with practical qualities, such as farmers could take account of; but it was a land provided by God—a land in which God should dwell with them, a land in which He should carry on His dealings with them as one who gives His people inheritance. A seed was given them— a seed multitudinous and mighty; but a seed raised up by God, given by God, to be made by Him the seat of blessing, and the tie between heaven and earth.[1] This was the element in the case that opened up the indefinite possibilities, that disclosed the certainty of unspeakable good. And then, trial and need, sharpening their discernment, raised new questions, suggested new answers, trained the heart to a nearer approximation to God's thought. That land, and that seed, took their meaning from that God. 'O God, Thou art my God.'

It is important to attend to the genius and way of working of this method of dealing with men. *Instances*, we have said, arising in their earthly experience, were made the occasion of divine transactions with them, and so built up the scenes of their life, and furnished their deepest and most lasting impressions. Now an idea is often entertained, that the main business of believers in those days, so far as regards the exercise of their minds, was to make use of the dispensations of God, by drawing analogical or typological inferences from them. So we are to conceive them arriving at the contemplation of the permanent principles applicable to the relations of men as sinners

[1] Note K.

and as believers; so we are to conceive them getting sight of the future benefits of the redemption that was to be achieved. And so, also, their benefit or profit is supposed to be measured by the degree in which they discerned the symbolical or typical reference of the arrangements in which they were involved, by the degree of skill they had in reading their picture Bible.[1] Surely to think so would be a great mistake. They found themselves dealing with God about some earthly thing, which God had been pleased to make the matter of promise, and the occasion of practical transactions. It was the possession of a land, let us say. It was no more than a temporal thing. Well, temporal things are of great weight and moment in the exercise and discipline of us the children of time. But, moreover, the land claimed their interest, and called out their concern about it, in a way that was quite peculiar, because God had made it the instance and token of His goodwill. Here was the great thing, that it was with God the Living One they had to do about it,— with Him, so great, so pure, so true—so present, yet so arduous to be dealt with; they had to close, to walk with Him, to trust Him. In making good their hold on God about these earthly and temporal things, in many a trying conjuncture, in many a time of fear without, and of burdened heart and conscience within, they were by God's wise disposal cast into such exercises of mind about the blessing, into

---

[1] Or it is assumed by opponents, that the identity or continuity of Old Testament faith with that of the New Testament can only be brought out on some such theory, which is then made a means of assault.

such attitudes and postures of faith, into such a consciousness of who and what God is, and how related to them, that in dealing with Him about that particular benefit, they did at the same time grasp and embrace the substantial benefits of the everlasting covenant. That is to say, they realized God as theirs in such a manner, and with such an impression of what He is in promise and covenant, that they rested on His present mercy all their want, and they looked to the future and coming mercy as mercy that should express and bring to light the whole goodness of a pardoning and life-giving God.

I do not doubt that by types and figures, apprehended to be such, men might discern somewhat of the spiritual benefit to which they pointed. And much more frequently, men might reason analogically, from the earthly instance of God's care to the higher form of blessing which they must seek from the same goodness.[1] But no doubt, in many a case, the faith of believers, in the exercise that arose about those earthly things, grasped implicitly the spiritual blessing along with the earthly good thing, without ever in their minds making distinction between them, or opposing them to one another, as type or antitype. That is to say, they laid hold of that in God which is the substance and heart of the evangelical blessing, even when their whole soul was absorbed in dealing aright with Him about those things in which their connection with Him for the present was illustrated and expressed.

---

[1] According to the apostle's logic : 'He that hath done *so*, how shall he not *much more*,' etc.

Out of these elements an amazing multiplicity and complexity of teaching, or at any rate of training, was made to emerge. A great variety of relations to God, and of intercourse with God corresponding to those relations, was brought about. Hence the principles brought into play became in the highest degree instructive; and the mental exercises of awakened men placed under that dispensation became singularly vivid and searching. The principles brought into play were, ultimately, those same which regulate the ways of God with men, through Christ, under all economies. Still, they were brought out commonly in the concrete, not in the abstract. What found expression as distinct objects of mental contemplation and discernment, were mainly the various elements of the divine character: God's almightiness, His fidelity, His indignation at sin, His delight in righteousness, His mercy to those who sought and feared Him. For the rest, God's dispensations moved on,—conforming, indeed, to the principles which were to prove constituent of the gospel, and regulative of God's administrations in relation to it, but rather embodying these principles than revealing them. They stood before men embodied in impressive instances, yet so that the effect might be felt, rather than that the principle could be doctrinally disentangled and discerned.

Nor must we lose sight of the expectant attitude of the Church, and the progressive character of God's revelations. God was moving on, and the Church with Him—ever moving on. Believers were never allowed to think that they had come to the end of what God had in hand. There was more to be said, and more to be done. Men were thrown on the future for the full opening up of all that was *in* the mercy promised, and of all that bore proportion to man's need, and to the character of Him whom they were learning to know in many a particular as the Lord God, merciful and gracious. Their whole position trained them to feel that they should say not merely 'All this is true,' but 'All this, and more.' Hence quite another character, and a higher efficacy, accrue to much that seems to us imperfect and elementary.

It is well for us to strive to apprehend, along lines of thought like that now indicated, how it was that 'elements of this world,' as the apostle says, could be employed so freely, so constantly, as the material by means of which men were trained to the knowledge and service of God. And thus, also, we shall understand how rich might be the virtual knowledge of God, and how living and various the impressions, while there was comparatively little of explicit or exact doctrine.

Those elements of this world supplied a platform on which the intercourse between God and His children might go on. But they did more. They constituted a scaffolding within which the house might grow up, conformed on every side to its intended plan, and yet ultimately separable from it. But they were more. They were the very matters about which, for the time then present, God was dealing with men by word and deed,—palpable, historical, circumscribed in time and place,—occasioning the most practical thoughts and feelings. But they were such, and so arranged, that the faith in God, and the walk with God about these, learned the very goings of the faith that receives and holds eternal life.

Considerations such as these are very necessary to be kept in view when we go on to that great and very remarkable stage in the divine dealings—the Mosaic legislation and economy. The Abrahamic covenant, without this vast and elaborate appliance, administered by simple providential dispensations of fatherly goodness and fatherly chastisement, was suitable for a time. But when the family grew into a nation, it became suitable to take other methods.[1] And so came in that dispensation of law, significantly appealed to in the Epistles to Romans, Galatians, Hebrews, and elsewhere, which constitutes so large a part of the Old Testament economy, which entered so imperiously and prevailingly into the life of every Jew; which gave a character so unique, and in some respects so difficult to trace out, to the discipline and the exercise of Old Testament believers. I hardly need remind you how interpreters and expounders of theology, in its relation to the various economies, have laboured in illustrating the relation of the various parts of this system to the permanent principles of Law and of Gospel, nor how capable of intricate and difficult discussion some of the questions which here arise have proved to be. Into this wide field I shall not, of course, attempt to go. I will attempt no discussion of the way in which this whole

[1] Note L.

system was fitted to make due application of the principles of Law and Gospel to the case of men living under that dispensation. In this department it is probable, after all that has been done, that something yet remains to be performed. I shall hold it enough to say, that we are sure of many things we cannot particularly explain, and can confidently refer various elements of the system to their proper heads as cases or illustrations of great principles, where we cannot show, as yet, that these were all fitly placed in that remarkable system, so as to make a complete and harmonious whole, whether of teaching or impression. We are sure, from the New Testament and from the nature of the case, that in these arrangements the Divine Ruler was reaching on towards the pattern and the principles of things afterwards to be disclosed. And whatever difficulties there may be about a complete adjustment of the whole scheme, there is no difficulty in seeing a singularly solemn and awakening declaration of law, and a very constant application of it,—so that the purity and majesty of God, the rule of righteousness, the intolerable offensiveness of sin, are brought out in the most vivid and solemn way; nor is there any difficulty in seeing suggestions, embodiments, shadows, figures of the way of salvation by Jesus Christ, the crucified, such as it is vain to cavil at and impossible to overlook.

And yet, while there is so much in the law that irresistibly suggests to us principles of which the true and permanent embodiment is in the things that do not pass away, the letter of the law is even singularly void of anything to dispose or encourage the Israelites to look beyond it to something further. They are sent on their way with a significant *if* sounding in their ears: 'If ye will obey my voice indeed, and keep my covenant.' It is a covenant with stringent conditions, and with an elaborate mechanism for carrying out the details of administration and observance. And there is a marked abstinence from any indications that should lead the subject beyond these ordinances themselves. There is nothing to suggest that they existed not for their own sakes, but with a disciplinary and administrative purpose, as shadows of things not yet seen. This holds both of those requirements which seem purely legal, and of the ordinances which most obviously shadow forth the gospel way of atonement and reconciliation. With the sharpest distinctness, with the minutest specification, rule follows rule. All is given forth as if only the present were in view; as if the provision for the present regulation of the Israelite's life were exhausted in those minute mechanical provisions.

For, indeed, the object seems to have been to compel the people to realize in the sharpest and hardest way certain conditions, certain actual palpable relations to God. It seems to have been intended that they should be pressed right upon the edge of the most definite rules, and compelled to feel how, *according to these*, they stood related to God, or to God's service, or to God's congregation, or to God's promise. I say according to *these definite rules*, most literally. That was the first thing. Not according to certain remote and lofty principles, inferred by analogy, and apprehended in a dim uncertain way, were they to conceive their case; but according to peremptory rules, that come like a bar of iron into the commonest matters of every day's concern. We know how prone men are now to rest in the most vague conception, or no conception, of their relation to the unseen realities, even in this noonday of the gospel, after all the light that has been poured upon them, and all that is fitted to give them a constraining grasp upon the conscience. What, then, would have been the condition, in those days, of the men placed under that economy, had they been allowed or left to feel their way towards some dim and distant principle to which they should conceive themselves subject, by which they should be bound to be guided? Far otherwise was it ordered. A great Schoolmaster delivered them to laws. A man was made to feel himself definitely clean, or else unclean. His obligations, various, precise, minute, were made out to him most definitely. The responsibilities he incurred by mishap or by transgression were mapped and tabulated in stringent form; and that which vitalized the system, and lifted it above the rank of mere weary ceremonial, was not *first of all* the apprehended reference to further truths, but it was the God, the mighty God of Israel. To Him the Israelite found himself bound in these changing relations, in respect of small matters indeed in many cases, but always to a great and terrible God — the God of nature — the God of conscience — the God who had made the history of His people singular with signs and wonders, and who had it in hand still to carry it on. He might not see the reasons; he might not see to the end of that which was to be abolished. But as he found himself now near, but with risk of falling and being repelled, now excluded, but with a possibility of drawing near again by fixed provisions,—now clean, and now unclean,—now having to seek his sacrifice with all the qualities that must peremptorily attach to it, now offering it with the due succession of ordered rites,—a conception was formed in his mind, a praxis was drilled into the habit of the man, as to various forms of relation, various attitudes, various exercises toward God. And when the great reality of the Divine Existence filled his soul, then it overflowed in the inquiry after more in God, or in the apprehension and assertion of more in God, than the mere letter gave him,—after a nearness that was more than ceremonial, and a forgiveness that opened the way to more than an earthly temple, and a cleansing that reached deeper than only to the outer man; and the hope of his fathers became luminous, as he apprehended it to include some solid core of blessing, able to give rest to all these desires, and to satisfy them to the full.

But we cannot say that the array of doctrine towards which this system of ordinances pointed, and which in some sense it embodied, was as yet explicitly delivered. In order to disclose the meaning which it bore in that respect, it awaited a light that was not yet come.[1]

On the other hand, the heads of teaching which I spoke of before as brought into prominence,—God—sin—the hope,—continue to receive accessions of light, but not in equal degrees. The fundamental and per-

[1] Note M.

manent lines of the doctrine of human duty, and its relation to God's authority and will, and to His character as Judge of all the earth, are here laid down with the utmost clearness, to be filled up by an ample prophetic commentary in succeeding times. There is also a remarkable growth in the elements from which impressions might be drawn as to what is implied in the forgiveness of sin. With all the fresh light upon the immutable righteousness of God, and on the evil of sin, the truth that there is, notwithstanding, forgiveness with Him, stands out clear and bright; and the conception of sacrificial atonement as the way in which it should be sought and received, is wrought into the whole texture of Israel's thoughts and life. Then, as to the coming Hope, among other influences which tended to establish in the minds of men a central object in the midst of those bright expectations of diffused good which might be based upon the Abrahamic covenant, there was that notable promise of the great Prophet, whom God should raise up, and to whom Israel should hearken.

But the great means and occasion of giving vividness and development to the Messianic promise was to be provided at a later stage. For, following on the law came a great succession of providences, exercising the people by judgment and mercy in the knowledge of themselves, and in the knowledge of Him with whom they had to do,—in the knowledge of what it was to serve their King, and to walk with Him. And then the next great step onward in the ways of God was the setting up of the monarchy in David's house, accompanied as it was with new arrangements for the stability, order, and splendour of God's worship. The king's function, ideally, was to provide and maintain righteousness and peace. And no sooner was the kingdom set up, than we have the beginning and point of departure of an immense series of oracles and prophecies,—some directly pointing to the coming One, the true and effectual King; others shaping out, as it were, in various ways, the conception of what a King was needed for, and what sort of work God's true King must do.

The history of the kingdom proved to be to a lamentable extent a history of failure,—kings that sought not the Lord, a people that were content to have it so. And with alternations of occasional prosperity and recovery, a long decay succeeded the glorious days of David and of Solomon. And still God was near — still His hand came in — still His voice was heard—still His presence felt. Strange people, that could not be done with God, nor God with them! As the generations stretched out and passed away, how the question must have excited many a mind, What did God mean, then, what *was* His purpose, what was He to do, and what was He delaying for? For surely the result and scope of the great promises were not to be found in the existing state of things. If God had given them up, that could have been understood; but that was never so. The very specialty and severity of His judgments, as well as the signal mercy of His deliverances, marked them as a people whom He would not leave alone.

But chiefly His presence began now to be manifested, and His influence felt, through the prophetic ministry; one great effect of which was to make palpable and assured the mind and meaning of God in providence—so that the progress of providence, instead of wearing the aspect of a casual, impersonal thing, became instinct with the character and present purpose of God. And through the prophets, with the advancing development of God's ways, there came a more ample commentary upon them. The spiritual significance of the law was opened up, the place which God claimed in Israel's heart was vindicated. What God might be to them was made solemnly and pathetically plain in prophesyings, which drew upon the whole history of providence and of Revelation for its language and its imagery. And then, especially, turning to the future, what it was in God to be to His people was shown forth there. Often that future was dark with judgment; but the ultimate issues were to be the fulfilment of the covenant. Things were not to be conformed to the likelihoods which men might gather from passing appearances. Nor were all things to continue as they were. Nor was the decay that had fallen so sore on Israel to make God's promise vain. All should yet make way for the glory of the Lord.

Generally the picture of the future is drawn in colours and forms supplied by the scenery of the present. The people and the land rise into view purged from the defect and wrong that marred their state; and every element of good that Israel knew under that dispensation reappears with a strange brightness, and in a wonderful combination, expressive of peace, and grace, and of Jehovah's presence among His people. In this connection the assurance of Messianic blessing is presented, sometimes, as one may say, in a dispersed manner. Rule that is perfect in its administration, and secures its end; priestly work proceeding fitly and gloriously, and sacrifice accepted and returning in blessing; teaching that diffuses itself victoriously, and sways men from within; a new heart and mind, making men capable of successful walking with God;—these, or things like these, appear as incidents or aspects of a better state of things which God's mercy shall yet bring round.

But in various single passages, and in some whole tracts of prophecy, the personal Messiah rises into view; still as bearing one or other, or all, of these same blessings, but with an emphasis that cannot be mistaken, laid on the individual person who brings in the better hope. The prophetic eye rests on a Form around which all the elements that make up Israel's wonderful history seem to gather,—all the dark elements of conflict, all the bright elements of promise. The coming good for Israel and for all nations is seen hanging on the raising up of One who is to have the sorrow, the conflict, and the glory of achieving it. He is One who is to be raised up among the people; yet He is spoken of in terms that ascribe to Him an origin and a dignity not inferior to the Highest. Sometimes He is brought into view with great deliberation, and with a broad light shining on the scene. Sometimes He is only suddenly descried in the midst of scenes which give place, as it were for a moment, to let this brighter vision appear. Then the clouds descend again, and only the present or the immediate future is in sight.[1]

At the same time another function was going on. Modes of utterance were graciously provided for the experience of believers — modes of utterance calculated to create and reproduce the experience they uttered. This function is connected in the closest way with the prophetic function which I have just now referred to: for the one passes into the other. How much of prophecy is there in the Psalms! and what bursts of prayer, and song, and meditation in the Prophets! Those Psalms have been the guide and utterance of faith and love to this day. They are indeed unfathomed. No man has measured what may be in them. But looking at them, for the present, as provided for the utterance of the faith and love and penitence of men in those days, we see what thoughts were working in their minds, what feelings craved utterance, what impressions of God and of His ways were formed under the discipline through which they passed.[2]

Now from these materials also we see a continual growth and progress going on, and it takes shape to a certain extent in forms which may reasonably be called doctrinal. For instance, the fuller teaching about that fear and love of God in the heart which it is His nature to seek, and only in rendering which man truly meets Him; the hope of the new covenant, with its peculiar characteristics; the growing fulness in the reference to that form of God's presence and working which we associate with the special agency

[1] Note N.   [2] Note O.

of the Holy Spirit. These are only instances. They are sometimes brought in as necessities or blessings of the present, sometimes as hopes for the future, but at all events in a direct and explicit manner. And as I said but now, in looking forward to the Hope, the image of the coming One not only becomes clearer and more striking, but fuller intimations are given of the character in which He is to appear, and the manner in which He is to make His way to the possession of blessing, and to bring His people into the experience of it.

Still, many of these utterances could not be so definitely significant to the men who heard them as they are to us; and, for the most part, the prophetic teaching was not adapted to supply men with much of that furniture of definite conclusions which we call doctrinal positions. It was a teaching couched commonly in the language drawn from the mechanism of the dispensation, and from current providences. It tended always to deepen, widen, and illuminate men's thoughts of God; and as the illustration grew, both of the majesty of God's character, and also of the greatness and complexity of the purposes He had in hand concerning Israel, the sense of a growing pregnancy in the whole scheme, and in every element of it, must have arisen in the minds of believing men,— a deeper sense than ever of mighty issues moving to their accomplishment, of many toiling agencies co-operant to some great result. But it would appear that the course which had to be taken in order to enjoy the benefits which were then attainable, was not so much to draw out in any clear forms the scheme of the divine administration, its principles and ends, but to brood intensely on the instances, always multiplying, by which Israel's God was known, and on the illustration they afforded of His ways and of His gifts. These might be, many of them, earthly; yet the divine promise was charging them with a perpetuity and splendour of divine benefaction, which the future was hastening to disclose, and which was already brightening all the east.

So, also, the devout experience of the Psalmist expresses, usually, just a direct recourse to God, Israel's God, as known and recognised through the providences and the machinery of that dispensation. For instance, though there are some clear references to a future state after death, yet commonly the Psalmist, looking to the future, looks down the line of the temporal promises. God, sin, righteousness, the need of it, the assertion of it, the vanity of outward sacrifices, the future fulfilment of God's covenant, the wonders of His law, the rest and refreshment of His worship, the blessedness of adhering to God,—all this is set forth with wonderful, because with inspired energy. Yet how these things were related together, or how it could be all so singularly true and certain for men, was yet dark.

There was, then, so much of what we may call doctrinal teaching on some great articles which we have noticed, as to give to believing men the right point of departure for their faith and love; enough to give them a true conception of the drift of that divine process in which they were involved, a true impression of the meaning of the divine person with whom they were in contact. Nor was this teaching confined to those points of departure; it advanced and grew in various particulars, so that more full and definite views appear to have been attainable, and to have been attained, as the teaching advanced. Yet all this is seen, as it were, rising out of, and returning into, a historical process. A history built up of elements of this world, institutions and providences, is that which we see unfolded. In these, and about them, God is seen earnestly dealing with His people, and they are called earnestly to deal with Him. But then it is God more and more clearly revealed in the intense glory of His moral perfections, with whom they deal; and the dealings are ordered so as to bring out more and more what is involved in having to do with such a God. And in these dealings God is moving on, with a sedulous intent which never relaxes—He is moving on to what? What is He preparing to do? Perhaps the Israelite's best answer, after he had gathered all that was attainable, was to say—*More* than all our thoughts have reached. Eye hath not seen it, ear hath not heard it, it hath not entered into the heart of man.

In saying all this, I am speaking still of what we may gather to have been the sense of the teaching for those who lived under it. Certainly, in every step of this very remarkable process, the Divine Revealer and Ruler had in view His own ultimate counsel, and all He did was congruous to that. Doubtless He was working on the principles, and embodying the principles which regulate His procedure in the dispensation of grace through Christ; He was doing so in many a case in which not only the ancient saints could not discern it, but in which no New Testament student has discerned it either. Therefore I make not the least doubt that there are deep analogies underlying Old Testament arrangements and history which have never yet been found out; and that Christ speaks in many a passage where we commonly do not hear Him. Christ speaks; not because the inspired man supposed he was uttering the voice of the Messiah, but because the whole relation of the case was such that he could not speak at all what was fit for him to say in his position, without really uttering that which principally and properly belongs to Christ. It was God in Christ all through the Old Testament, and the footsteps of Christ coming are heard all along the way. But it is only in New Testament light that this is so clearly seen. Certainly, we under the New Testament may acquire a facility in discerning something of the connection of the whole, and of the scope and aim of the details, as related to God's ultimate purpose. We have advantages for penetrating the divine meaning of which it is full. Yet not so, but that we find it still beyond us; and we labour with a sense of unsatisfied desire to penetrate it more fully. We are fain often to find our way to the divine thoughts or the divine scheme, from the outside inwards, with a slow and faltering step. And we often turn aside and miss the true clue. So it has been from the beginning. One of our earliest pieces of uninspired Christian authorship is an attempt to assign the meaning of the Old Testament. It is not very successful; and we are at the task still.[1] However, the Old Testament is far from serving the purpose only of being spelt out into accordance with the New. It is the divine foundation of the New, and the proper preparation for it. The Church and the believer do well to be ever passing into the New Testament, by passing down through the Old; and this not only because the Old supplies the historical antecedents, but because it supplies the historical propædeutic. It gives us the tone; it furnishes us with the mould and scheme of thought; most of all, it gives us what God judged fit to be the initial discipline in the knowledge of Him, and in the knowledge of sin. It prepares us for the New Testament teaching, which is congruous to such a propædeutic, which discloses the eternal verities that were latent in the ancient scheme, and formative of it throughout.

What this rapid survey has suggested may now be summed up.

We find in the Old Testament a progressive teaching. The essential elements are present from the first; yet so that, beginning with simple elements, a visible amplification of the materials of knowledge takes place as we advance, and a progress is realized in the thoughts and the experience of the children of God. This was provided for by the series of divine revelations. God carried on the development by new steps of His providence, and new utterances of His will.

We find the Old Testament teaching, all along, made to rise out of the history of Divine acts, and of transactions between God and men. These advance and accumulate; and as they do so, the relation

[1] Note P.

between God and men is seen to include more numerous elements, to present more varied aspects, to require for its explanation a more profound and complex body of principles.

We find that, in these historical transactions, the objects especially brought into view, and made the matter of direct dealing between God and men, are elements of this world—earthly things, divinely chosen and ordained. It is in connection with these that God progressively brings out His character, and exhibits the tenor of His ways. These form the discipline under which men are trained, and they furnish the language and the lessons by which they are taught. This system, in its various departments of promise, providence, and ordinance or ceremonial, is charged throughout with a higher meaning. That is to say, it is pervaded by analogies to a system of things that does not pass away. But these analogies are far from being always understood by the men who, in those circumstances, learned to know God.

We find that a large part of the benefit and use arising from this system to those who lived under it, arose from a disciplinary and moulding operation; the instances of God's ways, and the experience of relations to Him made good under the system, produced impressions, and formed modes of view and feeling, in which an evangelical relation to God was felt and realized, even when the principles on which it was made possible, and was provided, were very imperfectly apprehended (if at all).

We find that this scheme, manifestly pregnant with a great divine purpose, and becoming more manifestly so as it advanced, comprehended in particular, from the very first, the word of promise, directing men to the future, and holding out a divine fulness of blessing connected with the seed which God was to raise up. One great effect of this, deserving notice as specially related to our subject, is, that in this way, men who lived by faith were always kept from thinking that their knowledge was complete, or that God's mind towards them could be adequately measured by any of His actual gifts. It became a duty to make all present teaching and all present experience the starting-point from which to look onward to greater things to come.

All this understood, we find that in this training a place was given to teaching so permanent in its matter, so direct and unambiguous in its terms, and so precise in the convictions it was fitted to produce, that we may reasonably call it doctrinal. However, it is not given in any systematic form; and it appears as rising out of the historical transactions, and out of the relations which they establish. It rises out of these, and returns into them again. The head of teaching, which is much the most fully illustrated in this form, is the character and glory of God.

These conclusions are fitted to impress upon us one or two general views which shall close this Lecture.

One is, that there may be a real identity of faith (*i.e.* of acquaintance with God, realization of relation to Him, and expectation of good from Him, according to His covenant mercy), where there are great differences of detailed knowledge and of theoretical insight,—such differences as obtained between the earliest and the latest Old Testament believers, or such as those which distinguish an Old Testament believer from one who uses well his advantages under the New.

Another is, that all along, as we mark the intercourse of God with men, there is a *much-more-ness* in His mind, as embodied in His revelation and proceedings, as compared with their mind, in dealing with the revelation, and engaging in the intercourse to which it called them. This *much-more-ness* is asserted not of God's mind as it is in itself merely, but as it is embodied in His present words and acts. Neither the thoughts, nor the prayers, nor the faith, nor the thanksgiving of God's people, have ever borne any proportion to the height, and depth, and length, and breadth of His thoughts which were towards them.

A third is this: The Old Testament system of dealing with the Church implies a fuller revelation of doctrine in reserve, awaiting the Church at some future stage. It does so, because it presents an order of things which requires such a revelation as its close and complement. It presents a manifold system, under which men were held, and through the elements of which they were obliged to pass,—a system not explicable from mere natural religion, not explicable from the declared principles of the dispensation itself, —awaiting, therefore, some further light. It implied and embodied principles of the divine government, truths and facts as to the ways of God, relations between God and men existing or made good, which were not disclosed. Now this state of things warranted the expectation of a revelation of truth on the points thus left dark. To leave all unexplained, to break off the mode of dealing with men thus provided, and substitute some other wholly unconnected with it, would be an inadmissible course. It would be to deprive the later generations of all interest in and profit by the earlier revelation, as something wholly irrelevant to them. To complete it or continue it, yet so as to leave all unexplained, would be not merely to hold the Church in perpetual childhood, but to order things so that the conclusive mercy, whatever in that case it might have been, which wound up the series of God's dealings, should permanently veil the ways of God, and leave the Church in ignorance of the real nature of the way by which God led them, or the end to which He had brought them. But this could not be. The end in view is the revealing of God; and the Church's fellowship with God was designed to be in a growing understanding of Him and of His ways.

Lastly, we find exemplified in the Old Testament, not only for Old Testament believers, but for ourselves, a manner of revelation of such a kind that, while much is instantly apprehensible, there are underlying principles necessary to a full solution of the questions that arise, to which we penetrate with difficulty. They are not furnished to us by way of direct definition, but must be gathered from instances and exemplifications; and these are understood not by the intellect alone, but by a moral sympathy. Some of these we may expect to find passing all calculations of ours, reaching out where we cannot follow. So that the elements of Scripture appear to be, like the elements of God's creation, real and palpable, in contact with us, such as can be verified and applied to practice, made matter of thought, source of feeling, occasion of use; and yet on some sides and aspects of them, down under our feet, and out on every side, and up to heaven, they stretch: we measure them, yet they cannot be measured; we know them, yet they are not comprehended.

LECTURE III.

ON THE DELIVERY OF DOCTRINE IN THE NEW TESTAMENT.

IF the task of assigning the method in which doctrine is revealed can be only partially and approximately discharged with reference to the Old Testament, that is still more the case with respect to the New Testament. It is still in the attitude of men approaching from below, and looking upward, that we must survey the subject, and describe it; whereas, to perform the task perfectly, one should have to mount up to the sources of the teaching, and follow it down as it passes into human thought and human speech, and claims to mingle with human faith. This wisdom is hidden from all living, saving Him who is in the bosom of the Father. For us, only the side of things that is next us is accessible; and even of this, our knowledge is fragmentary and mixed.

In the New Testament a great wealth of doctrinal teaching meets us. Yet let us remember, as we proceed, how much is in the New Testament also, that is distinguishable from doctrinal teaching, and has its own independent ways of acting on men, and on their life and destiny. We have narrative, that is meant to operate as historic fact dwelling in the memory; recorded events, great and small, that are to form the scenery of our mental vision as we look up the stream of time; influences that touch the heart, and operate by impression; a various inculcation of privilege and of duty, laying hold of the conscience—drawing the sympathies of the renewed heart—to be proved and made good in the actual life of men. These are great parts of our New Testament: they intertwine in the closest way with the doctrinal teaching, and depend on it for light and life; and it, in turn, conveys much of its meaning and finds much of its evidence through them.

But our concern now is with the one element only. In speaking of that, it will be best to mark some contrasts between the Old Testament and the New, the consideration of which will introduce what is most essential for our present purpose.

The Church of the Old Testament, then, was looking forward to good things to come. God was already their God—that was present. God was already blessing them—that also was present. But the mercy by which the goodwill of God to them, and His care for their welfare, should be adequately and conclusively expressed, had not yet arrived. It was a hope; serving God day and night, they hoped to come to it. Nothing was yet brought to pass by way of event, able either to express or explain the relation towards them which God assumed, or able to justify the trust in God which they were taught to cherish. So, also, nothing had come to pass adapted to countervail the power of evil working in the lot of man, and continually coming to light; nothing that carried in its bosom a manifest remedy for all. Yet they had God, the source of all events, of all resources; and in God a hope grounded on promise; and from God a continual earnest which held them looking forward. But we under the New Testament have received the promise. Those events, in which grace comes, conquers, and reigns, have become part of the world's history and of ours. Those greatest blessings, in which the mind and goodwill of God to His Church on earth are adequately unfolded and made effectual, have been revealed, have been imparted. Christ has come, lived, died, risen again, and ascended into glory.

Again, the Church under the Old Testament was trained under a progressive course of revelations. At each stage the revelation was incomplete, and seemed to leave the Church thankful, yet questioning, looking wistfully for something further. At no period of her history was any oracle given, adequate to guide her for many succeeding ages. As the Church passed into new circumstances and encountered new difficulties, new light was given, both for the purpose of directing her own course, and also to add some fresh illustration to the purposes of God concerning which faith should be cherished. Each communication of this kind admitted of being supplemented by another as time went on. With the New Testament Church it is otherwise. A manifestation has been made to us of the mind of God and of His ways, in which Revelation is complete. He has made that discovery of Himself in which, for men on the earth and for the Church in its earthly state, His whole counsel is embodied. He has no more to add. We have no more to receive. What God does for man, what He will have man to seek from Him, and do in His service, what His mind is concerning both, have been conclusively revealed. The Church must still move on through successive experiences; history does not stand still now, any more than in the days of old. New circumstances arise: transformations pass not only on the outward conditions of men and things, but on the inner conditions too; the intellectual and moral scenery of the mind of man shifts and varies; out of the depths of human nature, and from the ferment of social changes, new questions rise, new temptations are developed, the strain is applied to the Church's system in new directions. But we expect no new utterances to direct us in these particulars. There is still, indeed, the promise of the Spirit to be fulfilled: what that may contain, or may warrant us to expect, is for separate consideration. At all events, we have now not a developing and advancing, but a completed Revelation.[1]

Once more, in the case of the Church under the Old Testament, a great part of the meaning and mind of God was rather embodied in a discipline than exhibited in a doctrine. So there was communicated to the believers of those days, much of the benefit or fruit corresponding to many a truth which they were never distinctly taught. This benefit might come to them in one or both of two ways. The discipline might supply forms or types of thought, according to which the nature and the manner of bestowing of better blessings might be conceived; and the one might be received not merely as an image of the other, but as a pledge too. Or, again, it might come in this way,—

[1] Note A.

which was perhaps the more constant and powerful,— viz. as the discipline exerted a moulding influence on those who were under it, and obediently yielded to it, bringing them to an attitude and exercise of faith towards God which corresponded to an evangelical relation to Him. But now, under the New Testament, the Church receives a far more open declaration of the mind of God. It is true still, indeed, as it was under the Old Testament, that Revelation requires submission; and that great part of the insight (as well as the benefit) which it affords is to be attained along the path of obedience. Yet the contrast between the two Testaments remains. The revelation of the New Testament stands much more in *intelligible principles* of truth, applicable directly to the very agencies and events by which redemption is achieved, and to the relation on which redemption proceeds, or which redemption constitutes and brings into being. It calls us to understand these principles, to give effect to them, to enter into the meaning of them as fully and completely as we can. For all predicaments which now affect the Church, all predicaments in which a believer can find himself, are ruled by those relations, those revealed relations to the Redeemer, and to the great world of being and of principle of which He is the centre. It is no wonder, therefore, that doctrine holds a large place in the New Testament revelation, and in the history of the Church following upon it down to this hour. To understand the meaning and to assign the range and connection of principles, is one great part of the duty now laid on the Church and on believers; and it has a close connection with the enjoyment of spiritual blessings, and with the discharge of spiritual service towards God.[1]

Yet the manner in which this peculiarity of the New Testament is provided for deserves particular attention. For while the two great divisions of the Scriptures have their differences in point of method, there are great fundamental resemblances. If it be true that the Old Testament is essentially historical, its lessons rising out of transactions and events, the same is equally true of the New Testament. It consists essentially in the unveiling of divine transactions and events, in which man's nature and man's destiny are historically concerned. The essential elements with which we here have to do are persons, facts, events, presupposing history that goes before, necessitating and entailing historical consequences, or historical alternatives that are to follow after. The Lord Jesus Christ is announced, is incarnate, manifests His glory, is rejected, crucified, rises, ascends, gives the Spirit, and so forth. But the difference lies here: For the purposes of Old Testament teaching and training a provisional and preparatory history was evolved, and a provisional apparatus of facts and objects, standing much in elements of this world, was appointed and employed. But in the New Testament the great realities break into manifestation, the essential and decisive interpositions of God in the world's history come to pass. The persons and the facts that we have here to do with, are not provisional and temporary, but adequate and immutable. Here

[1] Note B.

we come face to face with the actual embodiments in a divine history of the divine counsels. Here we have the proper and complete expression of eternal principles, as they bear, and as they take effect, on man's state and on the earth's history. The mediation of Christ, for example, is the adequate and complete measure of the love and grace as well as of the truth and righteousness of God, in so far as mankind are concerned in these great attributes. Our knowledge may still fall short, our understanding may still labour ineffectually to grasp the great truths in their full compass; but if that is so, it is not because the objects set before us are mere earthly images, and the relations between them (to one another and God and us), poor shadows, inadequate to convey the truths to which they point. Here we are in the presence of the truth itself. And if, after all, we fail and falter, it is only because we are ourselves inadequate to reach the truth that stands right before us; partly also it is because human language, at its best, is able to give only a partial account of so great a history: though prepared and fitted for its work by all the processes of Old Testament development, it still struggles under the burden, and leaves much unsaid.

Thus, then, there is a continuous unity of principle in the method adopted throughout divine revelation, in Old Testament and New Testament alike. Always the historical is presupposed, and out of it the doctrine emerges, illustrating it, and becoming itself visible and substantial as it shines forth from the great array of facts. The constancy of this method, and the necessity of it with relation to the conditions of our race at least, are strongly illustrated by the reserve so manifestly practised with respect to the revelation of many important truths, until Christ had come, and lived, and died, and risen. Until those great facts had become historical, it was not possible to make fitting revelation of principles and relations which they embodied, and which they were to disclose. In the meantime, doubtless, the Church needed some guidance and influence such as truth transmits into the mind and life. But this was provided for, by providing facts and events of an intermediate, temporary, representative kind. Birth of children, inheritances, kings, priests, prophets, sacrifices, ceremonies, conflicts, providences of a hundred kinds, served the turn for the time of preparation. About these, and out of these, representations of truth could be made to emerge ; from them, evangelical impressions, or impressions corresponding to those which the gospel requires, could be derived ; and to the Church standing by them, looking forward, auguries of greater things, like these, yet to be realized, could be suggested or declared. But at last, in the order of the times, the great facts arise ; and from them breaks forth, and from them for ever shines clearly, the light of Christian doctrine—not dispersed into a train of slow successive lessons, but concentrated and gathered into one blaze of light around the incarnation and the cross of our Lord Jesus Christ.

So, first and last, the divine truth is designed to lead us into the understanding of divine history, in which history it calls us to confess and to claim our own place. The adoption of any other method seems inconsistent with the nature of man; possibly it may also be inconsistent with the nature of God. With a view to a fitting communication of the mind of God to our minds, some such method may be dictated by the very nature of our minds. It may be dictated also by the very nature of the divine mind, and of all divine truth. For God is the Living One; not a holy name and being only, but holy power and life. And divine truths are also divine forces, the light and the life being one. And when the Eternal Word would reveal God, He went forth to do it in great and marvellous works, in a universe full of force and movement, full of strange, intricate, ever progressive histories.[1]

Hence (altogether apart from the question of the comparative dates of the particular writings) the New Testament rightly begins with the Gospels. They are the foundation of the Epistles. A firm grasp of the history is the first essential of all sound Christian learning.

Yet this is not to be understood as if the facts did or could first of all rise into view as mere dry facts, afterwards to be invested with doctrinal interest and importance. It was not so in the Old Testament. It could not be so in the New Testament. The Epistles may open out further what is implied in the history, and what results from it; but the Christian story is already doctrinal at its very first proposal, and all Christian knowledge of it includes elements of doctrine as to what the facts mean, and how they are related. Those facts are from the first luminous, the

[1] Note C.

counsel of God coming to light through them, and through the divine words which accompany them. The Gospels are already all alive with doctrine before you come to the Epistles.

The Gospels were committed to writing, of course, at a time when the great facts of the Christian history had been accomplished, and the faith of them delivered to the Church, which was already walking in this light. The evangelists write as fully conscious of the meaning with which the facts were pregnant; and they speak so as to guide the readers on these points in cases where they might be in danger of being misled. At the same time, we have in their pages a selection of passages from the history, so told that we can see the impression produced by the events, while they were falling out, upon the minds of those with whom God was especially dealing. We mark how they were made to feel that the power of God was in movement, that the promises were hastening to fulfilment, and that the kingdom of God was at hand. We mark especially our Lord Jesus coming on the scene, and engaging in a ministry, in the course of which, in addition to most significant works, continual instruction was going on. Yet we see clearly that there were topics on which a certain reserve was used. Until the things concerning our Lord came to an end, there were topics on which much teaching could not be advantageously spent. And certainly, until then there seemed to be no recipiency for it. Solemn sayings, suggestive and weighty, with reference to coming events, seemed to be spoken in vain. They rather served the purpose of intimating that there were elements in the case which those about our Lord could little apprehend or estimate as yet, than of disclosing what these were. Thus, for example, it is clear that the essential truth as to our Lord's dignity had become certain to the minds of the apostles. But as to the manner in which His history should proceed to bring about the fulfilment of the promises, viz. by a dark and shameful death, their minds remained obstinately non-recipient; and behind that fact, which they would not open their minds to credit, how much of doctrine lay unreceived! Indeed, one cannot escape the impression that the apostles, for a time, were even less recipient of some of the truths bearing on these points, than many of their predecessors under the later portions of the Old Testament economy. They were held, as it were, and fascinated by the power of influence, by the fulness of light pouring on them from the living Lord; and they had no eyes or ears for what seemed strangely incongruous to all their thoughts of Him. The essential thing was, that the history, *as it fell out*, should lay hold of their minds, mould their thoughts and their impressions, and become a means of teaching, and a foundation for it, which nothing else could be.[1]

And so, when in their turn they become instructors, we find them intensely occupied (*e.g.* in the teaching recorded in the Acts) with calling first for the recognition of the Christian facts, along with the most simple elements of truth as to their meaning. That God had sent His Son for us, that it was He who was crucified in weakness, that God had raised Him

[1] Note D.

up, that the Spirit was now given, that repentance and forgiveness of sins were preached through Christ's name, and given for His sake, and that He should come again: these were the first points. Through these, men were led on to all that this history was fitted to disclose,—who this Son was,—in what sense He was the Son,—how forgiveness was His to bestow, and so on.

But in the Epistles especially, among other ends which are provided for, the manner in which the Christian faith is to be understood, and is to be made use of and applied by believing men, is variously explained. It has been remarked that the grand outlines of the New Testament Christian doctrine are already evident in the Gospels. And it might have been remarked, that already the Gospels throw back on the Old Testament a flood of light, under which, if not an increased significance, yet a very increased *explicitness* of significance, begins to attach to every page of it. But the Epistles make the great advance in this line. They add to the fulness of our doctrinal knowledge by their own statements. But besides that, they give us keys that unlock many chambers of deeper meaning in the Old Testament and in the Gospel history. In delivering their own Christian teaching, they instruct us at the same time how the whole history of redemption bears, and should be brought to bear, on this department, and how the mind of the great Prophet through all the Scriptures is to be gathered for the guidance of our thoughts. The person and work of Christ, the state and powers of man, the gracious counsel of Father, Son, and Holy

Ghost, the application of redemption, the means of grace, the ultimate issues of all, are set by them, not only in the light of their own statements, but in the collective light of all the Scriptures.

Some further considerations as to the manner in which this is done shall be added immediately. But I detain you for a moment to dwell on this as manifest fact, that a leading object in the Epistles especially is to deliver to us, and to teach us to apply, principles of truth for the regulation of our thoughts and of our actions through them. This is to be noticed the more, that it has sometimes been denied and obscured. The Epistles differ extremely in tone and character. Some of them expatiate on the development of doctrinal theses; others deal with practical interests or with Christian experience, seemingly, at times, in a fragmentary or desultory way. But of both classes the assertion now made holds. It is not merely that the writers take occasion to declare great truths. But they expect their readers to follow and sympathize with them in the freest and most various applications of those truths, in reasonings with them of every conceivable kind. They are not content to propound oracles to be listened to, as to faith, as to practice. But, as if feeling that the time was short, and the limits narrow, and the work of training the Church to the responsibilities that lay before her great, they are never weary of arguing, proving, deducing, corroborating, illustrating. The Galatians go wrong on a point of practice connected with an outward rite. It is an error symptomatic of grave perversions of the inner life; yet it is of a kind that might seem to require to be settled by definite prescription as to the outward thing. The apostle is not content to settle it so. 'O foolish Galatians, who hath bewitched you, that ye should not obey the truth?' The meaning of Christ's crucifixion, the principles that regulate the gift of the Holy Spirit, the way in which Abraham was justified, the relation between law and promise in the Old Testament, the difference between the dispensation that had not and the dispensation that had the unveiled grace of adoption,—all these must hasten together to set them right—all these should have prevented the error—all shall be drawn on now to remedy it. The Corinthians have a practical question about women's rights. The apostle could have settled it with a sentence; he settles it with a catena of principles from the very source: he would have them understand that the head of every man is Christ, and the head of the woman is the man, but the head of Christ is God. Meekness is to be pressed on the Philippians; the doctrine of the incarnation is called in to enforce it. The instances are innumerable, and I need not name more of this kind; but, in the Epistles which are more especially devoted to some set theme, every one knows how, instead of delivering a mere lesson, the writers ply an eager dialectic to compel their readers to plunge into the great connections of truth. They would have us labour to discern the bearings of that which is delivered on every side, not merely passively receive the utterances of an oracle, or gaze awe-struck, as the idolater at a fetish.

All this is congruous to the idea or position, that the Church is now, under the New Testament, as she never was before, delivered to a mould of doctrine. To understand and apply revealed principles, related to one another, and fruitful of applications and results in their bearing on cases which may arise, is a great part of the believer's duty, and a great element in his exercise and trial. It may still be true—it is—that there is the greatest reason for maintaining a lowly spirit in receiving God's revelations—yielding ourselves to be formed to the reception of that which it pleases God to reveal. It may be true also—certainly it is—that God's thoughts go unspeakably beyond ours; so that he who knows most knows but in part, and he knows best who feels most fully how little he can measure the counsels of God. Yet it remains true that we are now more eminently called to some fellowship with God's mind as well as with His will: we are called to know—to understand—in our measure. A leading object of revelation is, that those who receive it may enter into possession of intelligible principles of truth, so as to use and apply them in a manner conformed to their genuine sense.

But while the New Testament involves or comprehends a disclosure of principles into which it expects us to enter, and which it teaches us vigorously and watchfully to apply, yet certainly it does not present them as they are presented in creeds, or systems, or theological deliverances. That is to say, we do not find the New Testament dealing strictly and only with the question, What can be delivered to knowledge? and, How can it be measured by strict and instant definition? and, How concatenated, so that the intellect may have open passages scientifically cleared and measured from part to part, and from position to position? Not so. The New Testament has (in its narrow bounds) a great deal more to do than that.[1] And in its own peculiar method, it does a great deal more for theology, and for other weighty human interests as well, than it would have done had any such method as has now been suggested been in point of fact pursued.

It is a revelation of a great world of principles indeed, but not of principles only,—of persons, facts, forces. With that world we are already connected, are so in the very roots of our being, yet in a dark, dull, perverse manner. Partly, then, the object is to revive the lost or the decaying knowledge and sensibilities; partly to set before us the nature of the relations into which we have fallen unawares; partly to reveal to us the nature and effects of new interpositions, further explained on one side by their adaptation to experimental wants, further explained on the other by effects that are to follow from them. Then, even in so far as this involves revelation in the strictest sense, it is revelation that is not to open its meaning to mere intellect (if, indeed, there be any source of knowledge that does or can do so); no — but to feeling and to practice; to sorrow and to shame; to love, and to gladness, and to hope that goes thrilling into the ages to come; also to watchfulness, and to effort, and to conflict. It is such a great practical world which is revealed to us, not merely that it may be known, but that it may come in on us, under the influence of a great Agent, as a universal moving force, teaching, striving, quickening, strength-

[1] Note E.

ening, and so forth; and the revelation is adapted to all these ends. Therefore, so far as speech can do it, it is not scientific theory about the thing, but the various many-sided vitality of the thing itself, that strikes out upon us from the page of Scripture, soliciting and operating on every capability of our human nature.

It belongs to this object of the New Testament writers, as we find, that they should occasionally select some doctrinal thesis for more set and continuous discussion. But even when they do, what we find embodied in their treatment of the theme is something very different from a syllabus of dogmas, or even a theological exposition of the ideas that are taken in hand and constitute the writer's immediate subject. The most elaborate treatment of a connected theme, or set of themes, is probably that contained in the earlier chapters of the Epistle to the Romans. The apostle takes a plan or order of thought, the dialectical advantages of which are obvious on ordinary principles, and he advances by steps which such principles explain. But the material which fills his outline conforms to the common character of all the New Testament writings. It is in the first place more than doctrine, glowing as it does with an enthusiasm, and appealing for a response, in which doctrine fuses itself with other elements. But in so far as it is doctrinal,—and that is its leading character,—it is doctrine administered and delivered in a peculiar and, I will say, a divine method.

The peculiarity observable even in such passages is doubtless partly explained by this, that the writer is dealing, first of all, with the case and wants of the particular society to which he writes; and therefore what he dwells on and what he omits, his allusions and illustrations, the objections he supposes and the authorities he appeals to, are regulated in a measure by the case immediately before him. But this obvious condition explains only the more superficial characters of the phenomenon. It is more in point to say, that the apostle, in the spirit of his Master, discerns in a quite peculiar manner what the case *is* which is before him, what the condition of the audience he addresses. He views it in a direct light of truth, and sees into the roots of it, where its peculiarities spring out of permanent conditions of human nature. Hence, also, his treatment of it has permanent interest and value.

But then, in providing for the case, in administering to the wants, what source does the apostle draw from, and how does he proceed? Here I raise no debate as to the state of mind in which the inspired man should be conceived to be, or how far his insight extends. I neither know nor care. It is enough for me, that, speaking in the Spirit, he speaks out of the fulness of a supreme insight and a supreme wisdom. These are the resources, which, through whatever experiences and workings of his own mind, conscious or unconscious, are translated into the effects with which we deal. And when I ask again, What sources do the New Testament writers draw from, and in what method do they proceed?—I reply, Let those say who have felt how these writers, as from the centre of some bright world, of which they are a part, and which they perfectly behold, speak out to us, approaching from the outside and from below, apprehending feebly what they deliver so certainly and so fitly.[1]

Let us suppose that I have some experiences to go through, and that, in order to go through them successfully, an acquaintance is needed with the principles and applications of some science, some body of truth complex and far-reaching, involving abstract principles and concrete applications that branch out in all directions. Let me suppose that I have only the most vague and dim notions of this whole department of knowledge. Let me suppose that one who is a master of all science, and of this science, takes me in hand to meet this pressing difficulty. He says to me, Do not give way to bewilderment. I cannot make you in an hour or two a master of this science; yet, if you will attend to me, I will give you enough of what you need to know, to guide you through what lies before you, intelligently, advantageously, safely. So he begins, keeping always in view my practical exigency, my stage of knowledge, my degree of capacity, and measuring and proportioning his statements by this point of view. He tells me the facts and the processes, the forces and the conditions, with which I shall have to deal. That I may deal with them intelligently, he explains them as he goes, drawing forth principles, so far as I can take them in, so far as they are required with a view to my experiences. He does not always confine himself to what is barely necessary for the bare practical exigency. Partly because he respects my desire to understand, partly because gratified intellectual in-

[1] Note F.

terest fixes knowledge by illuminating and connecting it, he goes here and there a little further out into theory, and shows me lines of principles stretching away into regions which cannot for the present be explained. All through he dexterously adapts whatever he says to my actual state : he dovetails his instruction into my actual mental conditions; he links what he brings to what he knows me to have beforehand; familiar experiences of mine become analogies to illustrate, and fixed points by which to hold, the new knowledge; familiar applications are suggested, experiments that I might make, whereby to see with my eyes how the forces work. The lesson is a marvel of adaptive skill, and at the end he repeats : Now attend to what I have said, and it will take you safely through. But all these things which he has said, as he says them, are part of a complete world of ordered thought that dwells within him,—a knowledge not fragmentary, but complete. And even in his concrete illustrations, his condescensions to my ignorance, in his very phrasing of them, there are shades, and accuracies, and nice distinctions, that would be very significant, to one who knew a little more than I, how the operation of various principles that concur and limit one another is full before his mind, and is provided for in his speech. He is fetching out of the great array of ordered truth at his disposal, this here, and that there, which my exigency requires, and putting it in shapes that adapt it to me; yet so that the harmony and perspicuity of the rounded truth is nowhere really violated. For me, meanwhile, it is well if my provisional and imperfect perceptions so keep the tracks laid down for them, that I truly hold the facts and guiding notes delivered, and that I enter genuinely into the glimpses of science given me, so as to have my practice illuminated and made intelligent, and to have the spirit of research awakened for the days to come. Not very different from the case supposed is the case we have before us. For if our knowledge is not quite so hasty, and not quite so fragmentary, and not quite so provisional and occasional, as the illustration supposes, yet how far, on the other side, does His supreme insight, who is our teacher, rise above the measure of all masters of earthly knowledge! So, then, the apostles, speaking in the spirit of their Master, draw from a knowledge that is not in part, so much as shall serve the occasions of the life of faith for a few hundred or a few thousand years. They aim not at one department of the man only, but rather at the whole mood of mind that ought to be cherished, and the whole working of the man that ought to be set agoing. Into these dogma enters as an element, sometimes as the leading and prevailing element, but not as the only one. And then, it is generally not a single dogma singly analyzed and extricated, but a certain complex of beliefs in their mutual connection and influence, that is presented and inculcated. Resting on the facts of the divine history of redemption, they fetch down principles from above, as it were, the full bearings and relations of which are apparent to them, or are apparent to the Spirit in whom they speak; and they show to us some of these relations and bearings. They bring them to bear in the manner of direct insight. They do not speak like men following out patiently abstractions of their own minds, but like men who see the thing with their eyes; so that even their argumentative illustration is not in the way of painful analysis of thought, but is sudden, powerful, broken, hastening from point to point, as if some scene were rushing into view, and the connection of its parts not thought out, but seen. Hence, as in the case supposed, so in this, the sentences have a meaning so full and deep, that while the immediate intention for us is discernible, there is always room for further insight. Nor does this remark apply only to the mind of the author in his sentence. In the very utterance of it there is a pregnancy; not as of men paring down their words to the strictness of theory, but as of men filled with the complex greatness and fulness of the reality they see.

This supreme insight, with its direct effect on the utterance, characterizes all the Bible teaching. We also will utter our theology so when we are inspired—not till then in this world.

Now all this is brought to bear on the complex human being, as one alive, or that ought to be alive, through all his faculties, to the case presented. It is not the understanding alone that is dealt with, though the understanding is never neglected, and is sometimes the chief faculty called into play through long contexts. Still it is not the understanding alone. Every side of human nature that has an aspect towards the great elements of the divine economy is kept in view. The man with his conscience stirred, with his sense of relations towards God awakened, with his memory stored with the facts of a divine history, with his character moulded, and his mind furnished by the manifold experience of his own history,—the man drawn into sympathy with many past generations, that have been stirred, exercised, dealt with in the same way,—is beset by the Scripture teaching behind and before. And the doctrine (which is our present subject) is interpreted to him, not by symbols for the understanding only, nor in an order solely dictated by the exigencies of the understanding: it is interpreted to him through every aptitude that is supplied in all these complex conditions of his state.

In perfect harmony with the general method of administration, is the perfectly free and unrestrained manner in which language is employed. For the purpose of strict doctrinal disquisition, it is essential that words should be employed as much as possible in a uniform sense, determined by rigid definitions. It is not so with the New Testament writers. They make the freest use of the words of human speech, in any of the senses attaching to them, which serves the present purpose, and carries home the lesson that is in hand. These words have a certain meaning in each place in which they are employed; it is a sense fixed by the context, or by certain kinds of context and trains of thought. But the sense varies from context to context, according to the theme in hand or the object in view, so as to lay hold in the most direct and ready way of the practical human mind, in the variety of its practical conditions, and of its associations. Let it be considered in what various shades of sense such words occur as faith, law, love, sanctify,

G

and the like. Nay, the great name of God itself is not an exception: for He called them gods to whom the word of God came.

It is just because the manner of teaching is of this kind, that the Scriptures are on all necessary points clear; that while they exercise the intellect by various difficulties, their fundamental doctrines, and the general drift of their teaching, are apparent to honest and humble minds. Scripture conveys to such minds a satisfying sense of substantial and practical knowledge—knowledge of realities, and not of mere theory or abstraction. What men are to think about God, and Christ, and the Holy Spirit; on what principles God deals with them, and will have them deal with Him; what the results of the great history of redemption are; what men are to expect from God, and how they are to serve Him: on such points the Scriptures convey a teaching which is of no doubtful import to obedient minds. It is true, that, in following out the issues and relations of the various articles pertaining to it, questions arise which require further and more exact search, and necessitate discussions of various kinds. But on the great fundamental points, the manner of the Scripture teaching is fitted to bring about an instant appreciation of the meaning and bearing of a great system of substantial truth, and to supply, at the same time, means of further and more detailed determinations, in a degree which no other manner of teaching could accomplish.[1]

The occasional character of the Epistles has been appealed to, as proving that the New Testament was

[1] Note G.

never intended to be looked to as a complete or adequate rule of faith. These Epistles, connected with and adapted to the occasional wants of the early churches, are, it is urged, too thoroughly relative to that age to be suitable to meet the wants of all ages. But, in truth, it is this very feature or circumstance that secures the essential adaptation of the New Testament to its great office. Hence it comes that the teaching of principles takes the form of vivid practical illustration of the way in which they may be misunderstood, and the way in which they ought to be applied. I might urge—but I will not dwell upon it now—that the apostolic writers deal with the wants and dangers of the churches then existing with a peculiar insight, seeing deep into the very heart of them, so as to reach the common human ground of all analogous wants and dangers. Time fails for the illustration of this. It is enough to say, that, dealing with practical human nature, prepared in various different schools of prior training, and reacting in the freest way under the teaching and training of Christian revelation, the apostles find the occasion of just that administration of the truth which, first, helps us to ascertain its real meaning, by its declared tendencies and results ; and secondly, shows us how it is to take effect on human hearts, and lives, and societies, in all these bearing fruit unto God.[1]

We have seen, then, that the New Testament, following upon the Old, and completing it, delivers to us, along with all else that is required, a revelation of principles of truth, sufficient for the Church until the end

[1] Note H.

shall come. This is not delivered to us in a syllabus of dogmas. Such a syllabus must proceed by strict definition, and by single lines of connection, chosen in preference to others. The New Testament proceeds in another manner. It embodies a various and complex exhibition of the manner in which principles stand related to one another, to facts, interests, feelings, duty. In the Bible, as in creation, there is variety, seeming negligence, what may be called confusion. But there is real order; while the principles are brought out to us in the most familiar way, and by instances of the commonest kind.

Ere I close, let me vary the illustration of the points I have adduced, by putting them in another way.

Let it be supposed that the problem is to convey into men's minds an ample knowledge of principles of truth. Now the principles of divine truth are infinite. They rise from fathomless fountains, and go out to measureless issues. How can the right way of administering such truth, and of receiving it when administered, be ascertained? Would it not be well if some method could be selected which should regulate the measure and manner in which such truth is presented to us and unfolded? For, no doubt, there are regions of truth by us never yet entered; and, no doubt, every principle of truth with which we are acquainted has its outgoings where we cannot follow it.

Now the Scripture method subserves this end, and it does so in virtue of these two features in it.

The Christian doctrine rests upon and rises out of the Christian facts—the persons, the transactions, the events. These come before us in a purely historical way; and out of them, rising out of the history, comes the teaching: what we are to think of God, of man, of Christ; of that which He came to do and did; of the principles of truth that are honoured, illustrated, and made effectual by Him. So, also, all obligations and all hopes come before us as principles of truth flowing out of what man has shown himself to be, what God has done or is to do. Christian doctrine is the light that illuminates for us the transactions of a divine history, and the real persons, real powers, which in those transactions are made apparent. It rules the impressions we should form concerning the relations in which we stand, or may stand, with persons historically revealed, and events historically transacted.

The truths thus revealed are either simply manifested or exhibited, as, for instance, the nature of God; or they are truths established and generated, as it were, by the process of the divine history itself; as the redemption of sinners. But in the one case and the other alike, the grand distinction of the Christian revelation is, that the facts which lie at the foundation of *it* are the adequate and eternal embodiments of those truths, not imperfect and transient illustrations of them. They are, so to say, the native and appropriate expression of eternal principles as they bear on man's state and the earth's history, and in them God Himself rests. We are here, therefore, face to face with eternal realities and principles, passing into history. The doctrinal unfolding of the bearing of *these* facts and events is the direct unfolding of the unchanging truth. That we may understand such facts, that we may enter into them, and take up ground about them, explicit doctrinal statements are needed; and they are often of a very profound kind, demanding the most careful and earnest endeavours to apprehend it. And yet we do not lose ourselves in a world too vast for us. The fulness of divine truth is indeed infinite, and the range of divine principles of procedure goes beyond all compass of ours. Yet the doctrinal statements of Scripture are kept within bounds, so to say, by this, that they cleave to the facts of that divine history which has been transacted within the world. They are not, in general, orderly deductions from those first principles which would prove too high for us, but are directed to give us just views of the history. From these topics they do lead us out sometimes to heights where all thought reels, but evermore they lead us back to the facts. In the intelligence of them, all the teaching finds its proper end; in the holding, believing, and realizing of them, our hold of all the rest is verified, made real, human, and fruitful.

But, second, it is characteristic of Christian doctrine that it is delivered to be the light and guide of Christian life. It is not meant for mere gratification of speculative curiosity, or for rounding off a system. As it radiates from history—a divine history—so it is meant to pass over into another history, our own. In a word, it comes to illuminate and guide the life of renewed men. This does not imply that we are to measure our faith in the truth by our perception of its bearing on practice. It may well be that it has various bearings on practice, even in our own case, which our analysis is unable to detect or to assign. But the remark does imply that all our contemplations of truth should issue forth into faith, love, and obedience; and it does certainly afford us a guiding principle, illustrating the fitness of the method which the Scriptures pursue. Those truths and aspects of truth are brought before us which concern our faith and obedience, the due regulation of our thoughts, feelings, and actions. Our walking with God, and the reconciliation in which it begins, was meant to be lightsome; it was intended to involve the element of a mutual understanding. There is therefore a light of truth for us to appropriate and enjoy. But it is such as is fitted to direct practice, rather than abstract and speculative. We do indeed find heads of doctrine very exactly discussed. And this alone is sufficient to show that we are expected to use our utmost diligence to acquaint ourselves with the whole series of principles inculcated in the Scriptures, with their range and their connection. Yet, even in these cases, the discussion is so introduced, carried on, and applied, that we see the doctrine in all its branches bearing on life and experience; and by its bearing on these we find it interpreted and explained. It does not stand before us as an immutable formula; it moves, 'it has hands and feet;' we see whence it comes, and whither it goes. Now if it be so, that the method of Scripture limits and measures its communications, so as to give those truths which pass over into Christian life and worship, then be it noticed that this method ensures the exercise of the intellect (as well as other powers) far more profoundly than any other could. We are never allowed to take up mere forms of words, nor to sit gazing at abstract conceptions. Everywhere we are forced to enter livingly into the doctrine, so as to apprehend its relations to the vitalities of Christian life. If there *is* a limitation hence arising on the topics presented, there is anything rather than a limitation of the exercise of intelligence demanded, anything but a low rating of the importance of the results. A great field of duty, in the exercise of mind, is opened up, and room is made for endless progress, in having our conceptions brought to correspond more accurately and completely to the truth, as it is uttered to mind, heart, and conscience.

The complete Scriptures, then, exhibit the fulness of divine truth, as that is embodied and provided for in divine arrangements and transactions, and also as it is related to the variety of human experience, and the various modes and manifestations of the Christian life.

So we may say that the truth is set forth in the Scripture not statically, but dynamically; not in mere abstract conception, but as the rule of spiritual forces and the *rationale* of spiritual events.

This exposition was given forth in connection with the case of men and societies actually existing in the apostles' days. And so we find in the Scriptures not only an enumeration of articles of faith, but a directive exhibition of them, fitted, as nothing else could be, to give us a grasp of their true meaning, and to call out our interest in them.

With these views we may connect the fact that there is a distribution of doctrine among the inspired servants of God, so that we find ourselves, in some respects, in a different region as we pass from the writings of one to the writings of another. Words, phrases, doctrines, seem to assume a new turn, and to stand in new relations. This is very intelligible, if we remember that the divine fulness of the truth bears on human beings and their experience in ways that are very various. It is not a diversity in the being of truth that here appears, but a diversity in the manner of its going. The apostles, with a perfect harmony in the one truth, evolve, each as it was given to him, the bearings of what God is, and what He has done, on the diverse aspects of human existence, of Christian experience, privilege, and conflict. They were directed to do it, so as to complete among them the manifestation not only of truth, but of its applications, which men should require. They do it with incomparable freedom, fulness, power, and wealth of knowledge, with a certainty and explicitness of utterance which are due to the Spirit that spake by them; so that, however perfect the inner harmony between them may be, it is very far removed from mere outward mechanical harmonizing. We apprehend it partially, laboriously, gradually; not without the mixture of error, prejudice, and manifold imperfections. But we shall find that pregnant revelation ever fresh and adequate, able to guide the men of God at all new stages of the Church's history, until the very end shall come.

LECTURE IV

ON THE FUNCTION OF THE CHRISTIAN MIND WITH REFERENCE TO DOCTRINE.

FROM the topic of doctrine as it is delivered in the Scriptures, I pass now to that of doctrine as it is held and uttered by the believer. In passing to this topic, we shall do well to remember that the proper organ supposed to be engaged in searching the Scriptures, with a view to receive their teaching, is not merely the human intellect with its ordinary capacities, but the man, or the Church, considered as under the guidance of the Holy Spirit. The Holy Spirit is promised to enable us to deal aright with Scripture teaching;[1] and therefore His grace is a real condition of success, and an attainable aid towards it. In contemplating the form of human activity which concerns itself about doctrine, and the conditions under which that activity is exercised, we are to take it along with us, that the kind of success which we are encouraged to expect is promised to the spiritual man, and not to any other.

Doctrine, as it is set forth by the believer, is not in all respects the very same thing with doctrine as it is delivered in the Scriptures. This may be argued from the controversies that have arisen between those

[1] 1 John ii. 20, 27.

who agreed in regarding the teaching of the Scriptures as authoritative. But it appears more plainly from the mere survey of any of the forms of doctrinal statement put forth by Christian men or churches. These do, indeed, refer themselves to Divine Revelation as their source and authority; yet they are all visibly distinguishable from that Revelation, and stand at its bar to be judged. The case then stands thus: It is the part of the believer to receive as fully as may be the effect of that Scripture teaching, the character of which has in the last two Lectures been imperfectly described. This teaching, passing into his mind, takes shape there. As a matter of fact, we find that one of the results hence arising is the formation of doctrinal views and utterances. The believer is found sorting out and collecting what he judges to be truth, on points with respect to which the Scriptures, as he believes, have been teaching him. The statement of these conclusions is doctrine, in the sense in which it is now to occupy our attention. Doctrines, therefore, for our present purpose, are determinations of what men are led to hold to be true on the authority of Revelation. I say determinations, meaning to indicate that what claims the character of doctrine must have some clearness and precision. It must mark off what we mean from what we do not mean. Vague and dumb impressions existing in the mind are an extremely real and powerful element in human life. Such impressions form a part, and are far from being an inconsiderable or unimportant part, of the total effect due to divine revelation as it works in the world. They do not, however, come into consideration formally under the head of doctrine, although they may be all entitled to regard when we consider the conditions under which doctrine is moulded and developed.[1]

But in the sense now indicated, the right of doctrine to exist at all, or to claim an important place in the sphere of religious life, may be questioned. It may be said, Since we already have the teaching of the Scriptures,—teaching expressed in familiar human speech, yet incomparable and divine,—what are we to think of this new form of things, this 'doctrine,' in the sense and form in which it now comes into view? By what warrant or necessity does it arise? Why should we not be found, all of us, adhering merely to those words, and phrases, and sentences, and contexts, in which we profess to have the things most surely believed among us, declared by men who spoke as the Spirit gave them utterance? Whence only this activity which arrives at doctrines in the sense just explained?

In answer to this question, one might be tempted to plead the rights of science. Wherever there is knowledge, it may be argued, there is room for a science to sift and arrange it, to show its warrants, and estimate the degree of evidence of its various details, and trace its pervading principles. There is therefore room for science in the department of knowledge into which Scripture leads. Theology is a science, and doctrines and systems are its results. The scientific activity is as valid here as anywhere; the service of science is a tribute due to Christian

[1] Note A.

truth, and Christian doctrine is a department of science. I mention this, for the purpose of saying that it is not on this view that I am disposed to rely. I admit, indeed, that Christian knowledge, in all its degrees and stages, has a relation to science which it cannot and need not disclaim. For science is nothing else than the most strict, just, and thorough knowledge of things, according to their proper evidence, principles, and laws, which each department is found to exhibit. And all knowledge ultimately is amenable to those laws to which science is amenable, and which science studies most perfectly to obey. However, I do not think that it is the scientific interest which primarily calls out Christian doctrine; nor is it an obligation to comply with the formal conditions of science, which this activity properly obeys; nor do I think that the scientific impulse has been, historically, the creative force in this department. The results of this activity, as I believe, lend themselves to scientific treatment; how they do so we may afterwards consider. But I think it more fitting to approach the subject by an humbler avenue, viz. by considering what is involved in earnest dealing with the element of teaching in the Scripture, considered simply as so much teaching which it is binding on us to receive, and which ought to be dealt with in a manner corresponding to its own nature and genius.

For the illustration of this point, let me abstract from history so far as to suppose the case of a single mind dealing alone with Scripture teaching. In point of fact, the experience of believers is not solitary, but social; and great importance attaches to the manner in which they come to an understanding with one another, and influence one another, in this matter as in others. However, those elements in the case which come into view when the Church is considered collectively, may have their place afterwards. The hypothetical case of a single disciple is better to begin with.

In the Scriptures, then, such a disciple has the teaching which has been described. He may in one degree or another take up the meaning of it, and receive the impressions it is fitted to make. Its great array of lessons may gain upon him from day to day. He may feel himself standing before the great Teacher, or before His servants, hearkening to the teaching which they utter, sometimes perceiving a clear meaning, sometimes failing to catch the meaning, sometimes with a mixed consciousness of perception and failure. Amplify this sort of experience as much as you choose, and you will have, after all, but one aspect of the case. So far, he is mainly passive. But he cannot be allowed to be only passive. He has his own history to accomplish, inwardly and outwardly, —considering, choosing, acting. And the Revelation with which he deals, as was remarked in a previous Lecture, will not let him be only passive. It solicits, awakes, exhorts him; by influences which seize him on every side, it sets him in motion. He is called out to deal with this world of life and light, to take possession of it, to give effect to it. If it acts upon him, it is to the effect of leading him to react. Among the other faculties of the man, those which deal with truth are called out. And they are called into an exercise which is not merely recipient, but interrogative, investigative, positive.

Called out thus to deal with the meaning of the Divine Revelation, the disciple must deal with the various elements which it combines. There is what it recounts historically, there is what it would have him think doctrinally, there is what it would have him feel experimentally, there is what it would have him become and do practically. We have seen in what a remarkable and energetic combination these elements are presented in Scripture, each interpreting, each reinforcing the other. Even such a combination in the result, in human souls, is no doubt the last end aimed at by Him who brings this manifold influence to bear on men. The Bible was never intended to be treated as only a repository of materials out of which to make doctrines. The total effect due to the Divine Revelation (supposing the influence of the Holy Spirit to be present) is the illuminated life—is the quickened and purified man—is the harmonized and hallowed Church; or rather, it is the ideal towards which these tend, but which they never reach in this world. That is the end. But the endeavour to enter into possession of the Revelation is the way. In that endeavour we must deal with its various elements distinctly; we must ponder them one by one, that we may combine them in the end; we cannot grasp them all at once, so as to gauge the full significance of each. And so there comes into distinct consideration: How the Scriptures will have me think, as well as how they will have me feel or act. If I omit any leading element, or if I forget the great living combination in which all the elements should go forth again, so much the worse for me. Meanwhile it is a great part of the disciple's business to make sure of what the Scripture teaches. It is all the more important if the Divine Revelation be so eminently a revelation of truths and principles as it was maintained to be in the preceding Lecture.

Now, let this be observed: In any earnest effort to take in and appropriate the teaching of some one wiser than ourselves, one of the first steps we take is to put the meaning, as we understand it, into our own words. We put it into words of our own, and we bring the statement to the teacher, or to the book, if it be a book, for comparison. 'You teach this, as it appears to me;—is it so?' This putting of it in our own words belongs to the process of putting the meaning which we have perceived into relation with the habits of our own thought, and with the materials, the contents of our own minds. It is our way of taking possession of it, and making it our own. When we have so done, then we engage in scrutinies and comparisons, with a view to make sure that the meaning, thus re-embodied, is the same that was delivered—the same, or a part of it, at any rate, if not the whole.

If, now, the matter be a matter in which the ideas are simple and capable of instant and complete definition,—if, for instance, the axioms and the elementary propositions of mathematics be the subject of instruction, then we may speedily make sure of the whole meaning conveyed by the teacher's words. Though he is wiser than we, we have possession of *these* propositions as completely as he has himself. Moreover, we discern the perfect fitness of his words and sentences to measure out exactly so much meaning and no more. We therefore dismiss our own less perfect expressions, and adopt his, because we have thoroughly made them ours. The meaning and the expressions are both alike thoroughly appropriated, and the perfect fitness of the one to the other is ascertained. Our meaning is exactly equal to the teacher's meaning; and the words are the fittest of all to measure out that very meaning, whether as his or as ours, to all whom it may concern. They are especially fitted to record it to our own memory, and keep it clear to our own understanding. Henceforth, therefore, we rest in them.

But it is not necessarily so, if the teaching be of such a kind that the sense of the terms has to be collected from a usage, various and impressive, associated with many feelings and experiences, and from a long historical development; and if the teaching, touching many points which are wonderfully related together, interprets itself, not to one single category of the understanding alone, but to the whole man, and makes many of its approaches through the experience, and conscience, and heart. In short, the case is altered if the teaching be such as the Scripture presents to us. In this case, indeed, I am pressed by far more powerful motives than in the other, to give to myself strict and full account of the various elements of the world of truth which is to form a part of me, and of which I am to form a part. Also the teaching may possess me, instantly, with a clear impression of some leading truths, not as yet perhaps all sharply defined, but already filling my mind with their meaning, and operating within me. And I may already see the general direction of many a path of contemplation which opens out before me. But yet, when I proceed to put into my own words the meaning I can gather, I find myself otherwise situated than in the case supposed before.

For, first of all (granted that I am enabled to avoid error in the process), this meaning of mine, which I express in words of my own, is not equal to my Teacher's meaning, expressed in His words on the same point. It is a part of His meaning. It is, possibly, for me the essential part. It makes me participant with Him in His truth, not only in a measure, but in such a measure that I have solid footing in it henceforward. Yet my meaning, expressed in the way which most naturally measures out my thought for me, differs, at all events, by defect from His meaning, set forth in His words, in the way suitable for Him. Therefore I cannot take His words as the mere exact determination of my meaning. There is no such equation established between what I have learned on the one hand, and my Teacher's words on the other, as existed in the former case.

Moreover, in His words, commonly, the teaching appears implicated, more or less, with its significance for feeling, and life, and worship. In which more complete form I also probably should habitually present it if I were inspired, or if in me the unity of an enlightened understanding, and a sanctified heart, and a will at one with all goodness, were finally attained.

But as it is, I have to make my way into it, by realizing the separate elements of the case. I have to isolate and make sure of the exact fact, or relation, or principle to be believed for truth; and for the purpose of doing this, and presenting to myself what I seem to have learned on this side, I must select words which enable my mind to mark how it is taught to think, as well as how it is taught to feel or act. I am not to forget the great living combination into which they all should go forth again; if I do, the loss shall be sore indeed. Meanwhile it is a great part of my business to know well what the Scripture teaches. It is all the more so, if the revelation be indeed so eminently a revelation of truths and principles, as it was maintained to be in last Lecture.

Still further, the whole of truth on any point which the Scriptures give, they give not always in complete single statements; but in various statements which explain, and guard, and complete one another. Now, to settle what I have gained, I must gather up and present to myself the joint effect of the statements, so far as I have understood them. But this must be done by summing up that understanding of mine in words fitted to express it.

And this is all the more inevitable, for the following additional reason. In trying to penetrate into the meaning of the Scripture teaching, and to make sure of what it is, it has proved practically impossible to do otherwise than raise points, and questions about points, which serve as ladders or stepping-stones to climb up by, or waymarks where the paths divide. They are points about which Scripture has doctrine to teach; but it is not so taught that it can be disentangled and made sure of without difficulty; neither can it be easily ascertained and explained by us, unless we use for the purpose ideas suggested not so much by the direct teaching of Scripture, as by the necessities, or possibly the infirmities, of our own understanding. For example, the Scripture has very little to say, hardly anything, directly, about any such idea as that of 'person' or 'personality.' It is doubtful whether the Bible has any word that precisely expresses that conception. It teaches in a way so concrete and historical, that the doctrine is virtually given without the aid of any such abstraction. But we find it needful at a certain point to raise questions about divine persons, about the person of our Lord Jesus. We find immediately, that for our purpose it is an imperfect and provisional conception which is furnished to us by that word. We are obliged carefully to remember, that it is only with certain precautions, and deductions from, or qualifications of, its ordinary sense that we use it. Still, if we are to fix the sense in which we are to take many a Scripture teaching, we find that we must help ourselves by this conception, and raise alternatives about it between which we must choose, *e.g.* as to Godhead—as to our Lord's person. But in doing so, of course, we resign ourselves to express a meaning which we have gathered from the Scriptures, as *our* conclusion, to be measured forth and expressed in *our* words.

It does not follow, from what has now been said, that we are excluded from the use of the very words of Scripture for the purpose of determining and expressing the convictions which Scripture teaching may have produced within us. I may prefer to utter the doctrine which I hold in some sentence of the Scripture, which appears to me to declare adequately and precisely just what I mean to say. I may feel persuaded that the result of all my investigations is, simply, that I attach a more just and full sense to this sentence, and can now utter it, in its intended meaning, as my own faith. In expressing a doctrinal conviction so, I have the advantage of using words which are authoritative, and which are fragrant also with the associations that cleave to Scripture speech. This is true; although it is also true, that the use, on occasion, of other words, is suitable, not merely for the purpose of coming to an understanding with other minds, but in order to come to an understanding with my own mind. However, when the very words of some sentence of the Scripture are used by me, for the precise purpose of measuring and setting forth my conviction, they assume a new relation. Their sense now, and for this precise purpose, is measured by the definitions which I attach to them. These definitions, of course, I profess to be able to vindicate as just and accurate.

The tendency of these observations is to fix in our minds this view, viz. that doctrines, as they come into consideration in this Lecture, are the effect on believing minds due to one great element in Divine Revelation, separately considered and attended to. As held and uttered by the believer and the Church, doctrine is formally human. It is the human echo to the divine voice. It is the human response to the divine message. It is the human confession of the divine gift. It is our holding up as ours the truth, made ours, which the Father of Lights delivered to us as His. True, in the case of all doctrine justly gathered, and especially in the case of the great leading doctrines, the distinction is mainly formal. Still it is better to recognise it clearly.

The meaning of the Scripture teaching, as it delivers the doctrine that is according to godliness, is what God meant, what the inspired man meant, or the Spirit in which he spake. The meaning of the doctrine, as we confess it, is what we mean, what men mean, what the Church means. Therefore, when we inquire into the sense of the teaching as delivered by God, we search the Scripture (using all appropriate human aids) that we may more justly understand it. But when we inquire into the sense of the teaching as it is a doctrine believed in the world, we go into the field of historical theology, that we may more exactly determine what has been intended by believers and the Church in their successive utterances.

This distinction is in its own nature pervading. But in following the series of doctrines, we shall find it sometimes, for practical purposes, so nearly vanishing, that it would be little better than pedantry to refer to it; sometimes becoming so obvious as to be of great importance. As to the main articles of the Scripture message, the unambiguous statements of Holy Writ make their impression on the mind, at least on the humble and prayerful mind, so clearly, that the believer's thought and utterance about them is, and continues to be, a mere reduplication on what Scripture has said already. Round about those articles, no doubt, points arise with respect to which difficulty may be felt, and the peculiar human process becomes very sensible. But as to the main things themselves, the identity might seem to be perfect between the Scripture utterance and the believer's utterance. What more needless, it may be said, than to run any fine distinction between the unity of God as taught in the Scriptures, and as confessed by the believer? So, also, in spite of all the contradiction to which, unhappily, it has been exposed, the doctrine that the Lord Jesus is true God is merely a reiteration of statements to the same precise effect, *e.g.* in the fourth Gospel. It is of very great importance to remark this: for the fact that the distinction becomes so little obvious in regard to these points, is closely connected with the character of the Scriptures as a clear and sufficient rule of faith. At the same time, even on such points the distinction does not wholly vanish. The sense in which God is one (not *e.g.* the Mohammedan sense) has its own mystery, which we recall when we confess the Christian doctrine. And when we call Jesus God, we may well feel our incompetency to fill that great name with its just meaning. But when we try to give account to ourselves as to what exactly we believe on points more detailed and complex,—on points where the precise form of teaching must be determined by the comparison of the sense of many passages which throw light upon one another, —then we become more vividly conscious of the distinction which has been stated.

Yet it need hardly be said that the distinction

asserted implies no antagonism. The very object of the Scriptures as a revelation is to bring us to a fellowship with God in the truth. And therefore the meaning of the believer, as it is expressed in the forms by which he utters his belief, may and ought to agree with the meaning of the teaching which comes to him from on high. We cannot say that it always does, but it may and ought. His doctrine may be below the range and fulness of the Scripture meaning: it may represent one great element, severed and set apart, which in Scripture comes wedded to other elements dependent on it, and on which it depends. It may, in many of its features, bear token of the painful process by which we climb our arduous way, discarding one misleading alternative after another, analyzing, sifting, balancing, comparing, ere we come to rest in a final determination. For all that, it may, in its several articles, be the result legitimately due to the teaching received. It may express a participation in, and a possession of, the truth delivered,—'the truth which dwelleth in us, and shall be with us for ever.'

In point of fact, Scripture speaks of an assurance and certainty of knowledge as arising to believers, especially if they are duly profiting by the means of grace and by the unction of the Holy One.[1] And the measure of agreement among all the churches in which the teaching is drawn from the open Bible as the sole authoritative source of knowledge, is experimental proof to the same effect. It proves the Scripture to be so constructed as to make its main meaning clear to docile and diligent men.

[1] 1 John ii. 27.

It may be said, perhaps, that the distinction laid down between the doctrine as delivered and the doctrine as confessed rests on a confusion of thought. Such a distinction there is, it may be said, between doctrine as held and confessed by us, and the absolute truth as it dwells in the divine mind. But the absolute truth as it dwells in the divine mind is not here in question, but truth as dispensed, and therefore admeasured, in Revelation. We are here considering truth as it has been proposed in forms of human thought and feeling, clothed in human words, dwelling in the minds of human messengers, and bodied forth from their lips and pen. These human forms of thought and speech have been made use of with the utmost condescension, freedom, and plainness. Hence the truth bodied forth should not be represented as hanging over our heads, out of reach, but as conversant among us, standing on the level of our own minds. There is no reason, therefore, it may be said, why there should not be a full equation between the truth delivered and the truth received, at least on many points. There is no reason why the truth in the believer's mind, expressed in his doctrinal conclusions, should not be so fully identical with the truth set forth in Scripture as to deprive the distinction of all significance and use. Between the truth as it may exist in the believer's mind and as it exists in the divine mind, there is indeed a wide gap. But the precise thing which revelation has done, is to come across that gap, and speak wholly in the words of men. What is thus brought, may be wholly received. And, therefore, just as there is no need for making, and no propriety in making, a distinction between the meaning or sense of two believers who confess the same doctrine after full explanations with one another, though there may be shades of individuality in the manner of conceiving of each of them, so also there is no ground for asserting that what we confess is in thought to be held apart, as distinct from that which God has delivered by His messengers.

It is quite true that truth as it is in the divine mind is one thing, and truth as it is in Revelation is another. It may be admitted, that whatever is embodied in the forms of human thought and feeling, *i.e.* in human words, is intrinsically capable of being apprehended by human minds, although it should be remembered that many human words (such, for example, as the word God itself) designate things of which we have a knowledge that is imperfect, often most imperfect; and therefore those words, incapable of perfect definition, bring us into the presence of mystery as often as they are used. But that is not the main thing to be attended to. What is maintained is, that the use of human words, of forms of human thought and feeling, in the Scriptures, is such that the teaching, while in its own nature attainable, or commensurate with human faculties (for this is implied in Revelation), is never in point of fact fully attained. The attainment of the Church remains always below it.

This could not be asserted if the teaching of Scripture were to be regarded as only a lofty utterance of the experience, the views and feelings of believing men; if inspiration were nothing more than a powerful influence of the same kind with that which operates in every believer. In that case, there could be no reason for believing that the sense cannot be completely apprehended by some in every age. In point of fact, as is now more fully recognised than it used to be, it was generally through a powerful experience of truth that the inspired writers were fitted to declare it; and it is in the line of uttering what they arrived at by human tracks of thought and feeling that they teach us. But in this, and beyond it, there is a higher form of influence: it both formed the experience and guided the utterance; and it constitutes the Scriptures a divine revelation. The effect of this influence is, to charge the words with a weight and compass of meaning only to be perfectly apprehended when we have perfectly entered into the spirit of the Scriptures; or, to express it otherwise, the forms of human thought and feeling—capable only of carrying a measure of divine truth—have been used with a supreme wisdom and grace, so that their measure of communication still outgoes our measure of attainment and receptivity, and leaves us 'searching.'

This is best brought into view by considering the case of the Lord Jesus Christ. His words were human words, and indeed of the plainest; and the meaning they carried was such as existed in His mind in the form of human thought. However, it was human thought of such an order, and so related to eternal truth, and the words employed were chosen with so supreme dominion over the resources of expression, that while the history of His Church has been all along a history of human minds entering into

His mind, it remains that there is a contrast between the plenitude of His utterance and the measure of our insight. None of us has as yet entered into the full meaning genuinely intended and uttered, in so much as the one sentence : 'Blessed are the poor in spirit, for theirs is the kingdom of heaven.' But the distinction applies, not so much to the sense of single sentences, as to the sense of the whole teaching, in the complex relation to one another of its various parts and utterances.

What is asserted is, that while all believers enter into the expressed mind of Christ, so that they are in real and essential agreement with Him; and while, also, amid all varieties of attainment, their actual, or at least their possible, agreement with one another is such as to make it reasonable to regard them all as standing on common ground, and in a common attitude, there remains a disparity between them all, as to their attainment on the one hand, and their Teacher, as to His communication, on the other hand, —a disparity which is never to be forgotten. So that the measure of His communication is the ideal or the goal to which all the Christians and all the ages tend variously, but always with a distance and a shortcoming. There is a difference between the measure of attainment of an average believer, and that, let us say, of a Luther or an Athanasius. But this difference, very considerable in its own place, vanishes in comparison with that which obtains between the supreme wisdom and fulness of the Lord's communication, and the attainment of any or all of us. In presence of this teaching, the position of all may be regarded as a common position, and we all are called upon to pray, Open mine eyes, that I may see wonderful things out of Thy law.

So much has been said to illustrate and fix the conception of the manner in which doctrine should be conceived to emerge from the contact of the disciple's mind with the Divine Revelation,—doctrine, that is to say, considered formally as ours. Now here it may be said, 'If you have given a true account of what it is, and how it arises, one might expect it to take a more humble place, and to be more transient in its character, than it is. To put the meaning in your own words,—as a disciple does,—that may be very well. But having done that, and got every good of the process which it can impart, would it not be a step further, to leave your own words again, and enter on the very words of Scripture as better than yours, and as quite able to *hold* any valid meaning of yours, however much they may contain that is yet beyond you?' Well, I reply, so every wise Christian does. From his own words, and from men's words, doctrinal or practical, he comes back to the Scripture words, which, with all their unfathomed depth, are simpler and more effectual than any words of his. But there is nothing here to throw doubt on the use or to discredit the function of doctrine.

For let it be remembered, that it never was intended that believing men should be exercised merely in the way of rehearsing the teaching of Scripture, in any of its departments. They were intended so to work upon it, and so to have it working in them, as to *reproduce* it, so that every form of thought and every kind of illustration which their minds and their experience could furnish should lend itself to the service. Just so, a man must reproduce in works of his own, often decided on amid doubt and under temptation, the practical teaching of the Scriptures. Let a man be wakened up to any intensity of interest in the word of the Lord, and forthwith the process begins, and, according to the cast of his genius and training, out flow the explanations and illustrations which tell us what *he* is making of it. He does not substitute these for the Bible. They are his tribute to the Bible, or rather to the speaking Lord whose message it records. This is, beyond all comparison, worthier than if a man should rehearse only in Scripture sayings what Scripture teaches him. It involves a far intenser exercise of mind; it implies far more devotedness to the truth, more thorough and inward conversancy with it. And in so far as regards doctrine, it is worth observing, that what renders the process possible, and constrains me to it as inevitable, is just the structure of the Bible, as it is *not* a syllabus of dogmatic statements. If revelation delivered to me an article of faith, simply and only as a bare formal proposition,[1] I might be content to use it simply by cherishing in my mind that mysterious proposition as a pure dogma, affirming a mysterious predicate of a mysterious subject. I might think that the best and safest way. So I should believe it very much as I

---

[1] But in that case, consider the impossibility of getting the *terms* in which the proposition is expressed. The sense of the terms opens itself to us from the various usage of Scripture, with its historical and experimental cross-lights. No abstract definitions would supply the absence of this.

might believe an equation of two unknown quantities, that $fx=y$. The Bible will not let me do that. It is far too intensely faithful to the conception of truth, as an actual sense and meaning that passes from mind to mind, and becomes an inward possession, a light. Inevitably I am set agoing, and that with great earnestness, and with the sense of having something to say, to give account to myself and others of what this manifold teaching leads me to believe.

Yes, it will be said; nor is that objected to. Let men declare their minds freely, as a Christian man does in conversation, as a preacher does in his sermon. But how will you justify these set statements of doctrine, these exact and careful definitions? They do not serve their turn and pass, like a Christian man's remark: they are preserved, and recurred to, and handed down, and made the pivots of thought and the lawgivers of life. Here there is given to doctrine a fixity and persistence, as well as a prominence and influence, which do not agree with the former modest suggestions of the way in which it should be conceived to arise and to be made use of. In reply, it is admitted that human definitions of doctrine have often been put out of their place, used for ends and in a way which I certainly shall not undertake to vindicate. But it is maintained that a very assiduous care in the formation, verification, and application of such statements of doctrine, pertains to earnest and thorough dealing with the teaching of Scripture, and is called for by the necessities of the human mind.

This is true, whatever be the office or end which

we assign to our doctrinal statements. They may be regarded as summarizing (putting in summary form) the effect on our minds due to various Scripture statements, which occur in different connections, and which complete and limit one another. Or we may view them as analyzing that complex teaching which was described in last Lecture; so that, in addition to the broad and vivid impression which it makes, we penetrate into it to single out one element, and lay it by itself, as so much truth which we have been led to believe. Or, again, we may consider them as measuring how far we have been able to go on those topics on which Scripture teaching soars upwards, and suggests relations stretching far up out of sight. Or they may serve to bring out the connections indicated in the Scripture between truths that lend hand to hand, and give and take from one another, and join into an ordered intelligible whole, with inward harmony. Or I may find in them the means by which I bring the effect of Scripture teaching into comparison with the whole world of impressions, or views, or theories bred within me, or offered to me, in order that I may discern what must be dismissed, and what reformed, if the truth according to godliness is to bear rule within me. Whether these or whatever other offices be assigned to doctrinal statements, they arise out of necessities of the human mind, when brought into close and earnest dealing with the Scriptures. Now, when ripe results of this kind are reached, when modes of view and of statement that do this office well, have once been shaped out, they continue fit to serve the ends for which they were educed at first.

The value that may attach to them cannot be completely estimated until we speak of the Church, and for the present we are supposing the case of the individual. But what of ripe result the individual thus attains, result in which on repeated trial he still rests, he ought not to cast away. It is the attainment which the past has yielded, and which the future should employ.

At this point I should take into view, more distinctly than has yet been done, the peculiar influence and office of the Church. But before doing so, I wish to touch briefly—too briefly, it must be—on the conditions under which the exercise of the believing mind in reference to doctrine proceeds. Two conditions were mentioned in a former Lecture, as characterizing the method in which Revelation is delivered. The same considerations come into view again, when we contemplate the process of the believing mind in dealing with Revelation. They operate in the way of stimulating, and guiding, and guarding against error, the whole process of which we have been speaking now.

We saw that the foundation of the Scripture method is historical: a great history of divine transactions is set forth; it is bodied out to the eye with the utmost distinctness, and it rises to the crisis of its import and its interest in the history of our Lord. Now it is this, first of all, that lays hold of the disciple, and holds him to the end; and it does it in such a way as to question him that he may think, and yet steady him that he may not go far astray. For this history is not a spectacle to gaze at. It claims

I

part in us, and we are called on to claim our place in it. It is to become, as it were, a part of the disciple's own history, an earlier chapter of his own life, the very fountain from which that life derives. He is to give effect to it as bearing on himself; he is to realize the results of it, as daily coming into reckoning in the progress of his own affairs. So, then, questions arise such as these: What representations of it he is to carry into the particulars of his own life; what relations he is to discern in it; what influences he is to ascribe to it; what results and fruits he may expect from it. These questions have to be actively met, the answers to them have to be taken in hand, and carried consciously with him through his life. He cannot treat such questions as dim and distant. They keep rising out of the facts of Scripture,—facts so touching, vivid, familiar,—facts that take place as realities to the believing mind, and are felt to be charged with a great weight of divine meaning. So he is constrained to present to himself at least some distinct thought of their meaning and bearing. All this awakens, questions, stimulates the mind. Then, on the other side, whether his attainment in this direction be greater or less, a steadying and guiding influence is assured to him. That great array of monumental facts has been the means of saving many a man from the bewildering influence of his own speculations. As a believer dwells on what is disclosed of the character, and ways, and mighty acts of the Lord, from the beginning down to the coming, and death, and rising of the Son of God, he cannot easily mistake the general drift; he cannot easily misconstrue the great principles and connections; he cannot easily take flights of speculation that should carry him away from the faith by which men live.

Again, we saw that Christian doctrine is always delivered to be the light and guide of Christian life. The disciple finds himself called to practice and experience on the basis of the truth announced to him. He is called not merely to outward activities, but to the fellowship of an inward experience, which, with whatever diversities, is common in its general character to all believers. It is a life, a new life, the highest life. Faith, love, hope, repentance, and the rest, come into experience in connection with the objects and the truths revealed. Under the influence of the Spirit of God, the disciple finds this life a reality, and he feels it summoning him more and more to live it. But it is a life in the truth. To go forward in it, a man must realize the relations in which he stands, and the nature of that great world of Revelation in which he claims a part. So that here again he is stimulated, and yet here again he is steadied and restrained. For the truth is truth to live by. It must be granted, indeed, that men have erred in taking leave to dictate boundaries to God's teaching from a narrow experience. Yet surely there is a legitimate guiding influence to be found in this quarter. There is a verification of the truth in the life, and a congruity between the two, that moderates the boldness of theory, and recalls from undue licence either of thought or of feeling.

Indeed, Christianity, great and various as it is, is one whole. It is all of a piece. The whole of it may be said to be in the history, virtually given there. The whole of it may be said to be in every true Christian experience, virtually given and realized there. The whole Christian system is promised by the one, is demanded by the other. It does not follow, however, that human faculties can construe the developed Christianity, or the Christian system out of the history, far less out of the experience. But it does follow that the one and the other operate as guarding and guiding influences to keep believing men in the line of the genuine intent of Scripture teaching.

I must not be tempted to follow out the discussion of the relation in which these two sources of influence stand to what may be called the pure dogmatic of the Scriptures, and especially to the pure dogmatic process in the believing mind. The subject is full of interest, and leads into a variety of curious matter, both psychological and historical. Here it may be enough to say, that in so far as the dogmatic process offers an analogy to the scientific, or in so far as it takes on the character of science when more strictly and critically pursued, it may be conceived to find in these two fields what every human science needs, viz. its experimental verifications. Coming in contact with these, it comes out of the region of the abstract or of the unseen, and is tested against facts. The analogy is not perfect, indeed. There are differences between the cases on which I shall not enter. But still the statement has its truth. The theology must be such as shall enter into the great works of the Lord, as a key into the wards. And it must be such as can be preached, and lived, and prayed.

These necessities have sometimes constrained the working spirit of theological systems to return into the Scripture track, even when their letter has persisted in going astray.[1]

But at this point it becomes necessary to contemplate more directly the calling and office of the Church, as these bear upon the subject of this Lecture.

Generally, what has been said of the individual believer is applicable also to the Church, or to any of the societies which, as branches of the Church, claim to represent the Church in their own extent, and therefore own the obligations and claim the character of the Church. The function, and the kind of attainment, which have been spoken of with reference mainly to the individual believer, pertain still more manifestly to the company of believers. The Church has, or, to put it at the lowest, may have its common mind: for the members, however they differ from one another, all share the common conditions of human thought; and they all listen on substantially common ground to the revealed testimony, adapted to those common conditions. They exchange influences. They share attainments, which therefore become common. And when the Church sets forth a collective utterance on doctrine, she is to be understood as setting forth in her own language what she judges with a common consent to be the teaching of Revelation. In this effort, all, it may be, have benefited by the common ministry of all; the blessing jointly sought may crown the work with special success, and the result may be very ripe, safe, and profitable. But the Church is

[1] Note B.

neither perfect nor infallible. She is subject in her own way to the common imperfections on account of which each believer learns but partially, and his attainments are in some respects provisional. The Church embodies only on a larger scale the relation of the believing mind to the inspired Scriptures.

There is, however, this important difference, that the various functions relating to doctrine, which in the case of an individual are supposed to be all performed by himself, are eminently taken up in the Church by different individuals. The parts are distributed. Special aptitudes suggest different offices. There are fresh, investigative men, that seek for knowledge as for silver, and search for her as for hid treasure: these bring the ore clearly forth to many a mind that would have worked slowly and feebly for it, had it worked alone. There are the men who cling to the thoughts and the words which the past has delivered: these detain before the general mind the significance of teaching, which many, on account of its very familiarity, might be ready to let slip as unimportant. There are representative minds, that give voice to well-weighed, many-sided deliverances, deeper and wider than most could provide for themselves, yet such that most find satisfaction and rest in them. There are the question-raising minds: these take the doubts that may occur to the individual inquirer, and turn them into bold theories, so as to present in the sharpest way the questions that must be solved. And there are, of course, the sequacious or acquiescent minds—those which in this department at least are urged to no great activity, and feel no great wants.

All this, however, amounts to no more than to say that, in the actual fellowship of the Church or Churches, persons will be found, in whom each tendency or aptitude is represented, that contributes to doctrinal investigations or doctrinal determinations. But the Church acts more definitely and directly in this department, in virtue of its peculiar form as a society, and in virtue of the office which it has to discharge.

The Church of Christ is a community, the members of which are called out and called together by the common call to Christ; and claiming relation to Him, they claim and confess relation to one another, and interest in one another. This mutual relation and interest come to light in connection with the Church's special calling, which may be described in this way, viz. that the Lord has given to the Church truth to be confessed and proclaimed, and work to be done. In the use and enjoyment of the spiritual life which they have in Christ, and in which they are to grow, the Church through all its members is to be about its office. To confirm and build up the society, to promote the edification of its members, and to fit it for its functions, the Church has received appropriate gifts and institutions. The nature, ends, and means of the society shape the consciousness of mutual interest and mutual relation which the members of it ought to cherish, and which, in some degree at any rate, they cannot help entertaining. All this, in general, holds of the Church; and the same holds proportionally of all the smaller societies into which it is distributed, so far as they can vindicate for themselves a genuine interest in the calling, the faith, and the work which characterize the Church of Christ on earth.

This supposed, then it may be remarked, first, that all thought and expression of a doctrinal kind on the part of individual believers is strongly influenced by the relation in which they stand to the Church or Christian community.

The primary interest which a believer has in contemplating revealed trnth, is that he may know the mind of Christ, revealed to him by his Lord for faith and obedience. But a secondary stimulus which operates in rousing and directing more particular research, is the consciousness of having to reckon with other minds, including those of former generations as well as of the present. That others have been and are engaged in the same contemplation, by the same right which the individual believer pleads for himself; that they have been attaining their measure of success by the same blessing; that the results of their devout thoughts may and should be compared with the results of his devout thoughts; that consent and harmony in the faith, under the teaching of the same Spirit, is one of the forms of Christian fellowship and communion;—all this is an appropriate encouragement of individual effort; it tends powerfully to give such effort its special direction, because it imposes on each individual the necessity of weighing and testing his own thoughts against those of his fellow-Christians. More than this,—the consciousness of agreement with other believers gives to the mind a peculiar confirmation. The testimony of the Church, according to Protestant principles, is not the rule of faith. Yet, in regard to all those doctrines which explicate and determine particularly how the great objects of faith are understood, we take firm possession by taking joint possession, by testing the movement of our own mind against that of others. We most fully realize our own meaning, by realizing it in fellowship, not necessarily with every believer, but at least with some believers. Nay, even when an independent mind differs, on some points or on many, from those with which it is in contact, it does not even so escape the influence of the Church. Such a man frames his convictions with reference to those which exist around him; under their pressure his are moulded. Even our knowledge of our own thoughts, when they are most original and self-assertive, depends greatly on the distinction which we take between them and those which we find existing in other minds. The mould in which our difference sets, is determined largely by the form in which the common thought is moving, or the form in which it has been fixed. We understand ourselves through comparison and contrast with others.

Underlying all this is the great fact, that we all receive through the Church, and therefore in conformity with the faith prevailing in the Church, our training in the knowledge of Christianity. With the Scriptures, there comes over to us the outline of that which the Church believes to be taught there, as distinguished from what the Church regards as misconstruction and misbelief. It follows that, whatever may be the range of legitimate discretion afterwards to be claimed by the believer as he grows to manhood, and whatever independence he may practically assert, the influence of the prevailing views which trained and moulded him never can be dismissed. It never can be for him as if it had never been. Suppose him wholly to acquiesce—suppose him wholly and fundamentally to differ (which is apostasy, unless the Church herself is apostate)—suppose him only to vary in some particulars the mode of representing and connecting Scripture teaching,—a regard and a relation to the form of doctrine to which he was delivered cannot fail to mark his thinking.[1]

The peculiar relation, therefore, of each member to all the members of the Church has this for its result, that the mass of conviction generally prevalent exerts a powerful influence on each of the members, and solicits and stimulates the thought of many.

But the ties which knit the Church together, suggesting mutual dependence, and giving a right to mutual help, tend to communicate a special energy to the influence of some members of the Church. Reference was made a little while ago to the circumstance that, in the Christian society, various aptitudes exist in different members, fitting them to undertake different departments of work. But the ties which knit the Church together prepare the way for an intensified influence on the part of more powerful and gifted minds,—those, for instance, to keep to our present subject, whose specialty lies in the department of Christian thought and Christian teaching. For hence arises to them a peculiar right to be heard, as on a matter of common concern; and hence arises, on the

---

[1] Note C.

part of those about them, a peculiar disposition to listen, as on the part of those who desire all the help they can get. On these moral and spiritual predispositions is built the practical arrangement according to which a standing institute of Christian teachers is provided. Thus, whatever be the movement of those minds which are, or are taken to be, specially apt for discussion and teaching of doctrine, the liveliest interest in it, and a predisposition to take part, either by accepting or by criticising what may be proposed, is secured. It is secured in the case of a great number of minds, not fitted nor inclined to take any initiative, but competent to make their own position and convictions felt, when the waves of any doctrinal movement vibrate through the community.

For I fully admit that an intense exercise of mind about doctrines, and the defining of them, is not the calling, nor is it in practice the occupation, of all believers. Some are not greatly predisposed to it by faculty or taste. There are Christians whose main experience and duty is a glad receiving of simple certainties as they are directly set forth in Scripture; in which method the foundations may be laid of great attainments in fellowship with God. However, it is a mistake to think that, in such cases, doctrine is dispensed with. A formation of doctrine in the mind is really going on, and the capacity for all the great doctrinal determinations is present. But they are partly latent; partly they are sufficiently supplied by the common teaching, with which such a person finds no ground to quarrel. For him the mutual ministries of the Church supersede the necessity of strenuous independent activity in settling the modes in which doctrines are to be stated and understood. Nor is there anything in this mutual influence, and mutual dependence, which is not perfectly congruous to what we find in all departments of life. No man liveth to himself, and no man dieth to himself; our lives are intertwined. Maintaining the principle of individual responsibility, we must still acknowledge a communion that will not let us live apart. Meanwhile what is here specially intended is, that the constitution of the Church communicates impulse and energy to the aptitudes which are concerned with doctrine in the case of specially qualified minds. It does so, because it gives them a mission, it supplies them with channels of influence; and it facilitates the testing of all that is proposed against the conscience, the common convictions, and the spiritual experience of the general Christian community.

Lastly, the direct work of the Church, in following out her proper ends as an institution, leads her to make doctrine a function of her own. The mere existence of the Church tends, as we have seen, to intensify the activities which are occupied about doctrine; but, besides this, doctrine must become her direct care. Her work requires doctrine, and her work intensifies and energizes the doctrinal activity.

For the Church is a *teaching* institution, having to provide for the information and training in Christianity of her disciples and catechumens, of which training Christian truth is one great element. And the Church is an *uttering* or *proclaiming* institution, having to make known to the world, and to all whom it may concern, the message with which she is charged. And the Church is an institution which is called to self-government, and acts by way of *discipline* on her officers and members. A critical office has to be discharged towards some of their manifestations. This critical office, when it has to be applied to questions of faith, almost always makes severe demands on the capacity for wise doctrinal statement, and therefore applies the strongest stimulus to the faculties which are active in this department. In all these cases, the Church, whether in her corporate capacity or through her various agencies, has to convey the revealed truth to minds predisposed in very various ways; to minds which, in each generation, are moulded and seasoned by the common temper of their time. Now the process of interpretation which here comes in—the making of pervious roads into minds for truth, into truth for minds; the establishing of an understanding between the various minds concerned,—this is the very process of which, as already explained, doctrine is the indispensable medium.

It does not follow from this, that the activity of the Church must constantly tend to multiply her doctrinal utterances, or to maintain them at one uniform level. The amount of doctrinal statement for which the Church, or any branch of the Church, makes itself responsible in its corporate teaching capacity, or which it maintains as the basis of its discipline, may grow larger or may grow less as the Church, or the branch of it in question, pursues the lines of operation above referred to. But when those activities are vigorous and healthy, they will at least ensure a *care of doctrine*. It is conceivable that this care, becoming more intense, enlightened, and conscientious, may yet lead to the conclusion that the Church, instead of multiplying, should simplify and abridge the doctrinal statements which form her collective utterance, or which direct and sustain her discipline. Only, if the Church's activities are in a healthy state, this will arise, not from doctrinal indifference, but from an increasing sense of the importance of doctrine, and of a wise and right application of doctrine. It will be a new proof of care in this department; for, let it be repeated, the exercises of mind which express themselves by doctrine are part of the Church's life. The ends of the Church, as an institute of Christ, fix this to be so permanently and absolutely. In what form this care of doctrine on the part of the Church should manifest itself, is matter of separate consideration.[1]

We must not overlook, then, and we need not wonder at, the immense effect due to the Church in securing to the subject of doctrine the place it has had in the Christian mind and history. We assume that the effect thus produced is legitimate; that it is implied in the nature and design of the Christian society. With this legitimate effect it may well be that a great many illegitimate effects have been combined. It is indeed very plain that they have. Church action has often been utterly unjustifiable in the department of doctrine, as well as in others. Moreover, in addition to all particular cases of mis-

[1] See Lecture VI., *infra*.

take, either as to the doctrine maintained or as to the action taken about it, a further admission is to be made. A great standing source of temptation has opened in connection with the action of the Church, and in connection with the mutual ministry and the mutual dependence realized in the Church. There has been a constant tendency to allow the Church, or to allow agencies of one kind or other that come within the notion of the Christian fellowship, to intercept the fellowship with Christ, instead of helping and promoting it. The terrific force with which this tendency works in the hearts of men, is revealed in every page of Church history, and in the experience of every passing day. He knows little of his own heart who has not felt it. It has wrought, and it is working, to the effect of leading multitudes to take up with a professed faith on grounds which can never stand examination before the ultimate tribunal. I merely recognise this great fact here, without discussing it further. All that need here be said, is that the form of evil referred to affects not doctrine only, but every other department of Christian life and fruit-bearing. Whatever the amount of the evil may be, it is to be overcome by faith and by truth; but it is not to be overcome by denying the office of the Church. Meanwhile, as One shall be Judge in the end, who is able to disentangle each separate responsibility, and deal with it aright, so He now presides over the various currents of influence that are running in the world. And that which is committed to Him, He keeps perfectly.

PART II.

The line of statement which has occupied us up to this point tends to explain and vindicate the rise of great doctrinal determinations, and the importance attached to them. It would appear to be in the line of reason and of duty, that a series of positions should be laid down concerning God and the world; concerning the Father, and the Son, and the Holy Spirit; concerning the Saviour, His person, His offices, His work; concerning man as created, and as fallen; concerning forgiveness, holiness, and eternal life; concerning grace as it comes from God and bears on man; concerning the ultimate prospects which Scripture discloses. Also, that these positions should be sometimes, indeed, mere echoes of direct and numerous Scripture testimonies, whose obvious meaning and consent might be sufficiently fixed and indicated almost by the rehearsal of any one of them; but also should be sometimes of the nature of careful determinations of the sense to be assigned to Scripture teaching; or collection of its joint result; or should explain the relation in which it stands to modes of thought that have proved persistent in the human mind, that have claimed a relation to the sacred doctrine, and have challenged a decision upon their claims. The line of statement may explain how this, in general, should be. It was not intended to afford a criterion as to what the material contents of doctrine shall be, what shall be affirmed, and what denied. Neither was it intended to supply any canon by which to determine how far, *i.e.* to what degree of particularity, doctrinal statements must necessarily, or may legitimately, proceed. I do not believe in the possibility of laying down any such canon. I believe that each particular case must be decided, as to that question of *measure*, by a discreet consideration of all the elements, especially of the measure of light which Scripture seems to afford, and the way in which it seems to have been intended that it should be applied. However, it is too plain that, on the plea of doing justice to doctrine, men and churches have sadly transgressed the boundaries of a wise discretion. They have not only erred materially in some of their determinations; but they have erred in propounding determinations at all, in cases where the individual ought not to have determined, or where the Church ought not to have determined. As Christians, individually and collectively, have thus given occasion to offence and objection in their doctrinal manifestations, so a disposition to take offence and to make objection has not been wanting. An opposition to doctrine exists, and may be traced in all degrees of strength, from a reasonable jealousy of doctrinal excess, or a dissatisfaction with some ecclesiastical ways of applying doctrinal conclusions, up to a conviction that all doctrinal conclusions are unreliable, or a conviction that the whole doctrinal activity is a manifest mistake. We are led to ask, therefore, whether anything can be justly and usefully said on the measure to be observed in doctrinal statements and beliefs; and also what reply is to be made to the objections of those who, on various

K

grounds, would subvert our confidence in doctrine generally.

Let us begin with the latter—with those who from various points of view impeach the validity and the value of all that can be done in this department; not only charging infirmities, errors, excesses, on some or all of those who have laboured in it, but representing the very enterprise itself as in its own nature unreasonable: either so incompetent and inept, that it is a sheer mistake to enter on it; or else as so precarious and insecure in all its results, that no great value can be attached to it. To save time, the special modes of arguing the case adopted by different classes of these thinkers shall not be separately dealt with; but the main substance of what is common to them all shall be taken together, as it fairly may be. It is necessary to observe, however, that men of very different tendencies indeed are thus combined in one view. There are, on the one hand, those who really do not participate in the fundamental convictions of Christian believers. They regard those convictions as mistaken. In making out their case, they deny that the Scriptures should be regarded as embodying or containing a real revelation from God, although they may venerate them upon other accounts. So far as this part of their argument is concerned, we take no notice of it here. But besides this, they maintain that, whatever may be thought of the Scriptures, the topics with which theology is chiefly concerned are of such a nature that knowledge about them, capable of being set forth in definite and connected positions, is unattainable. Therefore, whether the Scriptures contain a revelation or not, they are misused when they are made the basis of doctrinal statements concerning supersensible things. This is the point at which they cross our path. Others, with whom we are also concerned, are of a wholly different class. They are devout believing Christians, who are far from wishing to sweep away the faith of the Church, who themselves receive the great fundamental verities, but who have been strongly impressed with the mischief, as they think, wrought by the over-activity and over-confidence of the theologians. They think it well, therefore, to moderate the interest felt in dogma, and to assuage the confidence about it by some general refrigeratory process. With this view, they apply much the same considerations which, in the hands of another class of men, are made to support more sweeping conclusions. Those we now speak of urge the argument but half way, or three-quarters. They admit that we are to submit our minds, frankly and devoutly, to the direct teaching of the Scripture, as bearing to us the message of God; but they maintain that, when we carry away a meaning or sense, made ours in the manner described above (p. 111), and when we treat this as reliable knowledge, capable of being combined with our other knowledge as part of the whole, this is for the most part a delusive process. I say, for the most part; because it does not appear to be intended to maintain the position as of universal application.

Now I think that there are two main lines of argument tending to the conclusions just described. Such arguments are drawn either from the nature of the sources of theology in the Scriptures,—it is said that they are not fitted to yield doctrinal conclusions that are valid and reliable: or it is drawn from the nature and limits of the human faculties,—doctrine, it is said, is a virtual claim on the part of the human mind to a kind of definite and assumed knowledge on divine subjects, from which it is by its own limits necessarily shut out. The two lines of argument are closely connected, and often run into one another. But perhaps it will subserve the purpose of clearness that we should hold them apart.

The first line of argument rests ultimately on this position, that the statements of Scripture which seem to support doctrinal positions are analogical only. The information is conveyed in terms which are applied by way of analogy to objects to which they are not applicable directly, or in the first intention. Now it is said, the mistake of those who form articles of doctrine and stand by them, is, that they take what is analogical as if it were direct; they take what is relative as if it were absolute. They mistake what they are dealing with. This is not the kind of knowledge that can be turned into doctrine. Between the truth as it is in itself, and the Scripture terms or expressions that convey it, there is a proportion. But what that proportion is cannot be precisely determined, and we can only say that we have indications of some divine things, but that all the outlines are vague. To make doctrine of it, as the churches have done, is worse than to turn poetry into prose. All we have is a picture-writing: it conveys impressions useful to direct practice; but we are not intended to presume that the pictures have prototypes behind them that are of one pattern with them : *c.g.*, when God has ascribed to Him hands and feet, no one now takes such passages in the anthropomorphic sense. But when mention is made of internal qualities of the divine mind, or of principles that regulate His procedure, it is as little reasonable to take the language in its obvious sense. There must or may be a likeness ; but there must, more certainly, be a difference between the case as it is, and the description of it which Scripture holds forth. And how great the difference may be no one can tell.

Considerations like these are urged by some who accept the Scriptures as the records of a real revelation, and cherish the impressions which they produce, but who think it best to live in these impressions, without caring to settle any doctrinal questions that may be raised. Practically, such persons do hold doctrines, because it is impossible to get on without them ; but recoiling as they do from the form or substance of most doctrines usually held, they find it a relief to throw doubt upon the whole department. More consistently and energetically, the argument is urged by men who take a hostile attitude towards Christianity, though they may regard the Scriptures as a great work of religious genius, important to the highest interests of the race. In order to get the real meaning of them, they urge, you must take what seems to be the teaching on things unseen, simply as words ' thrown out' at great objects of thought, believed to exist, but which no thoughts can compass, and no words describe. The latest labourer in this field, however, has very candidly admitted not only that the argument requires you to treat the Scripture writers as deceived and misled on many points, but that, in order to make it fully available, the belief in a personal God must be renounced. If that belief be admitted, there is a great deal, he admits, to be said for the position, that to deliver some such teaching about Him as Christians suppose, was really a main intention of the Scriptures. He therefore maintains that it was no part of the main intention of the Scriptures to propagate this belief, although it may be mixed up with their teaching, and no part of the essential glory and value of the Scriptures to have embodied it.[1]

I am not going to enter, in the corner of a lecture, into the intricate discussions into which, as is well known, this argument may lead. It may give occasion to a great deal of curious investigation into the nature and conditions of human knowledge—bordering on that last question of all questions, How do we know that we know? I confess, for my own part, that it has always appeared to me that there is no peculiar obligation on Christian divinity to sustain the burden of these discussions, and that a very simple statement is enough to expose the unreasonableness of trying to shut out doctrine by the aid of any such general and sweeping considerations.

It is true, certainly, that Scripture, speaking to us of God and things divine, makes statements into which analogy enters as an element. But then, in the first place, the mass of knowledge thus given is not merely descriptive—not merely a set of word-pictures. It is

[1] Arnold, *Literature and Dogma*, p. 312.

experimental. It is not merely delivered in propositions, the value of whose terms might be debated, but also in facts. It is explicated along the transactions of thousands of years, closing with the crowning transactions of our Lord's ministry. We are set to mark how the unseen forces and agencies interlock with the forces and agencies which make up our ordinary and palpable human experience. Now such a discipline of experience is the commonest means to enable men to estimate aright the meaning and amount of anything which is delivered to them for knowledge. There is not a surer way of growing to knowledge than is supplied by this way of imparting it.

Further, that analogy enters into the teaching is a fact to be taken account of: it may well suggest some cautions and limitations. But it is also true that our whole knowledge of our fellow-men (and therefore of all history), including our knowledge of our nearest friends, involves and rests on the analogical. We understand and construe them by the analogies of our own inward experience. And our outward historical experience teaches us to know how far the presumptions based on those analogies may safely be carried. Our knowledge, thus reached, is not at all unfit to be proceeded on in combination with other elements of knowledge. It is not what we call exact, such as our knowledge of the relations of number and magnitude may be. But it is of first-rate use and importance, and capable of being embodied in positions or articles of knowledge that are perfectly clear and perfectly reliable.

For, indeed, the knowledge we have by analogical teaching is the most real of all: it approaches more nearly to the vivacity of a complex and full experience than any other, and it may be so combined and varied as to avoid all risk of misleading. When we speak of a smile of providence, or a cloud with a silver lining, or the innumerable laughter of the waves, or of sounding a trumpet before us, we get a far more vivid and true conception of the thing than we should do otherwise. Parables instil perceptions into children with an ease and certainty which no other method could attain. Nay, the best of us are glad to sit down with the children, and get our perceptions corrected and vitalized in the same way.[1]

'Yes,' it will be said, 'in this way we may receive the right practical impressions—no one denied it ; but not in this way do we receive what we can set down for knowledge of the things and agencies unseen. This is but a parable of them, in images, differing from the originals who can tell how much ?' I answer, To which of the parts of Scripture teaching will this asserted character attach, which makes its value as knowledge so ambiguous ? Not to the account of what God in point of fact has done in the earth : there is no reason why that should be incapable of being told. Not to the account of the principles on which He has dealt, and will deal, with men : these may be really made known. Neither doings nor principles, indeed, are revealed completely. But so far as revealed, there is nothing to hinder their being delivered plainly. The ambiguity then will attach to the views given of God Himself, His nature and attributes. This inscrutable and incomprehensible One, we are to

[1] Note D.

suppose, remains unknown, even when images familiar to us are used to teach us what impression of His ways we may take up on this and that occasion. But why? If, indeed, God and man are so far apart that there is no fit foundation for instructive analogies to reveal God; if there can be no fit application of human terms to designate divine attributes, then the conclusion may hold. But the Scriptures assume and teach that there is a foundation. Man, they teach us, was made in God's image. Reversing the doctrine, some appear to hold that God, being in Himself absolutely indeterminate and indescribable for us, is in the Scripture usefully shaped into man's image. That, however, is not the scriptural assumption, and it ought not to be brought in to control the interpretation of the Scripture teaching.

There is a sublime distance between God and man. Whatever conceptions of Him are carried into our minds, ought to stir in us not only the perception of an instructive likeness, but also the sense of a sublime contrast. Yet this does not obliterate our knowledge; it only reminds us forcibly how much in this case remains unknown. The consideration that so much remains unknown ought to make us the more cautious in our use of what we do know, but it ought not to make us deny our knowledge. There is a boldness to turn our articles of attained knowledge into fountains of confident inference in all directions, which nothing but perfect knowledge will justify. That is to be put away from us. We must learn from Scripture what uses and applications of our articles of knowledge fall within the intention of the Revealer, and are justified by His method. But is limitation of this kind peculiar to theology? It applies as forcibly to the sciences of observation, say to chemistry. There also our attained knowledge must be cautiously used, must not be too confidently reasoned on. For we cannot foresee nor prescribe how the unknown facts and laws may unexpectedly traverse what seem to us good deductions from the known. It is maintained that the clear intention of Scripture (noway impeached by its analogical elements and methods) was to convey to us abiding convictions, such as take shape in doctrine. It is admitted, at the same time, that the question, How much doctrine? may competently be raised. For we may err not only by ascribing to the authority of the Scripture what is false doctrine,—rejected by the true sense of Scripture,—but also by fathering on Scripture simply too much doctrine, more and more precise than it ever meant to teach. This can be settled only by the discussion of concrete cases—of actual doctrines.

So far, we have been dealing with those who argue from the nature of the sources of theology in the Scriptures, representing them as not fitted to yield doctrinal conclusions. But I said, also, that an argument to the same effect is deduced from the nature and limits of the human faculties. How different, it is said, are the conditions of the divine thought, if we may ascribe conditions to it, from those of human thought! In what a modified manner must truth exist, when cast into the forms that make it receivable by man! Comparing the truth in the divine mind with the truth in the human one, must we not conceive it to be, in its second form, so purely relative to our low and limited faculties, that while it makes known in a manner what we may take to be true for certain purposes, it does not give any knowledge which we are entitled to treat as holding good in the general—as having the permanent and self-subsisting qualities of truth?

I might reply that there are diverse kinds of knowledge in the world; and of it all, how much is there that is not relative? It is relative to our faculties, our means of perceiving and discussing truth. However far we mean to go from home, we must always start from our own door. Yet we do not take this as precluding us from having real knowledge of its kind, which can be applied and used in that character. Neither need it hinder us here. But I do not care, I confess, to speculate on the nature of knowledge. A reply more concrete and conclusive is at hand.

For certainly the Scriptures, as was shown in last Lecture, deal with us in the way of furnishing principles which we are expected to apply, and revealing relations which we are expected to appreciate. They do warn us that we easily get beyond the bounds within which we enjoy safety and see the light. But they do not suggest that our faculties are such that, in dealing with Scripture teaching, we must be haunted by a perpetual doubt, and remain enveloped in a world of misty images through which we cannot pierce. They speak to us as if it were very possible for us to have an understanding, in the exercise of which we can correctly take the sense of what they deliver, and have it as part of the furniture of our own mind. They speak to us as if there were no reason why we should not be as well assured that we apprehend the great Teacher's meaning, as a child may be that he correctly takes his father's, when his words are earnestly and carefully adapted to his years and progress. For here, again, the historical structure of the Scripture fits it to afford us a guarantee that we do correctly catch its drift, and that when we read it we are dealing with teaching which is indeed 'in part' only, yet is firm, definite, and reliable.

But there is a more precise assurance still, that limited and imperfect as our knowledge may be, it is meant to be a true communion with the divine mind in knowledge, as well as in love and work. The objection contrasts the truth in the divine mind with the apprehension of it in the human one. But there are steps between the extremes, that assure us of a true community of thought between the Highest and the lowest; and that a true transmission of the divine thought is possible and is effected, great as the differences must be. For when the Scripture has duly printed its lesson on any of our minds, then our faith is but one note in a great harmony. It is truth in the divine mind, and truth in the mind of the God-man, and truth in the mind of His inspired servants, and truth in the mind of the believer whom the Spirit teaches—the truth that dwelleth in us, and shall be with us for ever.

We find in Scripture great assertions, pattern truths as it were, which furnish us with decisive specimens of the kind of truth which it meant to teach. They are such as these: That the Word was made flesh; that Jesus is the propitiation for our sins; that the Holy Spirit is given to those who ask. Laid hold of by these, and giving effect to them, we find that questions arise about other matters of the same kind, about which the Scripture seems to speak. Thus the doctrinal horizons extend. How much does the Scripture mean to say? What precisely does it warrant us to believe? A closer scrutiny may show that the Scripture, duly used, yields no such quantity and detail of precise and sharp-cut dogma as some have imagined. But whether that be so or not, the real question is, and always must be, not whether we shall have doctrine, but how much doctrine. What length does the Scripture itself warrant us in going, in our questions and our conclusions? Questions of extreme fineness will arise, about which there is the greatest possible reason for cautious and circumspect consideration. But we shall find no help from sweeping principles, intended to expel or to disguise doctrine as such. The questions must be reached by industriously bringing all legitimate considerations to bear on each particular case.

An acute and forcible writer,[1] desiring to moderate the confidence which men place in their doctrinal conclusions, has remarked that the Scripture admonitions which propose to us the example of children, have at least as immediate a bearing on our knowledge as on any other element in our life. We know as children, and are to bear ourselves accordingly. But how do children know? He replies that the knowledge of children is relative. They learn how persons and things are related to themselves; but the other relations in which those persons and things are

[1] Whately, *Peculiarities of Christian Religion*, p. 267 fol.

placed, or the nature of them in themselves, they apprehend very imperfectly or not at all. A child knows what his father is to him; but what he is as he stands at the helm of a state, or at the head of an army, he has no means of judging, or even imagining. Moreover, the knowledge of a child is very limited. Their ignorance is far greater than they themselves can estimate. And if they proceed upon their knowledge as if it were complete, they must fall into the most flagrant errors. On the whole, as he says, the child's knowledge is generally sufficient for practical purposes, enough to guide them in the usual and necessary details of their own life; but it is manifestly insufficient for any purpose of theorizing—of grounding inferences or forming systems.

An application of the lesson hence derivable to our knowledge of the ways of God, is, as I think, very just. We are very ignorant, and are very prone to over-estimate the amount of our knowledge. And yet this consideration will not relieve us from the duty of duly considering what we do know, and of making use of it as knowledge, in all its proper applications as such. For, in the first place, even a child's knowledge is knowledge. It has, as such, all the qualities that fit it to be made use of like any other knowledge. But what a child wants, is the habit of wielding and applying knowledge, with a due regard to its limits, and to the conditions under which it exists. In the second place, while our knowledge, compared with what it might be, and compared with what we hope it will be, does deserve indeed to be compared with the knowledge of children,—for, like them, we know in part,—there is another respect in which a certain manhood is to be ascribed to it. There was a time when the Church was in a kind of servitude, and knew not what her Lord did. But in this dispensation the Lord tells us plainly of the Father, and our calling is to take up the portion of those that are of full age: 'Ye *were* children, but now the fulness of the time is come.' It would be quite another thing to say that we always manifest this manhood as a quality attained; but the attainment is our present calling, and manhood must take up responsibilities with which childhood had no call to meddle. And just as a child, growing up under guiding rules and instinctive impulses, is trained to think, and to measure the worth of its thinking, until, ripening by degrees, he steps out into manhood, to apply as principles in his own possession what had heretofore been principles embodied in the conditions of his training, so the Church also is called to a certain manhood of the understanding, which must combine a certain courage with a certain caution, a confidence to assert with a wariness to scrutinize.

But, indeed still more to the point, I ask, thirdly, What is the true character of manhood as compared with childhood in this point of knowledge? It is not that the man's knowledge is perfect; for no man is omniscient, and in this world, at any rate, knowledge at its best is compassed by narrow bounds. It is not that the man's knowledge is absolute; for in a very great degree it is most manifestly relative,— a discernment of what things are to him, though he knows them not in themselves. But the characteristic of worthy and well-trained manhood is to estimate, as the child cannot do, how much he knows, and to give effect both to the reality of his knowledge and to the recognised limits of it. Thought and experience have taught him the boundaries of his own resources, at least approximately; and his exercised senses discern how his ignorance limits his knowledge without extinguishing it.

If then I have asserted, in one important sense, a manhood for the New Testament Church, which it ought to be our effort to attain and manifest, and if I ascribe to it, as a just attainment, a confidence to assert and to deny, I am all the more called upon to acknowledge the limits which ought to control our efforts, whether in forming doctrinal positions, or in systematizing these into ordered wholes of truth.

Here I revert to what was said of the constant risk, and the frequent exemplification of excess and over-confidence, in handling doctrine.

I have already said that I do not believe in the possibility of applying any general principle or canon to measure the extent to which the believing mind may validly proceed in laying down doctrinal conclusions. Generally, of course, the rule is, that one must go no further than he has warrant from the Scriptures. The mere recognition of this principle does not exclude excess, because the common case is, that men professing to rely on Scripture testimony, and having some show of it to produce, manipulate it in an unreasonable way, and base conclusions on it in a manner foreign to its genius and its divine intention. This being the nature of the case,—no general principle being produceable, and the matter depending very much on the application of good sense, combined with a humble Christian temper, and a general sympathy with the scope of the Scriptures,— it remains only to see whether any help can be derived from considering the causes that tend to produce excess in this department.

In order to avoid being led too far a-field, I will exclude from view whatever belongs to the merely exegetical misuse of Scripture, and will confine myself in fact to one point, viz. the use made of inference in reaching theological conclusions. No one will deny, probably, that theologizing may be overdone in the line of undue confidence in inferential processes; that the schoolmen, for instance, in addition to any sins committed by false reasoning, or by assumption of false premises, erred by mere prodigality of distinction and inference. On the other hand, inference has been maintained to be wholly a false method: either by those who wished to be purely Biblical Christians; or by those who wished to nullify Christian theology, by fixing on it the imputation of an inherent vice; or by those who thought that, without denying the right of inference to themselves, they could exclude their opponents from the benefit of it. By a very large and able body of men in all churches, —rather, one might say, by the general consent of the churches, exhibited in their practice, as well as vindicated by their systematic writers,—the use of inference, and its validity as a method, has been maintained, not without qualification, but within certain bounds.

There are, indeed, inferences so obvious and direct,

that they are rather cases or examples of a principle, than conclusions drawn from it or built upon it. If, for instance, it is assumed to be established as revealed truth that our race is fallen and sinful, then to assert that this or that individual, born in the ordinary course of things, is fallen and sinful, is not so much an inference, as a statement of part of that which was affirmed before. The denial of such an inference is the direct contradictory of the doctrine supposed to be admitted. To inferences of this kind no one objects. If a Romanist, admitting the doctrine, seems to contradict the inference, *e.g.*, in the case of the Virgin, he holds himself bound to meet the difficulty with a proper *distinguo*, and to show, partly that even in her case the inference is admitted, partly that exceptional causes operated to prevent the inference becoming applicable to her in the common form and measure. But when it is asserted that animal sacrifices were originally of divine institution, the assertion is based on inferences more remote and indirect. It is collected (whether validly or not, is not the present question) from considerations connected with God's dealings with Cain and Abel; from what is elsewhere revealed as to the conditions of acceptable worship; from the use made of sacrifices in the subsequent divine economies, and the like. In other cases, inferential argument comes in to fortify conclusions which rest also on what are, or are claimed to be, direct testimonies of Scripture.

First of all, it is clear that inference or argument cannot be excluded from the process by which doctrine is established; for doctrine, as we have seen, arises in virtue of the active exercise of mind upon Scripture. But no active exercise of mind on any subject can proceed without involving inference more or less express. The sense of passages of Scripture cannot be compared, the result cannot be summed up, false views cannot be confuted, nor their opposition to Scripture established, without processes of inference; many of which, indeed, are so easy and implicit that one is hardly conscious of them; but all of which, the more implicit as well as the more express, are referable to the same rational principle. Moreover, if doctrinal beliefs are in any sense ours, if we take possession of them by an internal act of perception and conviction, if they are beliefs which hold us, and so far illuminate us, then surely a possibility of *some* valid inference is involved in the nature of the case. Every truth is exclusive and inclusive. Every perception of truth, every vital possession of it, implies some perception of what it excludes and includes. Every such perception, then, is a perception of the virtue that is in it, when connected with some other truth, to evolve consequences more or less. To deny the possibility of valid inference, seems equivalent to denying the internal and intelligent possession of truth. Nor does any one who is in earnest with his convictions refuse himself the use of inference, however guarded and restrained, in explaining to himself what it is he holds by the consequences it entails, by the results emerging from the combination of its separate truths, by the alternatives which it excludes, and the propositions which it virtually and inferentially denies.

On the other side, however, there are considerations

which are strong to enforce the sense of dangers close at hand in this region, and the obligation of confining processes of inference within very narrow bounds. Nor, indeed, was more demanded by the Reformed theology than '*consequentiæ proximæ, necessariæ, evidentes.*' But everything depends upon the exposition given to such words in practice.

The practical limits are dictated by such considerations as the following:—First, the measure of truth revealed depends on the ends which the Revealer had in view. The knowledge conferred on us, sufficient for its own end, is in no sense complete knowledge, and for any end but that intended is insufficient knowledge. The moment our reasoning goes beyond the *intended* scope designed for us by the Teacher, and indicated by the general drift of Scripture, it stumbles into all the dangers of ignorance. For who can tell how the knowledge of something which is not revealed, would modify the process and the conclusion of the reasoning? Secondly, we reason by means of terms in which our doctrinal statements are expressed. Our confidence is, that those terms, as used by us, substantially express and interpret Scripture thoughts. They do so substantially, let us assume; but still not with perfect adequacy or exactness. In particular, as they are ours, defined and used by us, they are apt to combine with the Scripture sense which they are designed to carry, some tinge of meaning and association due to ourselves only—an unconscious or undesigned contribution from our fallible side of things. So long as we are looking at the doctrine, in connection with the various Scripture utterances the sense of which we explain and fix by means of it, this element, even if present, may exert no great influence, and do no great harm. We are marking how the Scripture teaching combines into a result which may be well expressed in such and such doctrinal terms. But when we turn round and begin to reason *from* our doctrinal position, the risk becomes greater. The inference may be drawing its strength from that excess or defect in our thought, or our term, wherein it fails, and betrays to a higher mind its weak and fallible origin. There is not a more plausible argument, looking at it by itself, than that which infers from the single personality of the Saviour the false conclusion of His single will and operation.[1] Here we have plentiful materials for guarding against the misleading inference. But a false conclusion may be as plausibly reached, where the means for correcting it are not so obvious and copious.

These considerations might suffice to show that reasoned conclusions in theology are not to be relied upon, unless we have reason to feel assured that they are not only within the premises, but *well* within them; lying fair in the main drift of the truth they are deduced from, considered as a portion of the Revelation by which God deals with us; and arising directly as demanded in an honest recognition of its plain meaning, not made out by precarious chains of inference. But the same lesson is dictated by experience in other fields. While experience affords ample and growing evidence of the value of reasoning processes duly used, it does, beyond all question, modify

[1] Note E.

very seriously the confidence to be placed in mere inference with respect to the constitution of nature, unless those inferences are confirmed by some counter-proof, such as that afforded by observation. The progress of science teems with illustrations of plausible inference refuted by experiment; and it is reasonable to admit the lesson in estimating the reliance to be placed on our faculties in theology. The method of theology in dealing with Revelation is not, as I think, to be identified wholly with the method of science as dealing with nature. But inferences from doctrines, which have been gathered and settled by the exercise of our minds upon Scripture materials, are analogous to inferences from positions established by scientific observation, so far as to justify a lesson. Now, in science, it has turned out that inferences from knowledge attained, intended to amplify and extend that knowledge, are unreliable by themselves, and require to be tested, and established by proof of another kind. This experience, which has taught modesty and circumspection to genuine men of science, ought to teach the same lessons to theologians also.

It is putting the same thing in another way, to say that, while theological reasoning is demonstrative in form, the strict necessity of demonstrative proof is often unattainable, owing to the nature of the matter, and owing to the weakness of our faculties and the limits of our knowledge. Therefore the argument which sets forth the inference ought, properly speaking, to be expressed in probable terms only in one premiss or both: *e.g.*, because A is B, and B is *probably* C, therefore A is C, *i.e.* probably. Now, according to the experience of science, the probability in such arguments is not to be reckoned as a very high probability, until some other kind of proof has intervened. The manifold depth of God's works and ways is so great, as very often to throw out our probable judgments in the sphere of nature. It is quite as likely, at least, that it should prove so in regard to those things, some aspects of which and some truths about which are disclosed by revelation.[1] And to all these considerations are to be added those which are suggested by the consciousness of our fallen state, the imperfection in the working of all our faculties in relation to spiritual truth, which is due to sin.

Two remarks may be added, however, for the purpose of suggesting that a too indiscriminate condemnation might pass on this ground.

1. A tolerably free, if only a reverent, use of inference and speculation seems to be legitimate, when it is directed, not to ground certainties for faith, or to form new doctrines, but to illustrate the drift of a theology, and the tendencies in which it may discern its own genius, or to suggest the mysterious possibilities which surround the boundaries of what we know, or to awaken the sense of wonder and the disposition to inquire. For such purposes one might speculate and infer without any very rigid attention to the cautions suggested, if only we remember what it is we are doing, and come back the more emphatically to those Christian certainties, as thoughts of another quality and of a higher warrant.

2. It is to be remembered that a great part of the

[1] Note F.

inferential argument in point of fact employed by theologians, is not for the purpose of setting up theological conclusions by that sole process, but for the purpose of throwing light on the sense in which testimonies, or classes of testimonies, from Scripture are to be taken. If the sense is disputed, then the likelihoods arising from the impression produced on the mind by collateral and connected truths are brought into play. These, supposed to be already established, appear to infer or favour a given conclusion on the point disputed ; and this is advanced as fitted to throw light on the sense in which the Scripture teaching was meant to be taken in regard to it. This is in itself so legitimate, that every diligent student of the Bible must have brought the principle into play in the course of his studies. The danger at hand is that of allowing inferences from the general connection of doctrine, which seem to us well grounded, to press and force the text of Scripture. Just as in science a fact crops up which seems irreconcilable with well-established scientific doctrines, yet must be accepted, and by and by will be co-ordinated on some wider and deeper construction of the principle ; so also our duty may be to defer to a perplexing text in its plain meaning, even if it seems at present not well reconcilable, in that sense, with views grounded on other portions of Revelation. That may be our duty. But our practice may be to explain it away ; and so we shut up the pathway to a fuller understanding of the mind of God.

In connection with the topics just touched upon, we find ourselves dealing, manifestly enough, with aspects of a larger question, viz. What should be said, in relation to our subject, of the value and use of scientific theology? The substance of the answer to this question is virtually supplied, it is believed, in what has been already said. More particular explanations on the point will be offered elsewhere.[1] Let me close this Lecture by summing up what has been said.

Attention was drawn to arguments that make against the worth of doctrines as a result of human thought exercised upon the Scriptures. Those arguments, it is maintained, still leave this as the question, viz. whether the Scriptures, speaking to us of divine things, convey to us any real knowledge. It does not matter though the knowledge should not be so much, or not so definite, as has sometimes been supposed. If it be really knowledge, it can be made sure of in that character; and leaving uncertain whatever is uncertain, we may measure and declare what it is that we know. All arguments of this kind, unless they go the full length of denying the divine origin of the Scriptures, wholly fail to justify a slighting treatment of doctrine, as if it were a department of uncertain value, or too certainly worthless. Whatever truth lies at the basis of these arguments, is rather fitted to impose on us an added obligation to go into the examination of doctrine with the most close and resolute scrutiny. Doctrine is inevitable, if the Bible is to be earnestly dealt with; and whether fairly faced or looked at askance, it cannot be suppressed: it will form in the minds, and it will influence the thoughts, of all Christian students.

[1] Note G.

But there are considerations which may well dispose us to go about the task with special earnestness of feeling, and special tension of the mind. There are the possibilities of error that have led to the various controversies — of which it is not so much my business to speak here. But there are the possibilities of a false method. There is the possibility of too lightly and confidently reasoning out our conclusions. There is the possibility of not marking carefully enough, intelligently enough, lovingly enough, how Scripture deals with us about truth, how it seems to expect us to deal with it. There is the possibility of not giving due weight, in particular cases, to the cautions which the nature of divine truth and the structure of Scripture impose on us in our formulating of doctrine. There is the possibility of our not making a due estimate of our ignorance. There is the possibility of our not keeping doctrine, as we hold it, in a due relation to the teaching of the Scripture itself. So, in proportion to the reality and greatness of the interest involved, there is need of close scrutiny of what we hold for doctrine.

Doctrine, according to the account of it which has been given, represents the obedience of my thoughts to the collective Scriptures. I apprehend that the Scriptures guide me to think so and so. But the form in which I express this conclusion, the doctrinal utterance on any point, may begin to dwell idly in my mind, as a sort of self-hung sign, whose authority is in itself; or it may become a substitute for the Scriptures, superseding the further earnest contact of my mind with the living Scripture utterance, so far as that point is concerned; or it may come into the Scriptures with me, as I turn to study them, to domineer over the utterance of the one trustworthy teacher. What shall I do with it then? Shall I fling it away, that I may be as if it had not been? That would be to fling away the past, and whatever in and from the past I have been learning. Not so; let me keep it, subject to correction, addition, improvement of any kind, as it may be found to need. But let me keep it in its place. Its place when it first arose was, that it was the result in me of the complex teaching of the Scripture. Let it never be anything but what (if at all just) it was at first—a form of obedience. If it be really such, like every other obedience, it will be an aid to further and more glorious and more fruitful obedience. Wherein it has erred, let it be brought to more full obedience. But let it sit with me, at the feet of the great oracle, evermore learning obedience—my doctrine evermore my actual obedience.

At some period of our lives we become acquainted with the full Church doctrine about the Trinity, and with a summary of the argument by which it may be sustained. Feeling how necessary such a doctrine is in the system of an evangelical faith, we are noway disposed to quarrel with any part of it; rather we delight in the symmetry of the statement, and in the stimulus the whole argument imparts to the intellectual faculties. We feel, perhaps, as if we had a great furniture of clear peremptory knowledge, and we confidently wield the terms and clauses that so aptly and definitely set it forth. But a time comes, when partly through study of the Scriptures, partly through study of the controversies in which those creeds arose, we begin, as it were, to *feel* the clauses and the definitions arising between the Scripture teaching in its various elements on the one hand, and the human mind with its questions and alternatives and perplexities on the other—arising amid difficulties, amid hesitations at the alternatives, amid ponderings of words where it seemed so hard to find words. We feel how the use of οὐσία, and the ὑπόστασις, and the περιχώρησις, and the like, in every due use of them, are determined not by the pride of knowledge, but by the humbly-felt necessity of holding ourselves up against this and that tendency that would lead us far away from the just scope of Scripture; we feel how this and that question as to the teaching of Scripture, which either must arise, or may arise, called forth its answer; and the human form of doctrine takes a lower place, because the divine Three are felt to be nearer in the Scriptures than they were before: it takes a lower place, it ceases to be so absolutely identified with the truth, as it lives and moves in the Scripture, but it becomes clearly more real. With more feeling of feebleness and ignorance, with more faltering lips, and yet with an enhanced sense of the reality of that mystery of which our words come short, we confess Jesus Christ, our Saviour, our elder Brother, to be God of God, Light of Light, very God of very God, begotten, not made, of the substance of the Father.

In the scrutiny which is so necessary, this also is to be remembered. The just use of doctrine requires a constant recourse to the Scriptures, in order that the terms we use may be vitalized. In the previous Lectures there was occasion to show how the Scripture interprets its meaning, not to one faculty in the man, but to all his faculties, appealing to everything in him, and revealing a world to which every aspect of his being is related. But doctrinal terms are apt to become for us mere names, related, according to certain formulas, to other names. Then they become counters which we reckon with, as if they were thoroughly in our own power. It is in the Scriptures, when they are used so that doctrine does not control them, but is controlled by them, that we find the terms filling again with their great meaning. Then we become sensible of our inability to grasp that meaning wholly, or follow it to the end, and so we become sensible of our dependence on the Scripture for guiding our thoughts and words.

But the great limiting consideration—most necessary, and perhaps most difficult—that should keep us within bounds, both in forming and in using doctrine, should be a due regard to, and something like a just estimate of, our own ignorance. This is easily said, but it is a hard thing to achieve. Ignorance, just because it is ignorance, cannot be measured, and can hardly be estimated. And then dangers beset us on either side. The consciousness that in many things we are ignorant, must not be allowed to breed perpetual doubt, to suggest endless possible alternatives incapable of being verified, to paralyze the mind or to bewilder it. For we stand in the light, though the darkness be all around—the darkness is past, and the true light now shineth. Resting on what we perceive to be the scope of divine teaching, what it means to convey to us, and to possess us with, there ought to be a resoluteness to affirm, to give effect and weight to truth, so that it shall exclude what it ought to exclude, and not be bereaved of the consequences which are plainly due to it. And yet, in dealing with things unseen, how readily may men err, by relying on conclusions which draw all their plausibility from this, that the part which has not been revealed is left out of the calculation! How readily, also, by forgetting that things of which we have a knowledge may be incomprehensible in their principles! They may be such as can be duly known only if we look up to them as great incalculables, to which no measuring line of ours can set bounds.

This, after all, is the question: How much the Scripture—all things considered, due regard had to its structure, its apparent aims, its peculiar method—really supplies us with the means of *knowing* on each topic? No mere general presumptions will shake or sweep away the fabric of the general belief of Christians. But if there are sifting times before us, the effect will probably be, to compel us, with more stringency, with more discriminating regard to all the considerations bearing on each point, to determine how much we can really say we know, how far we can say Scripture designed to guide our thoughts to this result, to this alternative, to this resting-place. For God has many means by which to constrain His children to search the Scriptures.

LECTURE V.

ON THE DEVELOPMENT OF DOCTRINE.

OUGHT we to recognise development of doctrine as a legitimate function of the Church of Christ? and if in any sense it is to be so recognised, then in what sense? This was pointed out in the opening Lecture as a question lying before us, and it must now be more carefully examined. Development there certainly was under the Old Testament, the light shining more and more as the rising of the Sun of righteousness drew nearer. But this was provided for in those days by a progressive Revelation, which guaranteed what it gave. Development also may certainly be traced in the writings of the New Testament, brief as the period was during which they were given forth; but here, too, the inspiring Spirit, who guided the human element while He supplied the divine one, is to be confessed; and development becomes merely a new illustration of the way in which human conditions and processes can be made vehicles for the conveyance of the divine message.[1] But ought we to admit that, under the New Testament economy, and after the removal of inspired teachers, doctrines are unfolded and elaborated as the ages pass,—doctrines which were not unfolded at the first, and which

[1] Note A.

yet deserve a place in the system of the Church's faith? There need be no difficulty in admitting it on the part of those to whom the Scriptures are not completely authoritative, nor on the part of those who hold that they were intended to be supplemented by Revelation reaching us through other channels, and to be interpreted by an ever-present and infallible Judge. But by those who accept the Scriptures as the sole, complete, and adequate rule of faith, difficulty has been felt. For if Revelation was completed, once for all, when the canonical writings were given forth; and if the record of Revelation is sufficient to make the man of God perfect; and if it be clear, so that the sense in necessary things can be discerned by prayerful readers, where can the room be, not to say the need, for development? What more of Christian truth can men have, than the apostles delivered by word and writ to the early Christians? Or, if more be asserted, does not the assertion imply, first, that the Scriptures are by themselves insufficient; and second, that valid additions from other quarters (whatever these may be) have been made to the teaching which they contain?

Development has been powerfully asserted (as was noticed before) both by Rationalists and by some Romanists. Rationalists commonly regard and represent Christian doctrine as one branch of the general progress of the human mind. The Scriptures are, with them, not properly a rule of faith, much less a complete rule, but are rather the record of certain movements of the human mind, due to natural causes, or, as some of them would admit, due partly to causes which are in some sense supernatural. Those movements, with Scripture as the record which prolongs and perpetuates their influence, have communicated an extraordinary impulse to the religious thought and feeling of men, and have impressed on it a definite bent. Hence come forms of religious consciousness highly interesting and important, which, however, were destined to be elaborated in the furnace of history, in the reflections and discussions of many minds and many ages. They were to combine with all the elements of human thought, and with all the lessons of human experience; and all along the process they were to be freely acted on by human reason, and by human unreason too. This process has often gone on under conditions which hampered and impeded it, but the process itself was inevitable; and through whatever difficulties, it did and does work itself out. Development, therefore, was natural and valid. It could not be dispensed with, and it could not be arrested.

A companion theory has been brought out by some of the defenders of Rome. They have asserted, as necessary and valid, a development very like that of the Rationalists, in so far as the human forces are concerned which urge on the process; but they represent it as superintended by the infallible Church, which sifts the results, and guarantees them (those which are authentic) to the faith of Catholic Christians. The most brilliant and ingenious expounder of this theory has unquestionably been Dr. Newman. His singular combination of speculation and faith, with equal degrees of courage in both, and his peculiar style—or flavour, as one may say—of learning, which goes through antiquity, attracting like a magnet what it finds congenial, and passing all the rest as irrelevant matters,—these gifts and peculiarities perfectly fitted him for the task. The theory of development, not advanced by him alone, but by him more elaborately unfolded, stands unrebuked, as the more adventurous form of the Romish doctrine regarding the office of the Church, as the keeper of traditions and as the judge of controversies.

On the other hand, development as thus explained was not the old Romish doctrine of tradition, and it is regarded with dislike and suspicion by many influential persons in the Church of Rome. Neither was it the original Anglican or High Church doctrine. Indeed, that party, both in its ancient and in its recent or Tractarian form, proceeded on views totally inconsistent with any such theory. They relied on an alleged consent of the Fathers, as the explicit warrant for all they taught, and a sufficient ground of sentence against any later doctrines. Newman has told us how the break-down of this *via media* led him to embrace Romanism and the development theory both at once. What the High Church party, as a party, hold upon the subject now, I shall not undertake to say; but several of their writers seem to proceed on the notion of development, without explaining the principle or the limits of the development which they admit.

The old Protestant position in the polemic against Rome was not friendly to a theory of development. Not only was the original or primitive teaching of the Scriptures asserted as the proper test or standard; but it appeared suitable to assume and assert a corresponding original faith in the Church, which had been corrupted by Antichrist, but to which the Reformation had brought the Church back.[1] It was not intended by this, that the Church had at any time absorbed and exhausted the fulness of the Scriptures, so as to bring out all that is in them. The contrary was acknowledged. But yet the doctrinal platform (barring mere changes of forms of statement) was very commonly thought of as identical in pure times, and altered only by corruption. Hence some Protestant writers as well as Romish have laid it down, that a negative prescription runs against anything taught for Christian doctrine which was not taught in the early Church, seeing they had the Christian faith, and we can have no more. And every one knows how very freely they accepted, *ex abundanti*, the challenge to produce early authorities for all their teaching : not that early authority was binding on the conscience,—for only Scripture had that prerogative,—but because as a matter of fact, in a pure age of the Church, the pure doctrine must be presumed to have been extant. A somewhat different application of the same general mode of view was made by another party, the followers of Calixtus in Germany, and some of the Latitudinarians in England. They proposed to fix some period of time in the Church's history, say the first five centuries, during which all that the Church then believed must be supposed to have got into writing; and it was to be assumed that only doctrines recognised as important before the end of that period could ever be entitled to rank as important at any subsequent date. The

[1] Note B.

object was not to exalt the authority of the Church, but to limit the amount of dogmatic material which should be allowed to enter into confessions and creeds. And the principle resorted to for that purpose was, that the early Church was in possession of all the material of that description which it ever could be legitimate to employ.[1]

All these parties, indeed, or most of them, recognised —they could not but recognise—changes which had taken place from age to age in the colour and amount of the doctrinal deliverances pertaining to what themselves esteemed to be orthodox Christianity. Sometimes they made admissions upon this point which were hardly consistent with their own affirmations, in other places, of the explicit identity of the faith from first to last. But commonly they explained the matter by saying that the change was merely in the form or in the way of putting things; or it might be the change implied in evolving the contents of propositions by logical inference. This remark applies, for instance, to most if not all of those who argued on the Protestant side against Dr. Newman thirty years ago. They generally treated the assertion of any substantial development as if it were treason to the faith. None among them could more worthily represent the rest than the lamented Archer Butler. He lays it down expressly, that the only development he grants (setting aside the development of error) is that which may have taken place by strict logical inference from Scripture propositions. Such development he grants to be valid and real, and the conclusions thus reached

[1] Note C.

he accepts as binding our faith. But then he says this does not come to much, because happily in most cases those inferences themselves, when duly drawn, turn out to be propositions which have direct Scripture countenance more or less express, so that we are not reduced to the necessity of resting them on inference alone. They might have been developed, but are in fact supplied by a more direct delivery.[1]

Yet even those who were most rigid in excluding development have commonly been obliged to make concessions at some point in their argument. They have been obliged to admit that inevitable processes are at work in the Church, which often produce changes in the modes of statement and of explanation adopted; and often those who begin with decrying all development, proceed in their argument as if they objected not so much to development itself, as to the authority claimed for it. Abroad also, in Germany, theologians were well accustomed to represent the history of theology as a process of development; and if this began with the Rationalists, ere long the believing theologians followed in the same line.[2] In our own country, since the date of the publication of Newman's work, the tendency has much increased among men of different schools to admit and apply the idea of development; though it is often done with little regard to the grounds on which it should be placed, or to the consequences which may be involved in it.

[1] Note D.
[2] It is hardly necessary to give specimens; one may refer to Doctrine Histories generally. Dorner may be cited, *Lehre vom Person Christi*, i. 66, 68.

There can be no doubt, indeed, that considerations can be advanced, and are now-a-days more strongly felt, which powerfully attract the minds of students to the theory of development, whatever the difficulties may be which it has been thought to involve in relation to the sufficiency and clearness of Holy Scripture, and in relation to the unity and perpetuity of the faith. One of the most effective and ingenious parts of Newman's essay, is his illustration of the position, that the very constitution of the human mind, and of human society, seems to demand that room be made for some process of this kind, and that Christianity would hardly be well adapted to the condition of mankind, unless development made part of its divinely ordered and divinely guided history. While this theoretic consideration operates *à priori*, facts supply an experiential argument to the same effect. The great rationalistic movement of last century and of the present has produced, amid many evil consequences, this good one, that an appeal to facts and an investigation of them have been carried on with more resolute disregard of consequences than at any previous period. The results of modern historical research certainly exhibit a succession and growth in the history of doctrine which corroborate the belief, that development of some kind or other, explained by one principle or other, must be acknowledged. These facts of history, or the most important of them, must have been apparent to learned men ever since the revival of letters. But whereas at one time the tendency was to explain them away so as to intercept the influence they were fitted to exert upon men's conception of the general course of Christian history, that has now ceased to be the case. Where learned men still stand out for the old reading of the history, as a certain number in the Church of Rome still do, it must be at the cost of some effort, and not without a sharp strain on the dogmatic prepossessions which dispose and persuade them thus to keep their ground.

The object of this Lecture, then, is to assert and vindicate development of doctrine as a function of the Church of Christ, belonging to her duty, connected with a right use of her privileges, and indeed indispensable to her life. It is asserted as a source of change and advance, not sudden, impulsive, and fitful, but commonly slow, secular, and cumulative. It is asserted as consisting well with all that Protestants hold of the completeness, perfection, and clearness of the word of God, and therefore as free from implication with the principle of Rationalism on the one hand, and with the principle of Romanism upon the other—with both of which it has been represented as allied. It is asserted as necessitated *à priori*, by the nature of the case, and proved in fact *à posteriori*, from the evidence of history. However, within my limits, all that can be done is to explain what is meant. A great deal of proof and illustration must be passed by, and a good deal must be left to depend on the general coherence and credibility of the exposition given.

Now, when a process of development is asserted, everything depends on how we fix the starting-point. The main difficulty that has arisen, in point of fact, in connection with the subject, is due to some confusion and oversight on this point. It is very commonly taken for granted in a general way, that if there is such a thing as legitimate development, the starting-point must be the completed Revelation as delivered by apostolic men. As soon as this is assumed, all the difficulties are at once present in full force. How can the completed Revelation (whether recorded in Scripture alone, or partly preserved by tradition too) be a complete and adequate rule of faith, if it serves only as the point of departure of a development that was to fill all future history? Or, if the completed Revelation be an adequate rule of faith, then the development must be conceived to be extremely extraneous to the faith, lying in matters which concern the restless curiosity of the human mind rather than the earnest docility of the disciple of Christ. In this case, whatever falls into the development, ceases to concern the Christian as such. Or, lastly, the importance and worth of the developed doctrine may be conceived to be saved by such a theory as Newman's; viz., that as the fundamental Revelation was divine and adequate for its purpose, so also the development is sifted and guided by the divine mind, which through the Church presides over the whole process. So the Protestant doctrine of the Rule of Faith would have to be abandoned.

But the truth is, that the development does not start from the completed Revelation; that would be a lofty starting-point indeed. It starts from the measure of understanding which the Church had of the Revelation at the time when apostolic guidance ended: it starts from the measure of attainment in knowledge of the meaning, scope, and connection of the truth; from the thoughts, and especially the clear thoughts, which the Church then had of the truth set forth in apostolic teaching, and embodied with other elements in the Scriptures. There is a connection between these two—the completed Revelation, and the Church's attainment in knowledge by the means of it; but there is a very great difference between them, which it is quite wonderful to see so little appreciated by some who write on these subjects. Do men really suppose that the early Church, as it passed out of the apostles' hands, had actually received into its mind the doctrinal fulness of the Scriptures? The difference between the completed Revelation and the Church's apprehension of it, was as great as that between the brightness of the sun and the reflection of it in some imperfectly-polished surface, that gives it back again really, constantly, but with a diminished, imperfect, wavering lustre.

Consider the case of an individual among ourselves, who has ordinary intelligence and culture, who has not enjoyed the advantage of religious training, who is awakened to a sense of the weight of divine things, and led to embrace the gospel on some simple report of its divine meaning. Such a person has, in the Bible which he now begins to study, the whole truth already given to him which man is required to receive. He may be said to be, in a sense, in possession of it, as soon as he has attentively read over the Scriptures. But, in point of fact, it is only by degrees that he appreciates the scope and meaning and range of application of a great deal that he finds there; and if he really makes progress, the sense of the vast dimensions of his ignorance will gain ground continually within him. True indeed, if, as we have supposed, he has been led to catch some leading views which constitute the special message of the gospel, there may be a very rapid, almost an instantaneous clearing up to him of the general plan, and of his own position with relation to it. Yet room remains for a great deal of further attainment in distinct and comprehensive knowledge. It is attainment which he ought to make; to go forward in it belongs to his calling as a believer.

But now, let us suppose our disciple, not placed in circumstances such as we ever experience or observe, but led to the serious and prayerful study of the Scriptures by himself, either in a desert island or in the midst of a hostile, anti-Christian society. In such circumstances, he has no guidance from the experience of others; nor has he brought to him, through those who have been in Christ before him, the suggestions and helps arising from the Church's experiences of 1800 years. All his attainments have to be struck out between the Scriptures and his own mind. He has, in short, if I may use the illustration, to compose for himself his own catechism. Every one may see that, in such circumstances, his advance towards true, full, and well-proportioned knowledge of Scripture teaching will be gradual, and would be subject to various biassing influences arising from the state of things around him, and from the mistakes on various points into which, in the twilight of partial knowledge, he might be apt to fall.

No instance of the kind now adduced will perfectly illustrate the case of the early Church starting on her history, when the light of apostolic grace and wisdom died away. The social character of the Church's experience contrasts, of course, with that of any solitary believer. Christians are primarily dependent on their Lord, on His Spirit and His word. But as respects those acquisitions and attainments which may become common property, they are very largely dependent on one another; and the Church is dependent on the state and progress of her members collectively, but especially of the more gifted and holy minds. Besides, so far as the last form of the illustration is concerned, the difference is obvious between the case of a man who has never seen in another the living exemplification of Christian life, and of Christian thought exercised on Christian truth, and the early Church, through whose collective mind the influence was thrilling still of the most powerful Christian individualities, and of a burning teaching that was not only recorded in precious pages, but was echoing in the memories and prayers and homilies of the Christians in all the older churches. So that our friend in the desert island must rather be supposed to be one who has enjoyed for a time the society and training of some wise and advanced Christian, but has had it soon withdrawn again, and, with his elementary attainments and his Bible, is left now to himself. And it is also to be remembered, that some obstacles to the ready perception of the meaning of the inspired teaching, which obstruct the progress of any modern student who has to make way by himself, did not operate in that manner in the early Church. For the language of Revelation was the contemporary dialect familiar to the greater number of her members; and the circumstances which, to a large extent, determined the cast and tenor of apostolic communications, were the recent or the present circumstances of those same congregations. They were spared the labour of representing to themselves strange and ancient conditions, as the modern inquirer must sometimes do. Still, with whatever deductions, the illustrations which have been adduced do suggest characteristic features of the condition of the early Church. Coming from the twilight of Judaism, and from the darkness of Paganism, surrounded and acted on by influences derived from both, the Church had to deal with the completed Revelation. In the earliest days of post-apostolic history, the Church had not yet gathered up everywhere all the writings which were stamped with their authority. On the other hand, she still had, especially in some of the congregations, the recollection, fresh and powerful, of apostolic teaching verbally delivered. But if the early Christians had in this way, on the one hand less, on the other hand more, than the precise record as it stands in the writings of the New Testament, that makes little difference to the argument. Indeed, the argument is only strengthened if it be maintained that their sources of information were defective; but by far the most reasonable view is, that at a very early date indeed the main writings of the New Testament were current in the churches, although no pressing necessity might yet be felt that the boundaries of the canon should be precisely determined.[1] On the other hand, as regards the real teaching of the apostles, reasons have already been offered for the position, that we ought to regard it as perfectly homogeneous in character with the written teaching to which we have access in the New Testament writings. Those writings, along with the Old Testament, are for us the completed record of Divine Revelation; and what the early or the earliest Church had, was, as regards our present argument, practically the same thing—in no material respect distinguishable. She had in her hands, therefore, means of acquainting herself with divine truth, its nature and relations, substantially of the same kind with those which we still enjoy. And part of her calling was to understand and appropriate the fulness of this completed Revelation.

What was the effect and result of this? It was no doubt, first, this: that in the Church generally there was a thorough acquaintance with the history of the great facts of divine revelation—especially of those which concern our Lord Jesus Christ—the great acts of the Lord in which interposition was made for the salvation of sinners. There was also a very lively appreciation of the mercy of God set forth in these facts, and a strong impression, though certainly not a complete knowledge, of their bearing on our deliverance. Secondly, this included—it could not but include—a great deal that was in the strictest sense doctrinal: as, for instance, that the Lord Jesus was divine as well

---

[1] See Hofmann, *Die heilige Schrift neuen Testaments*, V. p. 25 fol.

as human; that His death was for our sins, and the like. The fundamentals of Christian truth, disclosed in the great facts which embody them, were doubtless so received, that instant way was made for the appropriation of gospel blessings, and for the enjoyment of fellowship with God. Thirdly, as this was connected with the inward grace of the Holy Spirit, so also it was sealed in the experience of Christian life. In the case of many, it was no doubt a most powerful and blessed experience; and it implied a deep practical insight into the world of Christian walking, into the relations in which Christians stood to old and new— to world, and Church, and Christ, and God. In this state of things they felt, no doubt, assuredly, that the darkness was past, and that the light of life was shining in their hearts. Yet, fourthly, there might remain, there must have remained, a great disparity between that which was delivered in the Scriptures, and that which the mind of the Church had as yet taken in and received.

Now this disproportion or defect may be traced to different causes, and so might exist in different ways. First, it might exist as an elementary way of conceiving things which ought to be looked upon as natural and blameless. The great world of truth opened in the gospel could not all at once be mastered as it is there delivered, but only attained to, as men grew to Christian stature, and as, aiding one another, they ripened the common attainments of the Church. Many a Christian has felt, in the course of his contemplations, as though the apostles, from the centre of a bright world of truth and life, were uttering a wealth of meaning, the bearing of which he, standing on the outside, could only imperfectly apprehend. We find ourselves mentally and spiritually too feeble to grasp and wield and follow the range of the great principles which they put in play. And so it is easy to understand how the early believers, rejoicing in the wealth that had come to them, might still be far from that insight into the ways of God which the Scriptures are capable of communicating, and might fall short of much which was afterwards attained. For instance, that Christ is the Son of God was then, as now, Christian truth believed and lived on. It was not only accepted, but, in the main meaning of it, it was understood too. For who that had received the Holy Spirit's teaching, could fail to see and be impressed with the glory of that perfect Sonship? And who could fail to own the preciousness of being called to the fellowship of Jesus Christ His Son? Yet it might be a time, and not a short time, ere men did full justice to all the information educible from the Scriptures as to what this adorable Sonship does or does not imply, and as to the way in which it stands related to our Lord's pre-existent divine nature on the one hand, or to His human birth and history on the other.[1] And yet this might be without any false or perverted views: without the denial, actual or virtual, of any truth afterwards to be attained; without any assumption that that which they knew was all that was to be known. It is the case of men who have not proceeded beyond elementary conceptions; especially, it is the case of a company of men, whose conscious agreement with one

[1] See page 212 *infra*, and Note I.

another, whose common perception of the great objects of faith, has not proceeded beyond elementary conceptions, which are true and sound as far as they go. Now this is precisely one of the features which strikes one most readily in the very earliest Christian literature. It is characterized by a strong and joyful hold of the Christian facts, and of the fundamental doctrines which these involve; it is characterized also by a fine perception as to the way in which these bear on practical life, as well as by an admirable enthusiasm for holiness. But there is a manifest feebleness and uncertainty in handling Christian *principles*, an inexpertness in this whole department, which offers the most striking contrast to the manner, so powerful and definite, in which the apostles bring to bear on any given point the fulness of Christian principles—the most lofty and recondite as readily as the most familiar.

Here there was room for progress; and progress grounded on this aspect of the Church's condition is a normal and legitimate progress. It belongs to the proper destiny of the Church, designed for her in virtue of the constitution of man, and of the character of the Revelation which God has been pleased to give.

But besides what I have called an elementary style of conceiving and contemplating the faith which is natural, and therefore blameless,—to grow *on* which and *from* which is the Church's proper calling,—there were defects arising from causes which were less innocent. There could not fail to be, in the case of men fallen and sinful, and in the case of a Church composed of such men not yet perfected. This, then, is blameworthy defect; and under this head may be ranked all the shortcoming in the understanding of the Scripture, and of the principles of truth revealed there, which deserves at our Lord's hand the rebuke, 'O fools, and slow of heart' (Luke xxiv. 25). For, first of all, an indocility cleaves to men, which revealed truth and the influence of grace do not perfectly remove. And secondly, a peculiar sluggishness embarrasses and obstructs the proper proficiency of Christians and of the Church. Men, even though they love the truth, are very apt to stand still in it; *i.e.*, they are apt to proceed to those views and applications of it only which special mental conflict or providential discipline have prepared them to welcome. Its further issues remain not worked out. The mind slides over them, or past them, or recognises them in an unappreciative, unintelligent way; and so we fail to see that which, if the eye were clear, would be seen to be written as with a sunbeam. Thirdly, men's minds were prepossessed. There had come over to the Christians from the old world in which they lived before, a mass of thought and impression and prejudice. It filled the air, it clung to all the words men used, it was in a manner the mould and method of their thinking, it was part of themselves. In the reception of the faith of Christ this previous structure went down, breached in many of its strongest parts, and room was made for the new faith. Wherever it was evident to the Christian mind that the old world of thought was contradictory of the new, the old might be freely sacrificed and banished. Wherever the instinct of the Christian heart or conscience suggested that the old was dangerously alien to the new, the same thing might take place. But the whole extent of contrast and contradiction could not be discerned. A leaven of the old, an influence of it, still remained,—whether old Paganism or old Judaism, or old Philosophy, or old Art, or old social life, pitched as it had been to a non-Christian key. In so far, discernment was hindered, and the mind fortified against the just and full effect of Scripture lessons; and so the other obstructing influences were reinforced. Such things as these did not operate sporadically only. They were common and pervading conditions of the Church's life; and so the result due to them was a more or less pervading and characteristic defect in the Church's attainment.[1]

It is true, indeed, that the mutual ministries which obtain in the Church tend to modify the effect due to causes such as those now specified. For one stirs up another; and what one neglects, another, disciplined by other providences, marks, and communicates as

---

[1] In these remarks, I proceed on the principle that just perception of the doctrinal teaching of Scripture depends, for one of the factors, on spiritual enlightenment; and therefore I take into consideration the degree of completeness in which that must be conceived to exist and operate. In assuming this principle, I am not at all insensible to the great place which cultivated intelligence has in the successful investigation and explanation of Christian doctrine. Nor do I forget, or wish to conceal, that high intelligence, though unhappily separated from a spiritual mind and a good conscience, may signalize itself greatly in a certain kind of work in this department. Equally true it is, that truth presented in the Scripture, or proved and illustrated from the Scriptures, becomes a real object of knowledge to multitudes of people who are radically unbelieving. Not forgetting all this, I keep to the assertion that in the Church of God *just* perception of Christian doctrine, which alone can secure just statement of it, depends, for one thing, on illuminating influences. This is a common principle of the Christian faith. Without any discussion of the grounds of it, I say merely that it is here in view.

common good. Still, backwardness and defect arising from these influences must be assumed. Nor is the working of them insignificant.

It does not seem reasonable to go further, and to argue that influences which were biassing and misleading, might give rise to positively mistaken views, and to statements formally erroneous, on particular points of doctrine. Such influences wrought plentifully and mischievously in the subsequent history of Christian doctrine. But we are here fixing the starting-point. Even at the beginning, as every one knows, false views existed, and were propounded by individuals and sects. But that positively wrong and unscriptural views on some points, even subordinate, prevailed throughout the Church so as to characterize its general state, is an idea which no one would wish to entertain, and it would be impossible to prove it. Predispositions there were, no doubt, which were dangerous, because they would in due time become temptations, not to be overcome but by watchfulness and grace.

In the light of these considerations, it is easy to see that the starting-point of a process of development is not the apostolic teaching, but something decidedly lower than that, viz. the initial attainments of the Church under that teaching. This once admitted, it will also be understood that the development ought to be not so much from the Scriptures as a point of departure, but rather towards the Scripture fulness as the goal and landing-place. However, as yet we are not speaking of the process, but only of the starting-point. Reasons have been assigned for concluding that this initial stage of attainment ought not to be placed too high. It is possible also to place it too low,—to regard the early Church as living under the influence of views so vague and meagre, that it is difficult to understand how Christian life could be maintained,—and to represent the subsequent history as a scene of changes and additions in the doctrinal department so considerable, that evolution becomes revolution; the doctrinal equipment of the Church from one stadium to another of its earlier history is virtually transformed. The school which followed Dr. Baur of Tübingen accepted both these conclusions, and both are contrary to the truth of history. The faith of the earliest Church was bright, definite, and glowing, conscious of a great wealth of peculiarly Christian knowledge. And the various stages of the Church's progress, whatever changes may have marked them, have been united in a regard to great doctrinal fundamentals of which the earliest period was already in possession, and which the latest simply inherits. Three elements or attributes of the mental state of the early Christians require distinct attention, if their position is not to be misunderstood, and if their attainments are not to be underrated.

First, we may underrate the amount of doctrinal belief which must exist in any society of persons who are in possession of the Scriptures, or of teaching equivalent to that of the Scriptures, and who enjoy at the same time the promised grace of God. Such societies may be conceived existing in a great variety of circumstances, and predisposed in a great variety of ways. Yet the amount of doctrine which must exist in the case supposed is very considerable, and the articles constituting it are most weighty. When I speak here of doctrines, I mean all convictions so clearly conceived, so much understood and agreed upon, so ready upon all occasions to be uttered and put in shape, that it is pedantry to discriminate them from doctrines, even though they might want something as yet of the careful and exact minting which school treatment could give them. Certainly to the earliest Church we must ascribe no scanty furniture of such convictions. It may be difficult to draw the line precisely, difficult to prescribe the exact 'how much' to which these scattered societies of early Christians attained. But let us only consider what they knew—could not but know—of the Father and the Son and the Holy Spirit, of the fall from a better state, of redemption, of judgment, and of the hope of glory. Can we doubt that they must be conceived as in possession of the kernel, at least the pith and essence, of all those great doctrines which are the framework of Christian thought, and which determine the character of Christian experience? All we know of the earliest Christian literature, scanty as it is, agrees with this view of the case. The whole fundamentals, therefore, of Christian doctrine were already given, not merely in the Divine Revelation, but also in the believing mind of the Church. And they existed not merely in a virtual and implicit manner, but explicitly, present to the mind as luminous truths; only they were conceived, probably, and expressed, in a very simple elementary manner. And many determinations which afterwards came to be regarded as essential had not yet emerged, far less become matter of common consciousness.

But, secondly, let us not suppose that the doctrine which had become clear to them, existed in the Christian mind in a bare and dry manner. Let us not underrate the just sense of resource, of plentiful wisdom in store, as it were, which those early Christians doubtless had, and which we also should humbly cherish. Could they fail to feel that they had great abundance more of truth in their hands, of which they had not yet exactly searched out the bounds, nor could see to the bottom of it? What questions might be coming they knew not. But that they had ample resource to answer any question it ever should be needful for them to answer, of that they were sure, for it was a point of Christian faith to be sure of it. Therefore their state of mind is never to be conceived as analogous to the negative condition of him who says, 'So much I believe, *and no more.*' Round about the truth, which they could at once produce in explicit declarations, stretched wide and glorious all that wealth of inspired teaching, of which for the present it might seem better to take the good in direct impression, than to put it into any articles. The articles would come as they were needed. Meanwhile the unbounded trust in Christ, and the unbounded sense of obligation to Him, gave, so to say, a potential expansion to all they did distinctly hold, which ought never to be forgotten.

Thirdly, it is to be remembered that the Church, virtually and instinctively, had and held truths which had not been explicitly developed. The Church had such truths, virtually, at a time when she could not produce them, had never been distinctly conscious of them, nay, perhaps, would not have recognised them on a first statement had they been suddenly proposed. A liberal estimate of what should be set down under this head, is necessary in order to form correct impressions of the early Church.

How the Church could be in virtual possession of truth which had never yet come into view, may be illustrated by an experience which has befallen us all. On a subject that interested you,—one perhaps connected with the habits and experience of your life,—you have known what it is to have more in your mind, in some way, than you can express, nay, more than by strenuous effort you can produce to your own thought. You have found, for instance, that a view was offered to you, or a course of proceeding recommended, and you felt distinctly moved to reject it, to repel it; yet you could not tell why. You could not explain it to another; you could not make it clear to yourself—you had no doctrine about it; *but you had a position.* Studying and meditating, you get hold perhaps of the considerations by which you extricate into light this sentiment of yours, due probably to tendencies and impressions of many different kinds which predisposed you to a certain verdict. Your thought, your reasons, become apparent to you; you can try what they are worth, whether they are prejudices or more; and you can trace out the tracks of sentiment that concurred to predispose you, and see what they point to. Yet you had a position before the question arose, before the point was proposed which set the process agoing. You had a position, which was the result of your whole life, and of the general connection of your convictions or your practical principles. You had a position; but you had not, at that time, a doctrine. After the process has been gone through, however, there may come fresh light, not merely on the one point in hand, but on the connected points. You may acquire a new intellectual possession of the whole array of reasons bearing on that department of truth or life.

So the believing mind, having Christianity in its great fundamentals rooted in it, and plied with Biblical teaching, acquires a position which virtually anticipates questions not yet raised or thought of. And so the mind of the Christian Church, at a given stage, in addition to the doctrines which it embraces and propounds, may virtually be already regulated in a conformity with doctrines not yet distinctly contemplated or descried.[1] Neither man nor Church is hereby guaranteed against some measure of error at the very next step; for there is no certain consistency in the working of men's minds, even at their best state in this world, nor can there be as long as there are contending elements in their state. The actual development may be marred or misled by various forces. It is enough, for the present, to have spoken of what that state of things includes from which the process starts.

The possibility of such an initial state of things, and of progress from it, depends upon two conditions which have already been referred to; I mean the

[1] Note E.

structure of Revelation, and the structure of the Church itself.

As regards the structure and method of Revelation, it was shown that in its completed state it is emphatically, or embodies, a disclosure of principles which are to be understood and used in the manner appropriate to principles. Yet it was pointed out that these are not set forth merely in bare abstract form; nor was it fit that they should be. These principles prove to be such as have respect to living persons — God, Christ, man, the Holy Spirit; and to historical forces and events—sin, grace, salvation, judgment, and the like. They are exhibited to us arising into view out of historical facts and transactions, from which they shine upon us; they are exhibited also as they pass over into history and life, making plain their meaning in their results,—for instance, in the lives of those who receive them, in their faith, love, service, victories over sin and temptation, etc. Hence we perceive what the work to be done was. Those truths shine from the blessed history of redemption, so simply that they guide a child. Yet a complete acquaintance, or say even a tolerably full acquaintance, with any department of the great whole, involves a tolerably full perception of the manner in which the principles are combined in the history, and also of the manner in which they come into experience in Christian hearts and lives. Such are some of the materials on which the Church must work, in order to arrive at steady and clear perception of the whole truth revealed.

If this account of the method of Scripture be at all a true one, then, along with what it teaches at once, there is plainly combined something which it teaches only by degrees. Questions arise, and lines of investigation open, in connection with which a deep perspective is revealed in the Scripture teaching. As men begin to consider particular points, it turns out that, in order to success, many acquisitions are necessary: as, for example, a discriminating knowledge of the truth taught on other points, and a ripe familiarity with the various relations of the transactions which build up the great history of redemption, and insight into the bearing which the gospel, in its various aspects, was meant to have on sin, and need, and duty—on the human heart and the human conscience. Here is a wide field. Yet it may have to be traversed, in order that one may be prepared to understand and combine aright the various utterances of the Scripture, so as to ascribe to them their just scope and weight. To take in a sufficiently comprehensive view of all the elements; to gauge and test their relation to one another; to settle, also, the relations in which they stand to those modes of human thought by which we strive to explain them to ourselves or to one another: this is a great work. And it is a gradual work, in which no man, and no Church, and not the whole Church, is perfect all at once.

But the structure of the Church, as well as the structure of Revelation, was appealed to. This also prepares the way for the process of which we speak. The Church is composed of individuals. According to the Reformation doctrine of the Church, the revealed truth is intended for each of them; to find its verification in the conscience of each; and to set in motion in the case of each, by God's blessing, the workings of his own spiritual life. The members do not receive their spiritual life from one another, nor impart it to one another. Each draws directly from the living Head, on whom each is primarily dependent. Yet, as the Church is the appointed means for carrying the message to all whom it concerns, so also, in the Church, the members have a certain dependence on one another, and on the whole society, because they are appointed to receive important influences in that way. They have fellowship in truth and love, and they minister to one another's edification. More particularly, as regards our subject, the members of the Church have a common interest in the truth, and they have also a mutual ministry to discharge in communicating to one another what they have received. The organization of the Church provides means, especially, whereby the attainments of the more gifted, or more proficient, may be communicated to all. Hence doctrinal enlightenment does or may become common property. It *does or may*. We state it no higher; for what is called the Church, or portions of it, may prove largely non-recipient of the truth, or may oppose it. Hence doctrinal darkness and perversity may be diffused in the room of truth. All that can be said is, that by the means mentioned doctrinal enlightenment does or may, in a measure, and according to the capacities of men, become common property. Well, now, the Church is not only a fellowship of many in one age, but it continues in a succession of generations. One generation cannot hand over its spiritual life to another. Yet, just as men may extend helps and advantages to other Christians living at the same time, so one generation may hand over the like advantage to the next. Handing over the Scriptures, they hand over also what they have attained in the way of interpreting its meaning to the consciousness of their own time, and discerning how it bears on the questions of their own time. Hence, if things went always in a normal or ideal order, the Church might be conceived to make progress by a regular succession of slow but onward steps. In point of fact, it is not thus. Many forces that are, or seem to us, irregular and irrational, sway the Church to and fro. All one can say is, that progress is rendered possible, and incumbent.

Before proceeding further, I will notice one or two grounds of difficulty or prejudice which may occur to some minds. To assert a relatively defective measure of attainment as the initial stage of the Church's history, from which progress was to be made, may seem to convey a very unwelcome impression of the Church in the earliest age. It seems to say that the early Church was inferior to ourselves, and that we may look down on her from our own superior height. But this is not a seemly attitude, and the view which justifies it may be thought sufficiently condemned by that very circumstance.

To such a difficulty I have only to reply, that if the Church of our day does not know more of the full and just scope of the teaching of the Scripture than the Church of the sub-apostolic times, it has very great cause to be ashamed. In that point, the attainments of those early Christians were presumably inferior, as it may be hoped the attainments of our successors will in due time surpass ours. But superior advantage, in the form of additions in one kind of knowledge (even if it be very valuable), is not the sole nor the chief measure of men in the Church of God. And if in those early ages such knowledge as they had dwelt in a more intense and inward manner upon the great central verities—if it was more thoroughly mixed with faith—if God by His grace enabled them to attain a more adequate impression of the priceless worth of His own love in Christ—if He graced them with greater simplicity of spirit to count all loss for Christ —if He blessed their knowledge to beget in them a practical acquaintance with God, so that they had, more than we have, the instinctive perception of what it became them to expect from God, and how it became them to walk with God, and what it was reasonable to do and suffer for His name—if the recent glory of our Lord's incarnate life, and the hope of His return, so filled their hearts as to divide them greatly from the world, and bind them to one another, and lift and consecrate their common lives,—then, with a knowledge in some respects narrower, theirs was a deeper and diviner wisdom. Then, if so, we had better take our knowledge (which, whether it be more or less, could easily be surpassed) and sit down with it at their feet. For if any man love God, the same is known of Him. Whether in all these respects they so manifestly excelled us, I do not take upon me to assert. It becomes us to think that they may well have done so.[1]

[1] Note F.

It may seem, however, a difficult thing to understand how the questions could fail to arise and to demand an answer, which are in fact answered by the doctrinal deliverances of the churches as they now exist. No formal deliverances were given, it may be said, because happily they were not wanted. But the questions and the answers must have been current: the intelligent interest which inquires was there; and the teaching which replies, all the authentic teaching we yet have, was also there. Now, no doubt, all those questions seem to us, now that they have been raised, and have intensely occupied the Christian mind, to be natural and inevitable for the disciples of every age. Yet nothing is more certain, than that questions rise successively and gradually; and, in the Church, the questions which explicate the subordinate detail of Christian doctrine did so arise. It may be difficult for us to imagine a state of lively and fruitful converse with Scripture teaching, and yet a state in which those questions were not yet pressing on the mind. But however difficult to conceive, it is yet a fact, realized at the present time in the case of large sections of the existing members of all churches. It is the case of those who, being young, or being in humble life, or being converts in mission fields, have not had transmitted to them so fully the effect which the modern mind inherits from the conflicts and the meditations of eighteen centuries. There is no reason to suppose that apostolic teaching instantly disclosed to the early believers all that it might on due examination disclose to some; nor that it instantly revealed the range of questions and alternatives that were to open from it for the exercise of thoughtful minds.

Once more, the representation offered may give offence, on the ground that it does wrong to the great thought of the Unity of the Faith. A virtual and implicit unity of faith is common to the believers of all ages and all dispensations. But it may be said, under the Christian dispensation, an explicit unity of faith ought to be—is believed to be—the common possession of all, in every place and in every time,—the same truths, the same apprehensions of God's mercy in Christ, the acceptance by the early believer and the latest of the same clear and perfect teaching. For with the Christian dispensation came the clear shining of the light; and surely it is the same light, in which all rejoice together. Such may be the difficulty. It has been met already (p. 197). It was urged that the great fundamentals at least were in the possession of the early Church, unambiguous and explicit. Now in these the faith is determined, and by these its unity is secured.[1] The objects which faith should regard, the relations to them which faith ought to accept and verify, are fixed from the first; but distinct and discriminating knowledge of the objects and of the relations may be deepened and increased.

So far, then, it has been shown that development of doctrine was possible, and was incumbent. Now such development might be conceived to take place simply in virtue of the existence of successive generations of Christians exercising their minds upon the faith;. some of whom were charged officially with the duty of

[1] Note G.

teaching. That might be conceived to ensure successive acquisitions. And this other consideration might be added, that as generations passed, God's providence, carrying the Church into different positions, would supply new points of view, from which clues to fresh paths of Christian thought might be seen and seized. However, impulses of a more definite kind may be specified as having much to do with the actual movement of the Church. For the Church is very apt to be sluggish and contented, unless difficulties and trials wake her to her work.

One source of impulse is to be found in the collision of the faith with the mass of impression and opinion pre-existing in the world.

There was in the world, *i.e.* in the minds of men, a great mass of material, which was heterogeneous enough, no doubt, and yet it had a kind of common character, and was referable for the most part to a few fundamental positions.[1] The materials might be various; but the result to which they all tended, and the habit of thought and feeling which they all suggested, turned out in the end to be pretty uniform. There was, for instance, Philosophy in its various forms, comprehending a good deal of Natural Theology and a great deal of Ethics,—setting forth a great mass of thinking concerning God, man, will, duty, and destiny. On all these subjects a wealth of conception existed in the world. It was inherited from the past; it clung to the very words which men employed, many of which the Scripture also uses; it was embodied in the mental habits and tendencies of men as then exist-

[1] Note H.

ing. Now it was far from being obvious at once, how far Christianity must modify and transform all this, or must eject it. How far might it leave these actual possessions and predispositions of human minds unaltered? How far must it require them to be modified or to be renounced? This was a great question, singularly extensive and difficult. It began at once to be dealt with in every Christian mind in a practical way, as soon as faith took place: and the principle applied was of course this, that the views which Christianity brought with it must rule the thoughts as well as the life. This went on in a practical way. An adjustment was taking place unconsciously, or half consciously, between the floating conceptions and mental methods of the age on the one hand, and the new thoughts of Christianity upon the other. When it was distinctly seen that a Christian doctrine came into collision with an old idea or an old view, the latter might be distinctly and cheerfully renounced. With faithful Christians it would be so. But there were a thousand cases in the middle ground between Christianity on the one hand, and conscience or natural religion on the other, in which there might be no instant clear collision between the two tendencies, and yet a real incompatibility. In the minds of many men in such cases, a rough adjustment might silently take place, in which one force or the other was unconsciously abridged or modified. Now in some minds, a desire to look into these questions distinctly, and clear them up, was sure to arise; and so the issue was raised as to the relations between Christianity and the philosophy of the day. Those who undertook this task had to settle their conceptions of the nature and bearing of Christian principles, in order to bring them into a comparison with the principles of the schools. When they did so, they might earn the character of good servants of the Church, whose labours aided the common cause; or they might be regarded as misstating the problem, and as betraying the Christian interests which they meant to guard. Their exposition might be accepted, or on specific grounds it might be challenged. Either way, the enterprise advanced and matured the thinking of the Church. The chief instance in this kind is the Christian school of Alexandria. It supplied the first great deliberate, yet only provisional, adjustment.

But under this head of collision with the impressions and opinions of the age, another class of phenomena may be ranked. There were current in the minds of men various fancies as to the likelihoods according to which one might explain the origin of this manifold world, its inner nature, its use and destiny. These likelihoods were suggested to men by what they saw or guessed of the world's existing state, and of the elements which combine and contend within it. What ruled in this department was not theory, so much as feeling or impression. The fancies adopted received their animus from that which men chose to contemplate as a desirable or a probable destiny for the world, or for human beings. Had these fancies simply stood on their own ground, as non-Christian, they would have faded and died out. But they rushed in, as it were, to borrow the name of Christianity itself, and to turn to their own account

Christian materials. Ideas concerning God and Christ, and heaven and things to come, which Christianity supplied, were eagerly laid hold of and woven into the strangest speculations; and these speculations were given forth as authentic versions of the Christian faith. Such were the wilder—what we may call the more Pagan—heresies. In dealing with them, the Church had to test and expose their teaching; and in doing so, she became more fully aware of the proper genius and bearing of her own.

Another of the sources of influence to which I have referred as stimulating and guiding the development of doctrine, was the collision of the Church's faith with the heresies as they successively arose. Here I refer especially to those heresies which may be classed as more Christian, or less unchristian, than the Gnostic aberrations of which I have just spoken.

Commonly, as has often been remarked, these heresies arose in some such way as this: Some Christian idea, or some one aspect of a Christian principle, was laid hold of in an intense, exclusive manner. It began to be urged wilfully and impatiently. It was developed extravagantly, and conclusions were urged as needful in order to its being duly recognised and held, which were perverse and erroneous, and traversed some other principle of Scripture teaching; and finally, the process was crowned by the explicit denial of the part of Scripture teaching which thus interfered with the tendencies that were at work. The Church, meanwhile, could win a complete and real victory over such a heresy only in one way: namely, by doing justice to whatever truth the diverging tendency represented, but at the same time evincing its consistency with the other truths which that tendency had neglected or opposed. Such a process could not possibly fail to educate the Church's mind, and force her on to a more full, exact, and fruitful acquaintance with the whole relations of truth as unfolded in the Scriptures. And it developed doctrine, leading it out from less complete to more complete positions.

When the Arian heresy came to be discussed, one effect was practically to decide that certain modes of speaking and of helping men's conceptions in contemplating the Son of God, as at once one with the Father, and yet another from the Father, must be given up. Those expressions had been very current, had been used without offence, and with no important bad effects. They proceeded on the faith of our Lord's true Godhead; and yet they suggested the idea of the emergence of the Second Person as an event, and also the idea of a relation on His part to time and to the creatures, which entangled the thinking, or at least the language, of those who employed them, in inconsistencies. Arius, by the manner in which he brought forward his heresy, became the means of forcing into clearer view the alternatives which had to be decided. It came to this, that the Church must speak more clearly and connectedly. The risk of confusion between Creator and creature, by ascribing to the divine nature properties or vicissitudes that are applicable only to creatures, must be more carefully avoided. This had become necessary, and Arius made it so. There was really no tenable, no consistent line to take against Arius, now that he had broached his subversive error, but this : viz., (1) to acknowledge his fundamental position, that the true God is divided by a fundamental contrast from all His creatures, even the most glorious; then (2) to assert, against him, that the Son is divine, is God, is identified with that one God, is fundamentally contrasted with all creatures; and (3) to deny, still as against Arius, that we are to imagine, or impute to any creature, an attributive Godhead,—a Godhead founded on created and imitative perfections in a created nature, such as in words Arius was willing to ascribe to Christ; to deny that the name and glory of God are conceded to any who does not possess as his nature the divine nature, with all its essential attributes, all its incommunicable perfections. The line must henceforth be run clear and trenchant between what is proper to the Divine Being,—and this must be ascribed to the Son,—and what is proper to created natures,—and this must be denied of Him in His pre-existent state. This was all true. And the more clear perception of it, and of its grounds in Scripture, along with a more intelligent impression of the insufficiency and dubiousness of some ancient modes of speaking on these subjects, was part of the gain which the Church derived from the Arian heresy.[1]

A variety of influences came into operation as the history of the Church advanced, further complicated by the change that was taking place in the conception of the rule of faith, and of the manner and spirit in which it should be applied. One influence, it may be

[1] Note I.

observed, was not in early days particularly powerful, which was afterwards to work with very great force. I mean the systematic, or that which is connected with the desire and effort to connect the articles of the faith together in a reasoned and adjusted system. Doubtless, in the discussions already referred to, men did not, and could not, lose sight of the argumentative force to be derived, on the one side, from the harmonies of a consistent scheme; or the weakness, on the other, which a successful charge of internal inconsistency entailed on any cause. Still, it can hardly be said that the systematic impulse told directly to any great extent, at an early period, in advancing the development of the Church's teaching. As time went on, however,—as the positions acquired and defended as points of ecclesiastical orthodoxy increased in number,—the idea of formal system lay nearer at hand; and the suggestion tended to become more attractive, that points of doctrine fitted to complete the scheme, though supported by slender and indirect evidence of Scripture, might be corroborated by systematic considerations. However, until the opening of the scholastic period, no very striking results, manifestly due to this cause, made their appearance. Once in operation, it wrought powerfully in connection with very different schools of theology, as long as the systematic tendency continued to prevail.[1] For a century past, however, a strong tendency has been manifested to suspect whatever savours of systematic consistency in theology. This tendency is certainly in unabated strength at the present moment, at least in so far as

[1] Note J.

regards systematic representation of *revealed* doctrines. In the department of Natural Theology, system would probably be more freely tolerated.

So far of the designed room for development, and of the manner in which the Church, cross-questioned by the rise of controversies, and stimulated by successive points of view which her providential circumstances supplied, was urged into the work. Those questions which have successively quickened the examination of Scripture, those topics which have risen specially into view to exercise the minds of Christians, could not, it would appear, at least in general, be anticipated. Each rises in its time, prepared for by those which precede, and specifically presented to view in virtue of many causes, some of which probably work too deep to be detected or discerned. So, also, when a question once has been fairly raised, when a line of doctrine has strongly engaged the attention of the Church, and an issue has been presented, then, unless it be intrinsically irrelevant to the Scripture teaching, unless it be a mere extraneous matter, it cannot be let go again, and treated as though it had not been. Its importance may be differently estimated at different periods, the answer to be given in connection with it may be differently conceived, the ecclesiastical effect to be given to it may be differently assigned; but it cannot be wholly dismissed. It has come into view, and it remains in view. The elements of Scripture which have revealed some part of their significance in connection with the questions put, and the suggestions made, continue vocal on the point to the succeeding generations. The process gone through is become part of that past which underlies us all. It is part of what leads up to and explains the manifold present in which we have our actual being.

So, in some great landscape, the general forms, especially the greater ones, stand out incapable of being misinterpreted by any true eye. But on all sides there are portions where the detail is nearly lost in a general outline or a general tint. Through a haze in the air, or a dulness in the eye, or an intent preoccupation to make out precisely the line of march in one direction, only a general impression, or not much more, is made, and we are content with that. But some new interest — a question, a hope, a danger — attracts our attention strongly in a new direction. As the eye or the telescope fixes on the new points, a meaning begins to attach to the lines, to the tints, to the distinctions that seemed so faint. Presently the sunlight, breaking through, streams full upon the object of our gaze. Lights and shadows come out, the detail becomes animated and intelligible, the objects which were merged in one dim distance fall into many planes of nearer and farther relation, the scene is developed, so that far more than before is known and can be said. Afterwards the eye may turn away, its special interest being demanded elsewhere, and the light may cease to be so specially bright on that one spot. But a knowledge remains. Henceforth, even to our casual glance, those tints and lines have a meaning and significance. Not unless the same earnest gaze is fixed again, and the same light falls, will the same fulness and charm of knowledge present itself to the sense. But something is gained which the mind does not, nay, which it cannot again abjure.

But while influences like those to which reference has been made urged on the process of the Church's mind, they had no right to become her guides. They might awaken the believing mind to demands made upon it; but what resources should be drawn upon in order to meet that demand? According to the principles on which we proceed, the true resource was the teaching of Scripture, prayerfully studied with all possible diligence. Now this, in truth, was resorted to as the great and decisive rule and source of knowledge throughout the early controversies. There were, indeed, peculiarities in the method in which this was sometimes done. These may be taken advantage of, by those who choose, in order to obscure the evidence of the Church's reliance on the Scripture as the proper rule. But the fact is too broad and palpable to be got rid of.[1]

But it does not follow that the rule should always be applied with perfect success. Nor does it follow that the main body of professed believers, or of their teachers, should always keep true to right views of the rule itself, what it was, and how it should be used. Hence, while room existed for genuine developments, as we have seen, that was by no means the only possibility; and while genuine development has taken place, that has been by no means the only process disclosed by history. False developments— away from the truth—were possible, and have been

[1] In order to disembarrass the text of matter which might impede the reader, the necessary explanations are thrown into Note K.

actual, as well as those which might imply a fuller understanding and application of it. The existence of heresies is the existence of such developments, some of them exercising wide influence, over long periods of time. But it is not only of sects and fractions of the Church that this possibility is to be affirmed. The general body of believers may come under the influence of misleading views on points of great importance. And though we believe that God always has had, and will have, a Church to serve Him, which He will preserve from falling into fatal error on fundamental points, yet, however strictly the conception of its membership may be limited (in order to uphold the belief of its purity), there is no motive to maintain, and in fact there is no ground to believe, that the members of it are so set above the general bias of their time, and so fenced from its influences, that they never participate, yes, largely participate, in erroneous doctrines which are plausible and prevalent. The Church generally, and true branches of it, are liable to be betrayed into false developments, and have been so betrayed.

The preparation for this lay in causes, the operation of which, doubtless, God might have averted, if it had pleased Him to exempt the company of His people, or some among them, from the possibility of mistake, that is, to render them infallible. As He has not seen meet to do so, those causes have been allowed to operate, but never so overwhelmingly as to extinguish the knowledge and profession of the central truths of His gospel. The preparation for false developments lay in the mixed and imperfect condition of the Church on earth, and of all its members, even the best of them, in consequence of which their thoughts are prone to go astray, and erroneous tendencies are prone to be generated. It lay also in the rudimentary condition of the Church's initial attainments, already referred to. For though that might have existed innocently, yet in practice, as time went on, it involved a culpable inattention or inadvertence to the significance of Scripture teaching in some of its aspects and bearings. Important departments of truth were left unexamined; and so, as to these, men floated insecure, ready to drift with the influences that happened to prevail.

It was chiefly in connection with topics that were not discussed, at least not thoroughly and resolutely discussed, that tendencies to false development gathered head. Generally, they were topics about which a tone of sentiment could form and grow that professed to be Christian, that connected itself with Christian feeling and aspiration, and which could thus claim to be regarded as genuine and admirable. The tendencies, intellectual or æsthetic, embodied themselves, so to say, in parasitical, imitative methods of *christianizing*, simulating the characters of Christian devoutness, and promising to open a way for the fullest exercise of Christian virtues. Meanwhile the concentration of thought and debate upon other questions diverted attention, and secured time for the consolidation of sentiment and habit. So the growing tone came to be recognised as the established one—the true Church tone, which ought not to be questioned. If any persons did arise to offer criticism or opposition, they might readily take wrong positions in doing so, and raise wrong issues; in which case it was easy to disgrace them and put them down. Such, in general, seems to be the history of that steady drift in one direction on the subject of Church and sacraments, which constitutes one of the most remarkable developments in Church history, and one of the most baleful. Members of churches which are separated from Rome may differ as to the exact type of doctrine to be preferred on this subject; but none of them can consistently deny that the course of development here referred to crossed the right line at some point of its course, and ran into unscriptural excess. And most of them will be of opinion that it began to assume this character pretty early. In this instance we see how 'false development,' implying defective intelligence of Scripture teaching, and perverse apprehension of it, and exerting in turn a darkening and perverting influence, could spread through large bodies of Christians, and through the Church at large, ultimately going near to destroy the Christian life, with the working of which it had seemed at one time to be so closely connected. It is right to add, that it never could have gone to such mischievous excess but for the alteration of the prevailing view as to the rule of faith — which was, indeed, itself a part of the same development—in virtue of which the Church superseded the Bible. It has been pointed out[1] in what a gradual way this alteration was prepared, and the later history of the Church shows to what it grew.

[1] Note K.

The instance just cited is a conspicuous one. It must not be thought, however, that false developments arise only under influences similar to those now described. Misleading influences are indefinitely various. They may act and gather strength in innumerable ways. In whatever direction the circumstances of their time bring a strain on the minds of Christians, temptations arise, which may be overcome, but which may also manifest their prevalence by their results. Doctrinal divisions are the proofs of the existence of this infirmity. And it is very reasonable to think that all branches of the Church, without any exception, not only share the infirmity, but have manifested the effects of it in their dealings with doctrine.

The history of the Church in this department, then, has not proceeded according to any theoretical or ideal programme. It has included much that did not spring from her proper destiny of privilege; not only sound development, but unsound and erroneous divergence. Melancholy aberrations led her at last into a wilderness of error, so as greatly to mar the fruit even of those sound attainments in doctrinal truth which were still retained. I say that those aberrations led *the Church;* for, as I have already remarked, whatever we may hold of a remnant preserved when general apostasy had fallen upon Christendom, we cannot doubt that the prevailing condition of things involved them also in great darkness and bewilderment. Very remarkable divine discipline was needed in order to produce in men's minds an adequate sense of their own bewilderment. And very remarkable interpositions, providential and gracious, opened the way to regain much that had been lost, as well as to attain much that never had been so well understood before.

For the Reformation was a great doctrinal development. It was not merely and only a clearing away of corruptions and superstitions, and a regress to some standard of early attainment. Nay, it was not only a regress to the Scriptures themselves; it was also a progress in the Scriptures. It involved a positive hold on truth doctrinally, especially on some truths, such as constituted a positive advance and progress in insight into the Scriptures, as compared with anything that had been attained before in the history of the Church.[1] That this great providential blessing was not duly improved, that it was in various ways mismanaged and marred by the generation on which it fell, and others that came after, is but too like the common history of God's best gifts. Nevertheless, the attainments of the Reformation go down to all following generations, placing them in a different position with reference to doctrinal knowledge from that occupied by any generation which went before.

So, then, the developments in the history of the Church have been mixed, as man is mixed. We believe that the gracious presence and working of the Holy Spirit does not forsake the Church. He so presides and influences, as to secure that the whole course of things shall be a history of grace dealing with men in a manner worthy of God's mercy and patience. There is a proper progress in the divine conduct of all

[1] Note L.

human affairs, but most eminently of those of His Church. However, the manner in which it is made good is hidden from us. And it is a vain thing to talk of fixing, by any internal test or criterion, which are the legitimate and which are the spurious developments. True, indeed, all legitimate development of doctrine has its intrinsic congruities and evidences. But these are best seen when all is brought to another test, the true and permanent one. Each man on his own responsibility, the Church in each branch, and each age, on its own, must bring all to the test of the word of God, studying the teaching of it in connection with all the best lights that can be prayerfully applied.

What has been said may now be summed up. According to the constitution of things under which the New Testament Church was placed, there was room for doctrinal progress or development. Such development was not to consist merely in deductive inference from principles established by Scripture, although inference, like other mental processes, may enter into the general movement of mind by which development is carried on. But it consists in a more full, exact, and detailed acquaintance with the teaching of Scripture, embodied in the form of doctrine. This was a function which lay before the Church in her path of duty: provision was made for it in grace and in providence; and it was to be pursued under the eye and with the expectation of the blessing of the Lord. But failure as well as success might follow: wrong paths as well as right ones might be entered and followed. Much of the work which in point of fact has proved to be needful, has been reformatory. It has been directed to undo corruption and error into which the Church, or sections of it, have gone astray.

In connection with this function there are permanent acquisitions—attained results in theology; meaning by theology, the exact and orderly declaration of the human understanding of God's Revelation. Steps of progress are made good; nor is each generation precisely in the state of that which first started under the completed Revelation. Past decisions do not bind the faith of any one before God. Yet true it is, that at successive periods one question after another, that is of permanent importance for the human mind as engaged in the study of divine truth, is raised into special prominence. It engages the attention and concentrates the labour of qualified minds. And it is a possible thing, to take the lowest ground, that, amid all the imperfections attendant on human studies and debates, the question so raised may receive its substantial answer, on which no material alteration can henceforth be made. Thus the decisions regarding the Trinity and the Person of Christ in the fourth and fifth centuries, and those in the Pelagian controversy in the fifth, were great steps in the doctrinal history of the Church. They brought a firmness and comprehensiveness, a light and order, into the views of the Church which did not exist before. They served the purpose of moving difficulties out of the path of the Christian learners of succeeding times, and clearing the way to fresh points of view for 'further lookings on.' They may be misused, probably they often are misused, by orthodox people who make binding traditions of them. But that should not hinder us from acknowledging, that truth attained with a general consent in one generation, should go over to the generation following as a benefit to them. It is a communicable attainment, which we receive from our predecessors, and ought to hand on revised and increased to those who come after us. The labour having been once gone through, the mental conflict achieved, the confusions cleared up, the partial views completed, those who follow may benefit by the process. They may come more speedily to a just perception of the way in which those debated questions ought to be disposed of; and so, reaping the fruit of past providence of God and toil of man, may pass on to the work and debate of their own day.

Therefore, also, it is reasonable to cherish a respectful regard to former judgments of the Church, not only because there is a common faith of all believers in all ages, in fellowship with which we desire to abide, but also because former believers are our fellow-labourers in this matter of doctrine, and we are theirs,—fellow-labourers not merely by mutual consent, but by divine calling.

However, in connection with the principles which have been explained, no fair presumption lies against a deliverance on a doctrinal matter, when ultimately reached, on the ground that the early teaching of the Church did not come up to it. That may be so, and yet the deliverance in question may be thoroughly well rooted in God's word. It is true, indeed, that all detail of doctrine, at whatever period brought out, will be found to be congruous to the Church's earliest and constant faith. It will be of a piece with that. Yet Scripture is the authoritative criterion, not any congruity of this kind, real or supposed. If the latter were the criterion, it would be impossible to apply it with success in any doubtful case.

Further still, the development here supposed is not a development outside of the Scriptures, or supplementary to them. It is a development up to the Scriptures; and the Scriptures always are above it, as the perfect standard never fully reached. There is ample room for it, just because the Scriptures, on grounds already stated, are so much more and deeper than all that man teaches out of them. Thus room is made for whatever of genuine growth and movement the history of mankind requires. Yet the perfection and sufficiency of Scripture remain. Nor is any necessity implied for a guarantee such as the infallible Church is supposed to supply.

It agrees with what has been said, that we should think of normal and genuine progress in this department as being not spasmodic and fitful, but in general secular and slow. It does not transform the Church's familiar faith, but widens and glorifies it. Yet no absolute rule can be laid down. For new convictions sometimes tarry long at the door, and break into men's minds at last in a sudden manner. This may be expected especially when the work to be done is to sever man's corruption from God's truth by a new and more intense realization and application of the latter. The world has seen in the Reformation how a force long preparing may sometimes suddenly break loose and set men forth, as it were, into a new world.

If the past is to be surveyed under the influence of these views, their application to the present, and the future also, is not to be excluded. The main duty, indeed, of believers, is to hold fast and use aright the great treasure of truth which is open in the Scriptures to all humble and upright souls, the report of which resounds in the Church of God, and which needs no new disclosure, except that which the Holy Spirit gives inwardly by His grace. Yet it would be simply profane to assume that nothing more is to be learned, or that nothing is to be unlearned, from the teaching of the Scripture. However, I would not have it thought that, from the views presented, one must conclude the developing of doctrine to be at all times the Church's especial work or calling. Even when the Church's work is development,—the unfolding in some new form of the resources with which she has been supplied,—it is a development in many different ways, in which now one force takes the lead, now another. The conditions of the human mind and the human race subject the Church to various kinds of discipline. In consequence, they prepare and dispose the Church to various kinds of effort, to which her energies are applied successively. It may be new light is thrown on duty; or it may be new intensity is communicated to practical life. Or if controversy and speculation call her out, it may not be that kind of controversy nor that walk of thought which tells directly on doctrine. In our own day, for instance, what meets us is the question, 'How will you face and what will you make of history—the history of the earth, the history of the race and of nations, the history of the human mind, the history of religions, the history of your own religion?' Here the question has regard, not so much to this doctrine or to that, but rather to the credibility of any and of all doctrines.

I am tempted to produce one topic among the objects of Christian thought, in connection with which labour has been spent ever since the gospel began to be received; in connection with which also, it may, I think, be made credible that there could not but be development, that there has been development, and that there is room for development still; and all this in consistency with the substantial continuity of the one faith, and constant reliance on the authority of Scripture as supreme and conclusive.

The New Testament teaching is led up to by the Old. In the Old Testament, the elements and grounds are prepared, by means of which the New Testament Revelation became possible. And while the New Testament throws back so great a flood of light on the Old, the full appreciation of the New— the full and exact perception of its whole teaching— depends greatly on attaining, as much as may be, the key to the peculiar method, the trains of thought and principles of dispensation and dealing embodied in the Old. There is, of course, a great deal in the Old Testament, the evangelical use of which for edification does not need to wait for perfect theories about it. It would be sheer pedantry to think so. But disciplined insight into the very tracks of Old Testament thought and deed, is no doubt a material condition of full intelligence of the whole detail of New Testament teaching. Any one must see it who will observe how much the minds of the apostles move in the region of Old Testament Scripture.

Very well. Now, from the very beginning, the Church has laboured at this question, 'What to think of the Old Testament?' She never doubted that the Old Testament was the promise and prophecy of the New, nor hesitated to take the Old Testament sayings in the sense and application which they suggested to New Testament ears and New Testament hearts. She never doubted that, all through the Old Testament, the voice and footfall of a coming Saviour were to be heard. She could not doubt that of the Old Testament, because she thoroughly believed the New. But how that was to be made out and shown historically, looking at the Old Testament as the actual system under which many generations had lived,— here was the question. How were the lines to be traced along which the Old Testament should be conceived advancing to the New? One of the earliest pieces of extant Christian literature, the epistle ascribed to Barnabas,—certainly not his, yet treated with great respect in the early Church, and probably belonging to the earliest part of the second century,[1]—is just an elaborate and a highly unsuccessful attempt to solve this question. And thoughtful men were never weary of it. The allegorical system of interpretation, in all its forms and degrees, just represents the interest that was felt in it. That system has

[1] Note M.

been spoken of, most unjustly in my opinion, as if it betokened the mere idle fancifulness, the unchastened dreaming of unwise interpreters. Certainly it gave occasion, in the best of hands, to much interpretation which can only be read with a smile or with a sigh. But at bottom it represented the conviction that there was a meaning in the Old Testament, lying deep, worthy of that God in whose heart it was all along, for His great love, not to spare His own Son, but give Him up to the death for us. They were sure there was such a meaning; and not being able always to find the door, they broke in through the wall, and carried out rubbish as well as gems. Many a contribution to the understanding of the problem has been made since then; and still we are working at the Old Testament. Still we feel that there are clues yet to be got hold of—that there is a method not thoroughly understood, fine connections going deeper than we have gone. We are still working at it, the one thoroughly incredible hypothesis being that it is a collection of merely human books, due to those religious geniuses the Jews. And always a man's way of conceiving the Old Testament gives a certain set and mode of adjustment to his theology; it modifies the attitude and the method in which he approaches the New Testament, and deals with the questions which may be raised respecting its teaching.

It must always remain the duty and privilege of those who live on the earth as believers, in any generation, to apply the word of God, according to the measure of insight they may attain, on the one hand to sift and separate true and permanent from false developments of Christian teaching; on the other, to unfold that teaching, if it may be, yet more fully in relation to the lessons and the trials of their own time. In doing so, their attitude towards the past (and here must be understood principally the past labours of those who have put confidence in the Scriptures, and not of those who have wholly or partially subjected their teaching to some foreign standard) will be independent, yet it will be respectful and sympathetic. It will be governed by the feeling that there is communion in the truth on the part of God's children; that the Church, whatever her infirmities, has been under a guidance higher and better than man's; that her past labours are a great providential aid towards an understanding of Scripture, and especially to our dealing aright with the questions which the past is bringing to birth in the present with which we have to do. There will be no anxious and fretful longing for originality; for the originality which rejoices the man of God, is not the originality of man, but rather that direct and fresh learning of truth from the fountain of it—were it even of the oldest truths—which brings our minds near to God. But there will be independence, for we are servants of a living and a present Lord. Therefore also the attitude towards the Scriptures will be that of trust and expectancy. Of trust; for what we have to do is not merely to prove or hold that certain things may be successfully argued out of the Scriptures, but to discern how the Spirit in the Scripture teaches these things; and only in the Scripture itself can we learn that. And expectancy;

for there is more in the Scriptures than man's teaching has unfolded, even as there is correction in the Scriptures, it may be, on points on which all schools have erred and failed. I suppose there never yet was a believing theologian who had not more in him by virtue of Scripture teaching than himself ever perceived the value and the bearing of, or was able to bring out. I suppose there never was an age of believing life in the Church, in which the Church had not impressions and virtual beliefs which remained unspoken. And I am sure that there are wonderful things in God's law which our eyes are not yet opened to see. For let it be remembered that, apart from new articles, or new modes of choosing between old alternatives, or progress towards reducing into rule and measure the mysterious elements of the faith, a new character may be given to knowledge already acquired, by more exquisite perception of the sense of terms and moral value of great thoughts, by juster appreciation of the degrees of evidence of its several parts, by fuller insight into its proportions and relations, by more adequate impressions of the degree in which we remain ignorant, by truer perception of the moral perspective and the moral harmonies of the whole. Towards the Scripture we must remain trusting, scrutinizing, expectant; not because it is necessary for every man or every age to make discoveries in theology, not because it would be good for every man or age that they should, but because we must be true to our one Teacher.

Nor should we forget, that all attainments and developments of which we speak, however secular and slow, are attainments in a state of things, important indeed, yet after all provisional and preparatory. For here we see through a glass, darkly; but when that which is perfect is come, then that which is in part shall be done away.

LECTURE VI.

ON CREEDS.

WE need not be surprised if, in dealing with this matter of doctrine, or in dealing with one another about it, we meet with difficulties. Neither need we be surprised if we find all our methods imperfect, failing in one respect or another to reach the end which we aim at. Our ways of coming to an understanding with one another, and of applying that understanding when it has been arrived at, partake of the mechanical and the outward; they are approximative rather than exact. And such as they are, we never use them with perfect wisdom.

Creeds are among the matters in connection with which some degree of difficulty has always been experienced. The difficulties are both theoretical and practical. They vary with the different uses to which creeds, or documents partaking of the character of creeds, are applied. Now, in point of fact, the leading uses with a view to which creeds have been constructed, have arisen out of diversities of judgment about the right way of conceiving and stating Christian truth. There may be some uses of creeds, which are independent of divisions and controversies. But yet the question of creeds is so far entangled with the fact of division of judgment among people claiming to be Christians, as to make it fit for us to begin by considering how that fact is related to the calling of the Church and of Christians, and how it ought to be dealt with when at any time it occurs.

Christians are joined together in one faith, and so have fellowship in truth as well as in love. They come under the same authority, and they profess to receive the same teaching. Yet diversities of opinion regarding parts or aspects of Christian truth arise among them, which are of very different degrees of importance. Some are insignificant. But when they reach a certain point, they occasion trouble. They disturb and perplex the common life and the united functions, or they tend to do so. When that point is reached, the case falls under the general rules given us in Scripture for managing offences, as well as under the special directions with respect to keeping the teaching delivered to us. When cause of offence arises in the Church of Christ, means are to be used to remove it. If it cannot be removed— dealt with in such a way as to avert or dismiss the element of scandal — there is sin somewhere prevailing, to the detriment of the community and of the Christian cause. If, for example, the offence arise out of a diversity of judgment with respect to Christian truth, one side at least must be in the wrong; possibly both may be so to some extent; and this error of one or both is not without some degree of sin. The early Chiliasts, for example, were wrong in their anticipations of a fanciful and carnal millennium; and some of their opponents erred on the other side, in trying to cut the foundation from under Chiliasm by denying the authority of the Apocalypse. Then, supposing one side to be in the right entirely or mainly, it may fail to deal in a right and scriptural manner with those who are otherwise minded; and so sin arises on that account. The Church of Rome might be in the right against some of the Manichæan sects of the middle ages on the doctrinal difference; but she erred and sinned in dealing with them by a claim of absolute authority, and by bodily pains and penalties. Generally, the first duty, on occasion of a doctrinal difference that appears to be serious, is to try to remove it, in part or in whole, by a brotherly appeal to the supreme authority, with a view to friendly reconsideration of what is there set forth. Not very often has there proved to be, on both sides, so much faith, candour, and docility, as to secure a genuine use of this process, and to render it successful. It may be virtually accomplished, through the various forms of discussion, apart from formal and express conference. But however gone about, formally or informally, if it fails, the question comes to be, What next? The difference has taken shape; it has become more formal and obvious in virtue of discussion and comparison of opinions. What is to be done with it?

Here the first question that occurs is, whether the difference that occasions trouble may not be borne with—whether it may not be allowed to exist, by tolerance and forbearance on either hand. Christ's

Church was not meant to be a society in which men should be comfortably rid of all difficulties, by the process of turning them all out of doors. It was intended that much should be borne with, which it should require some trouble to adjust, some patience and magnanimity to tolerate, some wisdom to reconcile with fidelity on the one hand, and with peace on the other. As a matter of fact, many diversities of judgment have led to divisions, either because men judged, on one side or both, that to tolerate the diversity was a course not consistent with the duty of believers and of the Church; or because there was not enough of patience, good temper, and faith to take any other course. So there have been divisions, sometimes of individuals,—cast out as unsound and errant members,—sometimes of larger bodies. There have been divisions: some of them, in the end at least, necessary and imperative; others needless; all of them involving sin somewhere, and all of them involving also the existence of error, on one side or on both.

The rise of divisions in this way suggests two considerations, both bearing on the office of the Church about doctrines, but bearing upon it in different ways. On the one side, an increased care in the department of doctrine is naturally felt to be called for with every fresh experience of the fact that errors arise, and that irreducible misunderstandings are possible. This increased care tends towards fuller and more thoughtful explanation. It may produce greater sobriety of statement; it usually does produce greater amplitude and fulness of definition. On the other side, the very fact of divisions brings clearly out the possibility of error; it suggests the fallibility of human judgments, and reminds all parties of the appeal to a higher tribunal, where decisions are infallible and final.

These differences of opinion, and the divisions which have often followed upon them, do not exist simply as divisions between masses of Christians, greater or smaller. It is not merely that sets of men lean to different sides of contested questions, and in some cases break fellowship and part company. The action of the Church comes in at some point. The Church, whether by a virtual and approximate unanimity or by a majority, exercising or claiming to exercise functions entrusted to her by her Master, comes in at some point with her decision, and follows it up, commonly with some disciplinary application of it. Ultimately, indeed, Church powers and authority are generally claimed and exercised by each of the dividing parties, as Romanists and Protestants alike claim right to wield the keys, according to their several conceptions of the ends for which the keys were given. But often, before this last result is attained, there is a point at which a decision is pronounced in the name of the Church as previously organized,—a decision which can plead on its behalf the authority, less or more, of the ecclesiastical powers that be, proceeding according to their ordinary rules. The Nestorians had ultimately a hierarchy of their own; but a decision had previously gone against them from the Church authority of that time. It might be complained of on various grounds; but it could hardly be denied to be a decision which, upon the principles recognised by all parties before the dispute arose, was ecclesiastically valid. On the other hand, in the case of the disputes and the schism between East and West, there was no such decision. The two parties fell asunder, each carrying with it its own ecclesiastical resources, and its own ecclesiastical position. East could not produce against West, nor West against East, any ecclesiastical decision of the quarrels between them that had even a plausible pretence to be called Œcumenical, or to proceed from an authority once recognised by them both. But that is not the common case.

The respect due to such decisions, reached by what both parties in a difference or division have previously recognised as the Church, or as the regular and ordinary tribunal of the Church, is, of course, itself a matter of debate. The Romish and the Protestant communions, for instance, assign very differently the authority pertaining to such decisions, and the respect that is due to them. It follows that the Church of Rome is very differently situated from the Protestant communions, in reference to the question of giving effect, by disciplinary measures, to the judgments at which she has arrived. According to the Church of Rome, when a doctrinal question has been decided by the supreme ecclesiastical authority, the decision is divine information to all the members of the Church. There can be no doubt, therefore, about the propriety, or lawfulness at least, of exacting submission, and cutting off from the Church those who refuse it. They are directly rebelling against divine guidance. The propriety of disciplinary procedure hardly needs, on their principles, any separate or additional vindication. But, according to Protestants, Church decisions, whatever respect may be due to them, do not of themselves bind the conscience. Supposing, therefore, a Protestant Church, by the appropriate organs, to come to a decision of some disputed question, that decision may settle the view prevalent in the Church as to what the Scripture teaches upon the point, and so it settles the view on which the Church is to proceed in her practice. But it does not directly settle how the Church ought to proceed upon her view; it does not settle what effect she may and ought to give to it, *e.g.*, in the case of those members of the Church who are persuaded that the Scripture does *not* teach so. The Church must of course regard them as in error; but how they should be dealt with is a question not settled by the Church's authoritative utterance and publication of her own mind. Some further materials must be brought in : either direct Scripture teaching as to the way in which error should be dealt with; or information, from the same source, with respect to the ends which the Church is to aim at, and the way in which the fellowship of believers was intended to be regulated and maintained.

There is one fundamental division which at all events has to be reckoned with, viz. the division between Church and world, between the believers and the unbelievers. With respect to the contrast here implied, it is quite certain that it is part of the duty of believers, whether in the station of private Christians or of office-bearers, to hold out the truth to those without. It will not be denied that this ought to be done in such a way as to convey correct and full impressions of what the Christians believe. Every kind of legitimate explanation may be resorted to, and the mode of statement may be adapted to the wants, character, and training of those who are to be dealt with. If this be the duty of individuals, it can hardly be disputed that the whole society may do the same. They may sanction with the weight of their consent and approbation, given through the appropriate organs, statements that are intended for expository purposes. Again, one of the functions of the Christian Church is to carry on teaching—to administer, explain, and apply truth out of the Scriptures. This instruction ought, of course, to be adapted to the prevailing condition and temptations of the Church. It is carried on by the gospel ministry as well as by parents and others. And probably no one will dispute that, for this purpose also, the Church might set forth statements of views and principles generally assented to as taught in the Scriptures, in order to call attention to the points which might seem to require it most, and to provide a help and guide for the labours of individual teachers. The right of the Church to enforce such teaching, or to exclude contrary teaching on the part of its officebearers, may be doubted or denied. That, as implying division of judgment, will be spoken to presently. But the right of the Church as an organized society to have a mind in these things, to express it, to exhibit it as the belief in accordance with which all action on her part, in every sphere in which action is required of her, is regulated, can hardly be disputed. A statement so produced is a creed; it is a statement adapted to one of the ends of creeds. It has its authority partly from the prevailing consent which it expresses, partly from the official character of the Church as a witness of the truth. Even if constructed solely for the holding forth of positive belief, it will still be levelled at error in various articles; for one of the great influences which form doctrines into the shape they assume in individual minds and in Church decisions, is the rise of errors. But so far as creeds grow under the influence of the general object now under consideration, they tend to become expanded statements of positive determinations, put together so as to exhibit a full and orderly array of teaching. So considered, the creed is, as it were, the Church's answer to the world's question: 'You, who live with us in this changing world, have, as you profess, a divine revelation. What has it taught you?' The answer is partly in the Church's renewed life; partly it is summed up in the creed: 'It has taught us to hold, apply, and rely upon such truths as these.'

I do not think it necessary to waste time in vindicating the right of the Church to frame creeds for such purposes as these.[1] The topic may have to be referred to again in the course of this discussion. For the present, it serves to suggest that, even if no errors or heresies had embarrassed the Church's progress, creeds might still have had their use. Even in that case, conceivable, though impossible, the Church, or any branch of the Church, might have thought it right

---

[1] Not that it is universally admitted. See *The Confessional*, p. 58, 2d ed., Lond. 1767.

to set forth officially the faith of the whole society, in forms suggested by the point of progress reached, or by the existing state of human minds. But, on the supposition now made, it is not easy to suggest reasons for any great activity in the production of such forms. The necessities might probably be well enough provided for by the spontaneous activity of members and office-bearers in their mutual fellowship. At all events, the leading influence which in point of fact has determined the setting forth of creeds (those, that is to say, which state doctrine with any fulness or exactness), has been the existence of diversity of judgments, leading in the end to separation. The practical force which has stimulated and exercised the minds of men in their activity about doctrine has been the collision of opinion; and the practical work of the collective Church in this department has turned very much on these diversities of judgment, and on the divisions to which they led.

This remark may perhaps appear less applicable to the earlier forms of creed. If we take that which we call the Apostles' as an example,[1] we may be disposed to think it related to no differences among professing Christians, but only to the fundamental difference between Church and world,—a view perfectly agreeable to the fact that this creed was, or arose out of, the profession made by those who passed into the kingdom of light by baptism. It is occupied with setting forth very briefly the chief facts delivered to faith concerning Father, Son, and Holy Ghost, into

---

[1] A purpose which it may serve well enough, although its present form is not the earliest nor the simplest.

whose name the catechumen was baptized, combined with a reference to the great hopes which we cherish through grace. There may seem to be in it, therefore, no more than the simplest form of declaring that he, who erewhile had been a child of darkness, was now assuming the position and claiming the privileges of a child of light. That, no doubt, is the leading conception of it. Hence almost all Christians that are now in the world can accommodate themselves to the acceptance of it as the non-controversial creed; though it may be apprehended that the sense in which some of them must take it for this purpose is far from that originally intended, and originally felt to be in the words. However, what I wish now to say, is that the Apostles' Creed, however seemingly simple, does settle, and was probably meant to settle, some of the questions raised by the speculative sects of the second century. The words are silently chosen in such a way, that they bring up aspects of the faith sufficient to shut their speculations out. The very first article shuts out almost all, if not quite all, of the Gnostic sects, for it subverts and excludes the Gnostic doctrine of a Demiurge.[1] When we come to creeds like the Nicene,[2] the effect of controversy is of course apparent. The tendencies which might incline men to take a low view of our Lord's pre-existent nature, and to lay down a developed doctrine adverse to His true Godhead, had been felt; and therefore the old forms of setting forth the faith were modified by others intended to shut out

---

[1] Note A.
[2] Creeds considerably older might be specified, but the Nicene is better known.

the error, and to express, as the Church's faith, the affirmation of His Eternal Sonship in the divine uncreated nature. Still more elaborately and emphatically, the same character attaches to succeeding creeds, such as that which bears the name of Athanasius. Other conclusions and deliverances, which did not so decidedly take the creed form, were employed substantially in the same way and for the same purpose, that is, as instruments by which the Church made her collective voice felt, and gave effect to her influence in favour of what was regarded as the true view of disputed questions.

The Reformation confessions[1] adopt in substance the deliverances of the early creeds, sometimes reduplicating upon them in express terms. They take up, in addition, a large range of new questions; for the controversy with Rome had opened an immense line of discussion, and determinations on the chief points of difference passed naturally into the Reformation confessions, as counter determinations were embodied in due time in the decrees of Trent, and in the creed of Pius IV. It is to be remembered, however, that in drawing up the Reformation confessions, the object in view was not merely to utter an ecclesiastical decision of controverted questions, which might be ecclesiastically enforced. The object was to give an authentic account of the doctrine which each reformed church regarded as sanctioned by the Scriptures, and would be understood as prepared to teach among the people; and this in order to bring out clearly the Christian and evangelical character of the reformed teaching, and wipe off

[1] Note B.

aspersions and slanders. The earliest Reformation confession, that of Augsburg, which afterwards held so prominent a place in the body of Lutheran symbols, was originally intended, as is very well known, solely for this purpose of giving information. The application of it to regulate the teaching and discipline of Lutheran churches was a secondary and subsequent thing. On the contrary, the other leading Lutheran symbol, the Formula Concordiæ, was expressly planned to be an authoritative settlement of theological questions which divided the Lutheran Church, or which might be introduced into it; and it was intended to be enforced, as it was in fact, by ecclesiastical authority, and indeed by civil authority also. It served, of course, the purpose of informing the world how the Lutheran Church believed and taught; but the other was its original and direct design.[1] The object in view in those earlier Reformation confessions, that of giving information as to tenets in which the framers were in point of fact agreed, explains the range of subjects gone over, and the manner in which they are presented in those confessions. These are features in which they differ from the early creeds. At the same time, a very considerable influence must be ascribed to the fact that theological system had by this time entered powerfully into the habits of religious thought. This influence has communicated a special character to all the later efforts in the department of confession, as compared with those of the early Church.

[1] Similar remarks apply to some of the early Swiss confessions, as contrasted with the Formula Consensus Helvetici.

Whatever the original design of those confessions, they came to be applied ultimately, like the older creeds, for the purpose of regulating the discipline of the Church in the department of doctrine : either as containing the law which the Church was prepared to enforce, if in any case its intimations were disregarded ; or as expressing the personal faith and judgment which the Church expected to be uttered by those who were admitted to membership or to office. Some use of creeds, therefore, for such purposes has prevailed in almost every age of the Church. The precise application has varied. For example, it became usual, probably at a very early period, for catechumens at their baptism to express their faith in some brief summary, although the utterance of it was regarded rather as a Christian privilege and dignity than as a mere test. This plan has not been always followed. The objects which the Church has in view, viz. to see to the instruction of those who are received to full communion, and to ascertain that they receive the common faith, may be attained without the formal application of a creed. Those objects are provided for at present, in various branches of the Church, without that instrumentality. On the other hand, it is the reception of creeds by office-bearers that now-a-days claims precise regulation, and chiefly occasions discussion. Although the body of worshippers in many branches of the Church are called upon to recite the ancient creeds as part of divine service, it is the office-bearers alone, in general, who are placed under precise personal obligations by the application of creeds ; whereas in the earliest days it would be difficult to prove that any fixed creed, in addition to the baptismal formula, was anywhere in use for office-bearers. The churches satisfied themselves by other means that those who were chosen were trustworthy men.

The question arises, then, whether the formation and use of creeds, intended to be thus applied, is a legitimate office or function for the Church to undertake. The argument in behalf of the Church's right may be very briefly stated. It is assumed that Church fellowship includes, as one of its elements, the joint confession of the truth; also that one function of the Church—a function to which 'office power' ought to be applied—is to oversee this fellowship; and that another is to look to the maintenance of genuine Christian teaching, as distinguished from that which is spurious and subversive.[1] But the discharge of these functions implies that the Church shall pronounce upon certain doctrinal positions. It does not matter, at this point, whether the extent of doctrine which the Church ought to deal with in this form is great or small. Some such work, be it more or less, is implied in the function ascribed to the Church. A creed is the gathering together of determinations which may and must exist, in the same or equivalent terms, in the Church's action about individual cases of admission or deposition. Certain doctrines the Church cannot allow the want of; certain others she cannot allow the presence of. What they are, or what some of them are, is stated

---

[1] 2 Pet. ii. 1; Jude 4; Acts xx. 29, 31; Rom. xvi. 17; 1 Tim. v. 22, vi. 3, 5; 2 Tim. ii. 2; Tit. i. 9-13, iii. 10; Rev. ii. 20.

for the guidance of those it may concern. The statement being based on Revelation, becomes a creed. This is only the more formal, deliberate, and considerate performance of a duty involved in every authoritative act falling into the categories referred to above.

The main objections against creeds and confessions are embodied in the allegation that they prejudice the just authority of Scripture, and also the just liberty of members and ministers of the Church. Under the first branch of the allegation, it is maintained, not indeed that creeds, as used in Protestant churches, impeach the sole authority of Scripture plainly and directly, but that they do so virtually and practically. For, it is argued, they bring an immensely powerful influence to bear in favour of the reception of a human form of words as the authorized exposition of revealed truth. Their operation, therefore, tends to bind up the Church in a human system, and to hinder the proper influence of the inspired writings in moulding and swaying the thoughts of believers. This is represented as especially objectionable, because the influence employed for this purpose is a peculiar one. It is Church discipline, *i.e.* the administration of authority about ordinances instituted by Christ, ordinances in which all believers have a divinely-conferred interest and right. To apply this form of influence to the purpose now referred to, is represented as a bold misapplication of it. Hence, on the one hand, the proper standard, the word of God, is made to speak through the mouthpiece of a human summary; on the other hand, the liberty of the members of the Church is prejudiced: they are subjected to an abridgment of their rights, and also to a form of temptation which the Church has no right to inflict upon them. Various injurious consequences are represented as ensuing; among others, this, that the proper study of the word of God is impeded, and the proper fruits of such study are diminished. Men are compelled, or tempted, to confine their thoughts to a fixed mould which man has provided. This, it is said, is objectionable simply because the mould is human, apart from the possibility of its being distorted. This consequence, and many others, may be expanded and illustrated in various ways. The main strength of the objection, however, lies, I think, in the considerations just now stated. Some of the objectors connect their argument with the more extensive position, that the Church has no right to censure or exclude on account of any doctrinal opinions, or, at any rate, has no right to exact the acknowledgment of any but the most obvious, rudimentary, and uncontroverted Christian beliefs. Others, however, maintain the right of the Church to supervise the doctrinal teaching, and to censure serious errors; but they consider that this duty would be best discharged by a direct appeal to Scripture, interpreted by the present mind and heart of the Church as each case arises. Therefore they also, in the manner suited to their own point of view, appropriate and urge the objections to creeds which have been stated.

Before dealing with these objections, it is proper to make an admission. That creeds and confessions are warrantable and expedient, is the thesis which I maintain. But it is freely admitted that churches have existed, and do exist, which maintain scriptural doctrine and effective discipline without the aid of documents of this kind. The Congregational churches generally occupy this position.[1] In such cases, as we maintain, the very same work is done, in a less advantageous manner, which with us is done in a more advantageous. The creed is extemporized in each particular case in which doctrine comes into view; or rather the creed, which exists as an understanding in the minds of the community,—formed, under the guidance of Scripture, by the habit of dealing with the doctrinal responsibilities of church life,—is applied to each case by a somewhat rougher process than with us. In their practice, no doubt, they may sometimes escape the inconveniences attendant on precision. On the other hand, we, in ours, escape some of those which are connected with vagueness. From our point of view, it seems more than doubtful whether the system which our friends prefer could be extensively worked by any but Congregational churches.[2] We doubt also whether their system, in effect, promotes any enlarged degree of reliance on Scripture only, or any greater measure of individual liberty. However that may be, the admission remains, that formally documented creeds have been dispensed with altogether in churches which have continued to give rigorous effect to their doctrinal responsibilities. But it is not admitted that the application of one single principle of Church action, which we apply in our administration by a confession, is dispensed with by the churches now referred to. They also apply an interpretative subordinate standard, but it is not written.

[1] Note C. [2] Note D.

In reply to the objections urged against creeds, arguments are sometimes pleaded in a form too absolute and wide to be convincing. It has often been said, for instance, that the Church is surely as free as any society to fix her own terms of membership and office. No one is forced to become a member of the Church. Every one is free to judge for himself, whether or no he can comply with the terms. In these circumstances, to prohibit the Church to make her own rules, on pretext of maintaining the liberty of individuals, is in fact to assail liberty. It is to withhold from the Church, in the name of liberty, the liberty to give effect to her own constitution, and her own responsibilities, by effective administrative provisions and conditions,—a liberty inherent in every society, and a liberty which may be presumed to inhere especially in a society which derives authority from divine institution. To this the objector may reply, that the question of course is simply this, not whether the Church ought to have liberty, but what view the Church ought to take of her own liberty, and of the manner in which power should be exercised. The Church may hold herself free to do everything which she is ordained to do—everything that is plainly implied in her appointed functions. But she ought not to hold herself free to do anything that will prejudice the rights conferred on her members. It is a duty binding on believers to be members of the Church, and they have rights which ought not to be burdened or abridged without a plain warrant. It is argued, therefore, that to make the acceptance of any specific form of human words binding, is to impose a new burden on consciences. This, in the absence of clear Scripture authorizing it, must be regarded as an excess—a trespass which prejudices previous rights. On this state of the argument, it is to be admitted that the plea of the liberty inherent in voluntary societies to fix their own constitution and terms of membership is not sufficient. Nor is it even sufficient, in addition, to prove that the doctrines contained in the Church's confession can be each of them vindicated as to their truth from Scripture. It must be further shown that the application of some such method as this, materially identical with it, or equivalent to it, is required of the Church, or falls necessarily to her in the discharge of her appointed functions.

Another line of argument pursued by the defenders of confessions turns on the difference between members and office-bearers. In most branches of the Church, private members are not subjected to any precise or stringent testing by means of the Church's creed. Those only are subjected to this process who are admitted to office. Now, in regard to the allegations that creeds tend to stereotype the minds of men in traditional forms, and to obstruct that frank investigation of Scripture which might detect errors in received views, and open the way to new truth, it has been maintained that the membership at all events are free to search, canvas, and discover, even if those who take office for good and sufficient reasons submit to some abridgment of their liberty. Then, again, it is maintained that even in their case this abridgment is rather apparent than real. Office-bearers are not held bound to believe no more than the creed. Believing that, they may go on to build upon it whatever they find taught in Scripture. Moreover, if they are led to think that Scripture does not authorize, or positively condemns, the received teaching in any point, they are entitled and bound to follow the guidance of Scripture, only resigning their office if they cannot persuade the Church to agree with them. The pathways of Scripture investigation, therefore, lie open as before; the duty of searching out the meaning of Scripture, and the right to follow its guidance only, remain unimpeached and unobstructed by the use of creeds or confessions, at least in churches which are genuinely Protestant. Such is the argument. There is one part of it on which I should be indisposed to lay much stress in dealing with the objection now under consideration,—I mean the distinction taken between the case of ordinary members and that of office-bearers. The distinction between the position of these two classes, with reference to confessions, is certainly very important on some accounts; but in so far as concerns the duty of the Church to maintain the influence of Scripture on believing minds, and to do justice to Scripture teaching, it does not avail much to say that the ordinary members are free, even if the holders of office are in some sense bound. If the clergy are limited and confined, in their relation to Scripture, by subscription to confessions, then the whole Church is so. For that class is bound, as it is presumably qualified, to go before the people in the whole department of thoughtful investigation of revealed truth; and in point of fact, it is through the ministry in a very great degree that the contact of the average mind of the Church with revealed truth, and its working about revealed truth, is regulated. The question returns, therefore, with a force little diminished : *Are* the office-bearers of the Church limited and prejudiced in their relation to Scripture by the application of creeds and confessions ? And far the best, because the candid reply, is, that confessions so applied do operate as a temptation which it is not always easy to overcome. Confessions, as I believe, are practically indispensable to the Church. They confer also most important benefits on those who are called to accept them, first by the guidance which they supply, and secondly by the decision and precision which the necessity of reckoning with them brings into men's views. But they do unquestionably tend, and they may sometimes powerfully tend, to bias men's minds with reference to the single-eyed investigation of truth. On this point, it is quite truly said by opponents of confessions, that they operate not so often by disposing a man to conceal his formed opinions, but rather by disposing him to avoid frank and perfectly sincere investigation when doubts or questions arise which, as he foresees, might bring him into collision with confessional teaching. He is tempted to form a habit of undue deference to the human document, to the consent which it expresses, and the antiquity which invests it. He is tempted to let himself be paralyzed with reference to every movement that might eventually lead him out of the road which human hands have mapped out for him. The temptations which operate in this connection are not necessarily sordid. Most often they are not so. There need be no profound sympathy with a man whose temptations turn on the retention or the sacrifice of clerical income. But temptation may rise out of the strength and depth of the feelings with which he looks forward to the ministry as his life's work, or out of the habits and the ties which he has formed during years of life already devoted to it. Sacrifices of this kind may seem less capable of being borne; and interests of this order may seem to have a right to command out of their way the difficulties which investigation, if pursued, might be found to raise.

I do not understand, nor do I wish to understand, the state of mind of a man who has not felt temptation arising from this quarter. The existence of it ought to be admitted. The occasional strength of it ought not to be denied. And the answer to the argument grounded on it must be found simply in the position, that men were intended to deal with temptations, to feel the force of them, and to overcome them. When they come to us in a way of duty, we shall be the better for them, if we deal rightly with them. Sources of temptation wantonly or needlessly created are always to be condemned. If the use of confessions ranks in this category, let them be condemned. But if it falls in the line of the proper duty of the Church, then the fact that certain temptations prove to be connected with them, need neither surprise us nor frighten us. But it may certainly dispose us to show caution, more caution than has sometimes been exhibited by churches in this department.

Now the right of the Church to use creeds, with the view of sustaining them by discipline, will best appear by considering the case of heresy.

Heresy is doctrine persistently professed and maintained which subverts what is fundamental in Christianity. When any branch of the Church meets with doctrine which it deliberately judges to be thus subversive, that is, for it, a heresy. There may be doctrines not properly designated by so severe a word, even though they are judged to be wrong, and to call both for opposition and for the use of all possible influence with a view to correction. But when a doctrine appears, and is maintained, which is judged to subvert that which is fundamental, it is counted to be a heresy.[1] It is of course admitted that, according to the different points of view that may be assumed, men may differ in their appreciation of what is fundamental in Christianity; and in that case they will differ proportionally in their reckoning of what is properly to be called heresy. Men and churches will therefore make different applications of the idea which the term conveys; yet to each it is an important idea, and for each it has an important bearing on practice.

Even for the individual, the contact with heresy in the Church raises a serious question. He is partaker in a fellowship in which the one truth is rejoiced in together, and confessed together. That need not make him intolerant of all differences. Amid many divergences of judgment fellowship may go on, each member receiving the other (as he was himself received by Christ) with what appear to be his imperfections. But when the question comes to be of one who, professing to hold the Divine Revelation, teaches what appears to subvert it in the fundamentals, a

[1] Note E.

difficulty is at once raised. Can or ought the fellowship or the common profession to be continued in that case? Is it consistent with personal fidelity? Is it consistent with a true regard to the highest interests of the heretic himself?

The Church, at all events, in regulating and overseeing the fellowship of believers, as Church members, must take action in such cases. For her mission is to deal with sins and offences which break the communion of believers and deny the faith. The express maintenance of a doctrine which subverts the faith in fundamentals, can never be looked on as admissible in the communion that is built upon the faith, that lives in the profession of it, and that holds it forth to the world. Therefore the Church has always made it clear, that those who join in membership with her are expected to be one in faith, so far at least that errors of the kind now under consideration are not explicitly maintained. Beyond that point, it has never been usual to press hard on those who are only members of the Church, and are not entrusted with official influence. There are so many reasons, and so strong, for guarding their rights with peculiar care,—there is so much to suggest large allowances in the case of persons whose opportunities and attainments may vary indefinitely,—that acquiescence in the known teaching of the Church, or in its main articles, has generally been treated as sufficient. But in the case of those who occupy a representative position something more has been felt to be necessary. Some explicit evidence that they stand clear of heretical aberrations, it is reasonable to ask, and reasonable to render.

Now the manner in which creeds come into being and operation, with reference to this necessity, stands in close connection with what we have seen already of the office of the believer and the Church in the matter of doctrine. We saw that there grows up, among believers and in the Church, an utterance of that which the revealed teaching has led them to think and to say. A meaning has grown up in many minds under that teaching; it has assumed definite form, and it claims utterance. In a good degree, it is a consenting or united utterance. And when heresy comes upon the field, the various anxious processes which result in creeds are in fact the formation, by the Church, of a solemn judgment, that *so much* of this meaning, carefully expressed, must be regarded as belonging to the consent and fellowship of Christians; or at least the formal and explicit denial of it must be regarded as a revolt from divine teaching in fundamentals, and as breaking the fellowship of the Church in the one truth. In order to come to such a judgment, the Church need not pretend to be infallible. It is enough if there be such a persuasion as will bear the weight of the responsibility incurred in deciding the practical question. Nor is it implied that the *mere* words in which the decision happens to be couched are to be treated as sacred and essential. Athanasius was willing to be considerate and forbearing with reference to scruples at words in the Nicene Creed itself. Still, words carefully selected in such circumstances to express a meaning, commonly do express it aptly; so that, in practice, words and meaning have to go together.

Hence arise creeds, in so far as creeds are opposed to heresy. They express a portion of the *meaning* bred in Christian hearts and minds by revealed teaching. Concerning this portion, the Church has arrived at the conclusion that the denial of it must be treated as subverting the fundamentals, and as introducing into the Christian Church a discord that breaks communion. The application of creeds to office-bearers is first of all for the purpose of ascertaining that they are agreed with the Church in points of this kind. Assume that Arianism is a heresy; assume that the Nicene Creed is the counter-statement fitted to exclude it, and to affirm the fundamental truth which Arianism assails; then the application of this creed to office-bearers is for the purpose of ascertaining that on this fundamental at least, on which a difference has emerged which the Church judges to be intolerable, those admitted to teach and rule are not representatives of the heresy.

If it be part of the duty of the Church to see that those put in trust with the ministry are sound in the faith; if for this purpose it is right to enter into explanations, and to require them,—it does not appear unlawful or improper that a careful and well-considered explanation in selected words should be employed; nor that it should be agreed upon with some solemnity at the entrance into the ministry. This line of argument will not, indeed, vindicate any and every form of creed; for such forms may include a great deal more than what is simply fitted to affirm fundamentals against heresies, *i.e.* against forms of opinion which the Church feels bound to recognise and treat as heresies. But it does appear sufficient to vindicate the use of *some* form of creed.

Moreover, it suggests a consideration which establishes the same conclusion in another way. The Church does not exact, and ought not to exact, of her office-bearers complete uniformity of belief. Points are and ought to be left open on which men may differ; agreed in receiving the same rule of faith, they may differ in their understanding of some parts of its teaching. In order, then, to justify disciplinary procedure, it is not enough to show that a minister holds views which the Church in general, if called to decide, would judge to be not scriptural. It must also be shown that they are views which ought not to be borne with in a minister. Those who say that discipline in the matter of erroneous doctrine ought to proceed in the method of a direct appeal to Scripture, and to Scripture alone, virtually prescribe to the Church the duty of solving a double problem in each case. Not only the question, Is this view, in our conscientious judgment, erroneous?—but also this, Is it an error of such quality and magnitude that it ought not to be borne with?—demands an answer. The second question is often a delicate and difficult one. To leave it to be decided simply according to the impressions connected with each case, is to run the greatest hazard of arbitrary and inconsistent procedure. On the other hand, to form a judgment, under the influence of experience, as to the matters in which cognizance by discipline should proceed, and those in regard to which forbearance is expedient and right, and to record that judgment as the common understanding of the Church for the guidance of all parties, seems very expedient if not necessary. But this implies selection of topics and points; and the selection is virtually a creed. It gives you, not the whole Scriptures as interpreted by the Church, but something drawn out of the Scriptures as so interpreted. Something of the nature of a creed may thus be the proper protection against the imposition of an unqualified uniformity.

So far, I have spoken of the case of heresy. I have spoken of it separately, because in point of fact it illustrates the way in which the early creeds acquired doctrinal precision. Besides, heresy is in its own nature a constraining ground of procedure. The case is not one in which mere expediencies are involved, or questions of more or less edification. Considerations here urge to action which are definite and peremptory. The case, therefore, is distinguishable in principle from others which may be mingled with it in ecclesiastical practice. But I do not pretend that confessions and articles are commonly limited to material of this kind; neither will I maintain that they ought always to be so limited. Plainly, many points are determined in the Reformed confessions, of which no man will affirm that to decide them otherwise would be heresy in the sense in which I use the word. Confessions take a wider scope than the mere case of heresy.

This wider scope is perhaps hardly to be vindicated on general and permanent grounds. A special justification must be made out for it in each case. It might be well, therefore, for churches to cherish the consciousness that in their confessions there are two elements, or two strata of confessional matter. Those articles of the confession which exclude what the church in question is prepared to regard as heresy, constitute the solid core, which cannot alter unless the convictions of the whole Church should alter. Those articles which are not of this character may reasonably be regarded as the more variable element, which circumstances might require to be extended at one time and contracted at another.[1]

It would, indeed, be needless to advert to this distinction, if confessions were intended solely for the purpose of holding out to the world a statement of what the Church, with a general consent, holds for true on scriptural authority. For this purpose, all that is needed to vindicate any article is, that it be received as grounded on Revelation, and that it be regarded as sufficiently important to be distinctly stated. But we are at present dealing with confessions considered as tests of membership, and especially of office. In this view, there is reason for discrimination and for limitation. It is plain that, in placing limits on the admission of believers to membership and to office beyond what is called for by some plain necessity, the Church is assuming considerable responsibility. All her definitions are, admittedly, liable to imperfection; and the further she proceeds with them beyond the point indicated by such plain necessity, the more likely she is to manifest her fallibility. Besides, all such arrangements do no doubt tend, as already pointed out, to detain men's

[1] Note F.

minds somewhat in a human form of thought and speech, and to supply motives that sway them powerfully against forsaking it or varying from it. Although I have argued that this is no sufficient reason against forming and applying such documents, it is a reason against carrying the process beyond the point suggested by some clear justification.

But what that point is, can hardly, I fear, be determined by mere theory; certainly not by abstract and general theory, apart from consideration of the articles which it may be proposed to omit or to insert, their evidence, and their importance. Indeed, the extent to which symbolic writings shall be carried, must generally be regulated very much by a certain tact which, in applying Scripture materials to this purpose, decides what on the whole is reasonable, demanded by past and present necessities, and likely to work and to conduce to the various ends which are in view.

The motives which may induce the introduction of matter into confessions, beyond the bare utterance of fundamental truths as against clear heresies, are various. I still speak of confessions as designed to regulate admission to office, and exclude from view for the present the use of them for the mere purpose of declaring the prevailing persuasion of the Church, or of a branch of it.

Diversities of judgment on matters of doctrine, of which no enlightened man on either side will say that they involve the fundamentals, are sometimes attended with great practical perplexity. They do not hinder mutual recognition of one another as standing fast in the one faith; and yet they do sometimes obstruct practical communion. That is to say, the adherents of the divergent views find it difficult, or impossible, to get on together. The measure of light which they possess, and the points of view which they occupy, render this practically certain. With a prevailing spirit of indifference the attempt might be made, and made with some measure of success; but it would not be a desirable kind of success. Otherwise the attempt, if made, is found to issue in continual distrust, misunderstanding, and collision—in that serious kind of discomfort which partakes of the nature of scandal. It may be that the intensity of feeling connected with the points in dispute is too great. It may be that the truth held on either side inevitably suggests to the other a train of consequences in their view too necessary to be averted, and too repugnant to be endured. It may be that the difference runs into diverging views of practical duty too serious to be borne with. It may be that differences, which in a loosely constituted church give less trouble, would be fatal to the peace of one that is closely knit and organized for energetic action. A Wesleyan society may admit the Christian worth of decided Calvinists, but could hardly get on with such among its teachers. The Church of England can cohere, in its manner, notwithstanding many elements of contention; but it would probably explode if men in Presbyterian orders were received among the clergy; and their reception would be found unbearable by many, who would not maintain that ministrations by an episcopally ordained priesthood were absolutely necessary in order to salvation.

Again, there are schools of thought in theology—connected trains of view and of theological opinion, which for most minds go together. The mind that accepts the main positions in such a train or concatenation of doctrine, usually accepts the whole. The mind that decidedly rejects one of the positions, usually is led on ultimately, by the necessities of mental consistency, to reject the rest. They cannot all be said to be fundamental or of the first importance. The confession *might* therefore content itself with the statement of those which are considered primary, and proceed no further. Yet it is felt that a fuller declaration will more clearly ascertain what is meant; will guard against the annoyance of mere crotchet and inconsistency; will avert some of the troubles connected with incipient and half-conscious heresy. At the same time, for most men the fuller declaration will involve no additional burden, because, accepting the fundamental maxims, they will in all probability accept the detailed statements, which are connected and correlative. Considerations like these have operated silently, but powerfully, to introduce full statements on subordinate points into confessions; and not without reason, regard had to existing circumstances of the time when the confession was formed. Yet it must be owned that, just in these subordinate statements of detail, a profounder view of the whole department, should it be attainable, will by and by suggest palpable changes. The confession which embodies them acquires a school stamp, out of which unforeseen difficulties may arise after considerable periods have passed away.

Confessions, as applied to office-bearers, may be regarded as designed for the protection not only of the Church in general, but especially of ordinary members against teaching which might grieve and scandalize them. For unquestionably the Church has a regulative power, and may take cognizance of other failures in reference to doctrine besides that of a lapse into heresy. A minister might hold nothing which the Church should feel called upon to visit with condemnation, merely considered as his private opinions. And yet he might make such a use and application of some of these, that the Church which would tolerate the opinion, will not tolerate the mischief he makes by means of it. The question as between the Greek and the Latin view of the procession of the Holy Ghost ought not to have broken communion between East and West; and therefore, in certain circumstances, a Church might be right in avoiding the determination of that controversy in its confession. In point of fact, were it not that the point is determined in the creeds, most congregations now-a-days could not tell what views their pastors held upon the point, so little does it occur in public teaching. But in days when the interest in the subject was keen, when the East generally held, as it holds, one view, and the West another,—when each party recited its peculiar form of creed in worship, with a distinct consciousness of the special doctrine it involved,—the case was quite different. Suppose, then, that in those days a pastor in the East, becoming prepossessed in favour of Latin views, had begun to harp on the Western doctrine to his people with dogmatic pertinacity, ought the Church to have allowed him to persevere? Practically, they might have been saved the trouble of deciding, for the people would probably have stoned the priest. But, apart from that contingency, the clear duty of the Church would have been to restrain and suppress the indiscretion. Even if disposed (as the Eastern Church was not) to treat the question as one in which forbearance was proper, the Church authorities would be clearly right in forbidding the enthusiast to harass and irritate his flock. This is a consideration which legitimately enters into questions of discipline. It is not wonderful that it should affect the range taken in selecting materials for confessions.

There can be little doubt that a larger latitude might be practicable, as regards minor points, if any large degree of wisdom in the ordinary administration of Christian teaching could be ordinarily reckoned on. If one could count upon it, that a prevailing regard to the spirit and main scope of the gospel should uniformly regulate public teaching,—and a wise consideration of the convictions of those instructed,—and a modest estimate of the probable value of personal peculiarities of view,—then it might be easier to make room more freely for such peculiarities. But, in practice, a considerable amount of onesidedness and unwisdom, of pertinacious and senseless propagandism, must be reckoned on. With this in view, the protection of the congregations from what would vex and scandalize them, from what might raise irritating and bewildering discussion, demands more care. Not merely the existence of some diverging views in the minds of ministers and office-bearers, but the ardent or obstinate inculcation of them, requires to be contemplated, when the question is settled as to what shall be excluded, what treated as admissible. Sheer crotchetiness and unreason in the matter of doctrinal speculation, assertions which give scandal not so much because they affect anything of primary importance, but because they seem to disregard the plain and honest sense of Scripture,—these are forms of mischief against which it is reasonable to guard.

The churches have generally thought it well to give fair warning of what they expect, and feel entitled to exact, by calling on ministers and office-bearers to adopt statements by which they will abide. They have introduced into their creeds, on these grounds, statements and definitions which otherwise might possibly have been spared. Some material of this kind must probably have place. It is not easy to see how it can be avoided. It is not easy to represent to oneself how it is practically to be escaped. Nor is it a sufficient argument against it to say, or prove, that in the most perfect state of the Church, or in a conceivably perfect state, it would not be so. That may be true. And the latter state is to be striven after. Yet the existing state of the Church is a fact to which its arrangements must in some degree be adapted. The ideally perfect state is unity; yet all causes of division are not on that account to be overlooked. They exist, and must be recognised. So the Church may be in a state in which she is not yet qualified by considerateness, largeness of view, and love, to understand, tolerate, and put a charitable construction on differences, as at another period she may attain to do. Her confession may indicate the measure of her attainment. It may be an imperfect attainment; and yet it may be right that, such as it is, it should express itself. Certainly this should be accompanied by a sense of defect and of a standard of action as yet unattained.

There can be little doubt that, in modern times, ecclesiastical bodies have felt more free to embody in their confessions a tolerably full declaration of their peculiarities of view and action, and to bind this on all their office-bearers at least, because they are all aware of the existence of other communions. Let those, it is said or felt, who cannot accommodate themselves to our requirements, seek an ecclesiastical home elsewhere, under some ecclesiastical constitution which they may find more congenial. The notion is silently accepted, that churches are societies so arranged, that particular phases or types of Christian doctrine in which men are agreed may be cultivated and cherished, each in its own ecclesiastical compartment, on the understanding that for other types of view there are other churches. Now it would certainly be absurd to overlook the fact that there is such a variety of churches, or to deny that practically it settles with considerable convenience a number of problems, and so settles them as to leave no room for an appeal. I have never been able to see, however, that any church is at liberty to proceed in this matter on any principles but those which apply to the universal Church, or to accept any rule or mode of action which might not be adopted by the universal Church were it placed in the same circumstances. This does not imply that each church is to throw down its walls to admit all the others; but simply that the point of view of the universal Church ought to be accepted as the fundamental one. I admit that there are great difficulties in the way of practically applying such a rule. I am disposed to think, however, that they are difficulties which ought to be faced. If on special grounds it is held right to impose terms which the Catholic Church of Christ, as such, would not be warranted in imposing, this ought at least to be taken as marking an imperfection, indicating a barrier not yet surmounted in the way to the attainment of a more perfect state.

The argument has proceeded on the assumption that creeds are the utterance of the living, present Church. The revealed teaching which the Church receives, and on which she lives, she reproduces in her creed. Thus surely it ought to be. The Church has no right to speak, except out of present and actual conviction. The authority of Revelation is binding, but not that of any past age of the Church's own history. Only those who assert the existence of an infallible earthly authority, as interpreter of Scripture and judge of controversies, can dispute this. But then, as a matter of fact, creeds are commonly inherited. This age would be poorly provided unless the past furnished a supply. The ancient creeds have lasted since the third, fourth, or fifth centuries. The confessions are mostly of the Reformation age, or of the age which followed. It is natural, from a certain point of view, to look upon this circumstance with suspicion. Here is proof, it may be said, that the creeds either beget or express a slavish sequacious spirit, which makes the words of dead men the rule and standard of its thinking. Whether they beget it or express it, they are alike objectionable. You profess, it may be said, to believe in Scripture only as the binding rule; you repudiate the belief in the infallibility of human creeds. And yet you treat them as if it were inconceivable that you should actually find them fallible. The teaching and experience of hundreds of years does not enable you to find a single particular in which they ought to be altered, or are capable of being improved! Is this because their fallible authors made them perfect? Or is it because you count it enough to profess Protestant principles, and shrink from applying them?

I reply by affirming, in the first place, that there is reason for endeavouring, if it be possible, to utter the present faith so as to bring out the consent of past ages with our own. For while we are all fallible, and subject to the sway of time, even in our modes of apprehending and expressing truth eternal, yet there is a durable identity in the faith of believers. All is not in perpetual flux. The admonition to seek the truth implies that it may be found, and that we may know that we have found it.[1] An enlightened and established believer remains to the end of his days a learner. He is willing to believe that some measure of mistake, which further progress can correct, may cleave in many respects to the convictions he has formed, even his convictions on the most important questions. Yet he is quite sure that much of what he knows and believes never can be swept away. On points less certain and less important he may

[1] Note G.

have much to correct; and even with respect to the more certain and settled truths, some fresh adjustment of his thoughts may prove to be called for. But in the main, these last are his permanent acquisition, his fixed possession. It is no good sign of any man that he ceases to learn; but neither is it a good sign of any man that he fluctuates on all points to the last, and never reaches settled convictions. So also with the Church, or with any branch of the Church, in which the faith of the gospel dwells with power. There is truth attained which abides, though *all* be not truth which the Church in any one age may be disposed to take for truth. There is a consent which echoes from age to age, as well as from man to man; and the testimony of the Church is not merely the consent of the Church in one age, but also of the Church in sundry ages. It is well to feel this, and to make it felt, that believers, with whatever infirmities, drawing from one fountain of knowledge, and sitting at the feet of one teacher, have been learning the same lessons. It is well to make it felt, that the truth is not a fashion of our minds, but durable and perennial, and receives the same testimony from men in different times. All this is well, if it be possible; and for the reasons just given, it ought to be possible. Therefore we are glad to recognise in the early creeds the hand of God leading the Church to modes of utterance which we can take up and affirm. We rejoice in the harmony of the Reformation confessions, and we feel no cause to be ashamed of the strength and symmetry of that which we receive. But with all this, it must be affirmed unequivocally, that all these exist subject to correction. This concession must not be a mere idle flourish; it must exist in the Church as a living, practical, powerful principle. Loyalty to God's supreme word requires it; and where it is withdrawn or denied, the defence of creeds, on Protestant principles, becomes impossible.

Romanists may maintain the immutable authority of every utterance of the collective Church, or of its earthly head. They may do so consistently, so far, since they hold the Church to be infallible. We who deny the principle, reject also the inference. We assert not the right only, but the duty, of the Church, and every branch of it, to hold confessions and subordinate standards subject to correction. For as the inspired teaching is before the Church,[1] so the Church is before the confession. Therefore, if a case arise which proves to be not sufficiently provided for in the confession, we may add to it; and if we find Scripture so requiring, we may abridge or modify it; or we may take another in its room, if we find that likely to be more for edification.

This is generally admitted by Protestants; and the defence of creeds and confessions in Protestant churches is usually combined with that admission, or rather, is based upon it. It is the practice rather than the theory which admits of question in this respect; for opponents of creeds have some colour for asserting that no due effect is given in practice to what is admitted in theory. The inherited creeds, it is said, are retained; no effective method of revising them

[1] Note H.

exists. The consent of generations gives them a prestige on account of which no one will venture to question their authority. Those who feel only some dissatisfaction with their adaptation to present circumstances are content to let them alone, rather than encounter the responsibilities and face the questions which revision might entail. Those who see cause to entertain more serious objections are disabled morally, by the fact that subscription imposes on them an obligation to resign their positions, and so their right to influence a decision. At all events, a call for revision from those who object to material parts of the confessional teaching, tends always to rally on the old lines those who in general agree with it. They sink the opinions which might have led them to seek readjustment of details, in order that they may take the ground most convenient for fighting out the larger question. Thus the inherited confession comes to be treated as practically unalterable and irremovable, until perhaps a recoil takes place, and the Church, or a party in it too powerful to be controlled, breaks loose from it altogether. All this is unedifying and indefensible. Such is the view given of the practical operation of our creed system.

There is a measure of truth in it. In churches in which confessional writings are maintained and valued, while the right to revise is asserted, there is commonly great scrupulosity about the use of it. Tenderness and reverence are due to documents like these; and tenderness and reverence are due to the feelings with which they are regarded, on account of the interests with which they are connected, and the truths which they have been a mouthpiece to express. Instead of making difficulties, multiplying scruples, and readily entertaining projects for change, men are rather disposed to dwell on the advantages enjoyed in virtue of the existing system. And this, if only it is not carried so far as to lead us to forget more primary obligations, is the wiser and better temper. For it is not a reasonable assumption to start with, that the confession of a church should need much or frequent alteration. If it does, either the confession has been ill planned at the outset,—has been a failure as regards the proper qualities of this kind of performance,—or the church for which it is intended must be more than ordinarily unstable in its belief. Probably it would be better to be without any confessions, than to be always rebuilding them. These documents ought not to contain problematical matter, but rather that which is believed to be plentifully proved and surely fixed : they ought, therefore, to be so related to the central and durable convictions of the Church as to be likely to sustain the impression of the stability of Scripture teaching. Usually the circumstances of their origin secure in a good measure that they fulfil this condition.

Still it cannot be assumed that they have actually attained this character, especially when they are of some length and minuteness; and therefore it might be desirable to secure that, on any fair call, the Church's attention should be directed to any part of the confession supposed to require revision, not as a singular and revolutionary step, but as something belonging to her ordinary and recognised responsibilities. At present, any proposal to reconsider the confession would be felt in most of the Presbyterian churches as a revolutionary proposal, opening the way to unimaginable possibilities. Such a feeling is not consistent with the true position in which creeds and confessions ought to stand, nor with a right conception of the relation of the Church to her doctrinal teaching generally. And it is attended with danger; for, supposing a revision to become ultimately inevitable, it is apt to take the character of a revolutionary movement, which bursts through barriers long maintained, and effects a sweeping change. Regular provision for considering changes that might be proposed, would not, in all likelihood, lead to frequent actual changes. It would not do so in any case in which a branch of the Church possesses a wisely drawn confession to begin with, and continues to adhere in the main to the type of doctrine which it embodies. But in giving effect to modifications which might be generally agreed upon as clear improvements, and in ensuring deliberate consideration of suggestions, it would operate as a conservative arrangement. It would ease the pressure of the feeling, which constitutes half our danger, that men are held in the grasp of ancient formulas, received merely because they are ancient, from whose determinations, even of the smallest points, there is no real appeal. It would give to the confession an added weight and authority, as being more manifestly expressive of the actual and living mind of the Church. Finally, it would make it plain that confessions, as mere human compositions, are kept in their own place, and are not allowed to assume an immutability injurious to the sole authority of the word of God.[1]

Changes on an extant confession which is in authority may be desired on various grounds, and the changes proposed may be of different kinds. New determinations may be thought needful to be introduced, on the ground of errors arising which are not sufficiently provided for; or articles may be amended, to make them more scriptural or more clear; or articles may be wholly dismissed, on the ground that they have been ascertained to be not well grounded in the Scriptures. In all such cases the material merits are involved, and they shall not further occupy our attention. But it may be proposed simply to abridge, on the ground that, however scriptural the articles to be omitted may be, they are not fitly introduced into a confession; that the whole document is larger than churches are entitled to use, and makes statements in more detail than is suitable in formularies of this kind. At present this is one of the main points urged with respect to confessions and articles. The demand for a briefer creed may very likely receive an impulse in many cases from the objections entertained, upon the merits, to particular articles of the existing creed. But the argument is often urged, apart from those objections, on the ground of the mere unwarrantableness of burdening the access to office in the church with an obligation to make such an extensive profession of belief in articles drawn up by men. The question thus raised is a perfectly fair one, but frank and unembarrassed consideration is not easily procured for

[1] Note I.

it. Nor is this surprising. If the point were urged by those only who desire the great characteristic features of the faith of the churches to remain, and to be protected by the best possible kind of confession, an unprejudiced hearing would more readily be accorded. But since those also are in the field who have more serious objections in reserve, and contemplate more sweeping changes, the point before us is naturally treated as only the advanced guard of an invading enemy. Yet it is certainly entitled to be considered and judged upon its own merits.

It has already been remarked, that the Reformation confessions were intended for, or were applied to, two purposes. They were intended, in the first place, to announce what was held for truth with a general consent in each of the churches, and so to clear away all doubt as to the actual teaching. They were intended, in the next place, or were applied, to ascertain that candidates for office, especially for the ministry, held views sufficiently accordant with those of the Church to justify their being invested with office power. There is nothing unnatural in the same document being used for both these purposes. It may seem very fit that the statement which embodies the Church's testimony should be adopted by all who are to act as guides in the Church. An indisposition to make distinctions, and to provide for the two objects, as two, must indeed be expected. Minds that are strongly interested in doctrine always desire to give practical expression to the sense which they cherish of its importance. If ten statements have been embodied in a church's testimony, it will seem to such minds to be something like advertising the unimportance of half of them, to make five, only, terms of office. Many will always regard such a distinction as invidious and unsafe. Still it does not follow that the same document must always equally well serve both purposes, or that whatever is fit for the one purpose must be fit also for the other.[1] The Church may be prepared to give the weight of its collective voice and influence in favour of a larger array of doctrinal statement, because in point of fact the whole of it has gained her general suffrage. It will naturally be desired that this extensive consent should continue. But the best, the safest, the most warrantable way of promoting that object, may quite conceivably be, to stand upon a more moderate statement as constituting the binding terms of office, and to trust for the rest to the influence of accepted truth in regulating the cast of a man's whole thinking, and also to the moulding influence of the cast of thought and the tone of piety prevailing in the body. Be all this as it may, no adequate discussion has been given to the question, Supposing a right in the Church to exact something as a condition of admission to office, how much is she justified in exacting? It has been superseded, for the most part, by the general question of the competency of creeds; as if enough were done when it had once been proved that the Church is entitled, collectively and in some permanent form, to give witness for what she judges to be divine truth.[2]

I have already indicated my conviction that the question now referred to cannot be disposed of by

[1] Note J.   [2] Note K.

general and theoretical considerations alone. It can be settled only by a discussion of the material merits of each confession, and of the range which it covers. Discussion of this order is not in view in these Lectures. But it is useful to observe that, from the nature of the case, there will always probably be room for some difference of opinion as to the proper border line, even among those who are generally agreed on the previous and more important question as to the scheme of doctrine which the Scriptures authorize. This is a consideration which may reasonably assuage the spirit of impatience which is apt to arise on both sides, when questions are pressed with reference to confessions. Nothing, indeed, exerts more influence in the way of disposing sober-minded men to be exceeding slow to stir such questions, than the sense, the just sense, of the difficulty of prescribing the new *limits*, and agreeing upon them as scriptural, defensible, and serviceable.

Yet we shall not be always able to escape questions because the solution of them involves difficulties. If the question now before us shall prove to be one which presses for fresh examination, I am disposed to think that it will prove to be of importance to keep separate and prominent the case of fundamentals already dwelt upon, with heresies as the correlative on the negative side. I do not propound this as sufficient to remove the difficulties. It is not so easy to agree precisely as to which are the fundamentals and which the heresies. And if it were agreed upon precisely, it is not to be assumed, as I have stated already, that confessions can or ought to be confined to just these points. But yet the citadel of symbols, considered as subordinate standards, will be found to lie in this quarter. There are fundamentals of Christian doctrine; and there are heresies—forms of doctrine which, professing to build on Christian Revelation, and appropriating its words, yet subvert the fundamentals. That will never be doubted by earnest Christians; nor will they fail to give effect to it in some shape when their attention is drawn to it. Now if such points are to be efficiently provided for in symbolical books, they must be provided for in precise and definite forms of expression. It is at this point that confessions assume those characteristic features of trenchant inclusion and exclusion, at which the ordinary objections are levelled which are brought against them. Those features or characteristics must be present, if we are to have confessions worth the having. Once that necessity is clearly accepted, the questions that remain, though they may be difficult, ought not to produce any fatal misunderstanding— ought not to be unsusceptible of a reasonable adjustment.

In the Presbyterian churches, more than one class of office-bearers has to be kept in view, and the practical relation of each to the existing confession must be differently estimated. Ministers, of course, and candidates for the ministry, are generally led to a more full and exact study of doctrine, and of the scope and bearing of the confession, than other office-bearers. It might be expected, perhaps, that difficulty would more frequently arise among them. I am not by any means sure that this is the case, at least if the question be of difficulties removable by any revision that is in the least likely to commend itself to the general mind and feeling of the Church. A certain number of men are stumbled and repelled by determinations on minor points which they cannot accept. Some more are repelled, probably, by the mere impression of having to deal with so large a range of points, and to make themselves formally responsible on them all. It strikes them as unreasonable and wrong. But in much the larger number of cases, the generally homogeneous character of the confession, as representing one coherent view of Scripture teaching, tells, in the end, in the way of removing difficulty. As the examination proceeds, the impression grows, that if some main positions can be cordially and thoroughly accepted, scruples about the rest become artificial and untenable. There remain, of course, cases in which able and conscientious men are led, as the result of their studies, to adopt alternatives on leading questions of theology different from those which the confession holds forth. But then, usually, the opposition to the teaching of the confession becomes so extensive and thorough, that revolution, not retrenchment, alone would meet the case.

With elders and deacons it is different. In Scotland, we have never been without elders and deacons of very considerable theological culture. Still the class, and not the exceptional individuals, are to be kept in view. As a class, these office-bearers are not called to the same kind of study of Christian doctrine which candidates for the ministry must undertake; their duties cannot be said to require it; their opportunities ordinarily do not admit of it. It often happens that men, who are otherwise fit for office, feel that particular determinations of the confession do not strike them as scriptural, or as falling in easily with the impressions they have been led to form. Others shrink from the mere extent of matter and variety of topics. In this way, a growing number of valuable men are lost to the service of the Church, and are harmed by finding no proper exercise for their gifts. Moreover, when no objection is made or felt, that sometimes proceeds from the fact that the confession, as too arduous for detailed examination, is taken *en bloc*, on the strength of its general character,—a compromise which no one will regard as desirable.[1]

The subject of this Lecture has been treated under a strong sense of the practical necessity of creeds and confessions, combined with a strong impression of the danger to which the defence of them will be exposed, unless it is conducted with a resolute readiness to keep them in their place as human compositions, and to meet frankly every fair call to reconsider the form and measure which their authors have given to them. It may appear, that since so much has been said of revision, no very strong impression of the difficulties or the dangers attendant on that enterprise can exist in the writer's mind. This idea, if it is entertained, is erroneous. I should find it difficult to express the sense which I entertain both of the difficulties and the dangers, mainly on account of considerations which shall be mentioned presently. I should find it difficult

[1] Note L.

to convey the importance which I attach, I do not say to retaining the faith of the divine truth, which is not here in question, but to a wise stedfastness in refusing to vary the confessional expression of it, except for grave causes, and in the calmest and most deliberate manner. But then I am convinced that all the dangers and the difficulties are greatly aggravated by the formation of a habit of church life to which the idea of revision becomes something strange, monstrous, almost sacrilegious. I am convinced that, to familiarize our minds with the topic, is the true way to diminish the dangers of it. To look upon it habitually as a task that may at any time become incumbent, consisting in the reconsideration of some point or points of our standard of doctrinal qualification for office, in connection with the maintenance of the divine unchangeable faith,—this is much more likely than the opposite habit, to avert inconsiderate changes, and the instability from which they spring.

For the most serious source of apprehension in connection with this subject is suggested by experience. There has been every variety of measure and manner, of sobriety and of the reverse, in the assertion of doctrine, and the embodiment of it in symbolical writings. But one thing cannot be doubted. A high Christian enthusiasm has usually been connected with strong and decided affirmation of doctrine, and with a disposition to speak it out ever *more* fully. That temper has been venturesome to speak, even as it has been venturesome to do; as little fearing to declare God's word in human speech, as to embody His will in human acts. It has not been disposed, for the most part, to moderate, or withdraw, or pare down doctrinal statements, unless indeed when it had to denounce them as materially erroneous, and to set against them what it judged true and sound. On the other hand, when a tendency has been shown to moderate and lower the Church's utterance, to reduce the number of its articles, or shape them in less peremptory words, that has proved to be due, not always, but too often, to just the reverse of Christian enthusiasm or earnestness—to a cold rationalistic temper, or to the influence of human prejudice and human insubordination. If other, more Christian, motives and influences have been at work, too often they have been merged in a larger stream of those just described, and have served only to give character and credit to them. One mourns, seeing the mischief done by indefensible creeds, that no fitter hands proved ready to readjust them, and that it was left to semi-Christian and to unchristian feeling to do, in their own way, what Christian feeling should have done in its way. One laments that the Lutheran creeds, for instance, utterly indefensible as documents intended for creed purposes, should have been upheld and kept standing till they simply became a mockery, instead of being timeously taken in hand for reconsideration by Christian zeal and discretion.[1] But clearly all this admonishes us what kind of forces (not those we wish for) are apt to be at work in the revision of creeds. No Protestant can shut out the question whether some alteration may not be desirable or incumbent. But would that the question might be faced, when it must be faced, with a

[1] Note M.

great power of Christian life—with a true Christian enthusiasm bringing forth its proper fruits,—an enthusiasm for Christian truth combined with enthusiasm for Scripture simplicity and for Christian love.

The work of the Church's Head is always perfect, but the work of His Church and people is always mixed. At the best it is mixed, and sometimes the mixture of alien elements is great and disastrous. There are divine gifts in the Church's hands; but as she lifts them up in thanksgiving to God, or in ministry to men, they always take some stain from the hands which hold them. Nor does the use of them ever correspond perfectly with the Lord's will.

Yet Christ has always had a Church on the earth, and He has never forsaken it. Through the whole train of works and functions in which the Church has been engaged, amid all the marks of human shallowness, waywardness, and error, we may yet trace the tokens of One who blesses. So, though we may not overlook the Church's failings, we may not deny the Lord's gifts. We must not deny them in His own hands; neither may we deny them in the hands of those on earth whom He has enabled to follow and to serve Him.

Such are some of the thoughts which occur in closing a survey of the questions which gather about the delivery and development of Christian doctrine.

NOTES.

T

LECTURE I.

Note A.—Page 6.

Ἀλλ' οὐ γέγραπται ταῦτα, φασὶν, καὶ ὡς ἀγράφους τὰς φωνὰς ἐκβάλλομεν. Ἀλλὰ καὶ τοῦτο πάλιν πρόφασίς ἐστιν αὐτοῖς ἀναίσχυντος. Εἰ γὰρ ἐκβλητέα νομίζουσι τὰ μὴ γεγραμμένα, διὰ τί τῶν περὶ Ἄρειον ἐξ ἀγράφων ἐπινοησάντων τοσοῦτον ῥηματίων συρφετὸν, τὸ, ἐξ οὐκ ὄντων, καὶ τὸ, οὐκ ἦν ὁ Υἱὸς πρὶν γεννηθῇ· καὶ, ἦν ποτε ὅτε οὐκ ἦν· καὶ, τρεπτός ἐστι· καὶ, ἄρρητος καὶ ἀόρατος ὁ Πατὴρ τῷ Υἱῷ· καὶ, ὁ Υἱὸς οὐκ οἶδεν οὐδὲ τὴν ἑαυτοῦ οὐσίαν· καὶ ὅσα ἐν τῇ γελοίῳ καὶ ἀσεβεῖ Θαλίᾳ ἑαυτοῦ φρονῶν ἐξήμεσεν Ἄρειος οὐκ ἀντειρήκασιν, ἀλλὰ καὶ μᾶλλον ὑπὲρ αὐτῶν ἀγωνίζονται, καὶ διὰ ταῦτα πρὸς τοὺς πατέρας ἑαυτῶν διαμάχονται. Ἐκ ποίας δὲ Γραφῆς καὶ αὐτοὶ εὑρόντες τὸ ἀγένητον, καὶ τὸ οὐσίας ὄνομα, καὶ, τρεῖς εἰσιν ὑποστάσεις, καὶ, οὐκ ἔστιν ἀληθινὸς Θεὸς ὁ Χριστὸς, καὶ, εἷς ἐστι τῶν ἑκατὸν προβάτων, καὶ, ἡ μὲν σοφία τοῦ Θεοῦ ἀγέννητος καὶ ἄναρχός ἐστι, πολλαὶ δέ εἰσιν αἱ κτισθεῖσαι δυνάμεις, ὧν μία ἐστὶν ὁ Χριστός; Ἢ πῶς ἐν τοῖς λεγομένοις Ἐγκαινίοις, ἀγράφοις χρησάμενοι λέξεσιν οἱ περὶ Ἀκάκιον καὶ Εὐσεβίον, καὶ εἰπόντες οὐσίας τε καὶ δυνάμεως, καὶ βουλῆς, καὶ δόξης ἀπαράλλακτον εἰκόνα τὸν πρωτότοκον τῆς κτίσεως, γογγύζουσι κατὰ τῶν Πατέρων, ὡς ἀγράφων αὐτῶν μνημονευσάντων; Ἔδει γὰρ αὐτοὺς ἢ καθ' ἑαυτῶν γογγύζειν, ἢ μηδὲν τοὺς Πατέρας αἰτιᾶσθαι.—ATHAN. *De Synodis*, § 36.

Note B.—Page 8.

'Non enim per alios, dispositionem salutis nostrae cognovimus, quam per eos, per quos evangelium pervenit ad nos; quod quidem tunc praeconaverunt, postea vero per Dei voluntatem in Scripturis nobis tradiderunt, fundamentum et columnam fidei nostrae. Nec enim fas est dicere, quoniam ante praedicaverunt quam perfectam haberent agnitionem sicut quidam audent dicere, gloriantes emendatores se esse apostolorum. . . . Quum enim ex Scripturis arguuntur in accusationem convertuntur ipsarum Scripturarum, quasi non recte habeant, neque sint ex auctoritate, et quia varie sint dictae, et quia non possit ex his inveniri veritas ab his qui nesciant traditionem. Non enim per literas traditam illam sed per vivam vocem. . . . Quum autem ad eam iterum traditionem, quae est ab apostolis, quae per successiones presbyterorum in ecclesiis custoditur, provocamus eos: adversantur traditioni, dicentes se non solum presbyteris, sed etiam apostolis exsistentes sapientiores, sinceram invenisse veritatem. . . . Traditionem itaque apostolorum in toto mundo manifestatam in omni ecclesia adest respicere omnibus qui vera velint videre, et habemus annumerare eos qui ab apostolis instituti sint episcopi in ecclesiis, et successores eorum usque ad nos, qui nihil tale docuerunt neque cognoverunt quale ab his deliratur. Etenim si recondita mysteria scissent apostoli, quae seorsim et latenter ab reliquis perfectos docebant, his vel maxime traderent ea quibus etiam ipsas ecclesias committebant. . . . Sed quoniam valde longum est in hoc tali volumine omnium ecclesiarum enumerare successiones; maximae et antiquissimae et omnibus cognitae, a gloriosissimis duobus apostolis Petro et Paulo Romae fundatae et constitutae ecclesiae, eam quam habet ab apostolis traditionem, et annuntiatam hominibus fidem, per successiones episcoporum pervenientem usque ad nos indicantes, confundimus omnes eos, qui quoque modo. . . . praeterquam oportet colligunt. Ad hanc enim ecclesiam propter potentiorem principalitatem necesse est omnem convenire ecclesiam, hoc est eos qui sunt undique fideles, in qua semper ab his, qui sunt undique, conservata est ea quae est ab apostolis traditio. . . . (Here follows notice of the Roman succession, and adduction of authority of Polycarp and the church of Smyrna.) . . . Tantae igitur ostensiones quum sint, non oportet adhuc quaerere apud alios veritatem, quam facile est ab ecclesia sumere; quum apostoli, quasi in depositorium dives, plenissime in eam contulerint omnia quae sunt veritatis. . . . Ante Valentinum enim non fuerunt qui sunt a Valentino, neque ante Marcionem qui sunt a Marcione ; neque omnino erant reliqui sensus maligni quos supra enumeravimus, antequam initiatores et inventores perversitatis eorum fierent. . . . Traditione igitur, quae est ab apostolis, sic se habente in ecclesia, et permanente apud nos, revertamur ad eam, quae est ex Scripturis ostensionem eorum qui evangelium conscripserunt apostolorum.'—IREN. *Contra Haer.* iii. c. 1–4. So much is quoted, to show the connection of the statements with the general argument.

Tertullian has caught sight more fully of the capabilities of this mode of pleading, and erects it into a universal extinguisher of heretical argument:—

'Scripturas obtendunt et hac sua audacia statim quosdam movent. . . . Hunc igitur potissimum gradum obstruimus non admittendi eos ad ullam de Scripturis disputationem. Si hae sunt illae vires eorum, uti eas habere possint, dispici debet cui competat possessio Scripturarum ne is admittatur ad eas cui nullo modo competit. . . . Ergo non ad Scripturas provocandum. . . . Ordo rerum desiderabat illud prius proponi quod nunc solum disputandum est : quibus competat fides ipsa, cujus sint Scripturae, a quo, et per quos, et quando, et quibus, sit tradita disciplina qua fiunt Christiani. Ubi enim apparuerit veritatem disciplinae et fidei Christianae, illic erit veritas Scripturarum et expositionum et omnium traditionum Christianarum.' Accordingly, having described the founding of churches by the apostles,—' Hinc igitur dirigimus *praescriptionem*, si dominus Christus Jesus apostolos misit ad praedicandum, alios non esse recipiendos praedicatores quam Christus instituit, quia nec alius patrem novit nisi filius et cui filius revelavit, nec aliis videtur revelasse filius quam apostolis quos misit ad praedicandum, utique quod illis revelavit. Quid autem praedicaverint, id est, quid illis Christus revelaverit, et hic *praescribam* non aliter probari debere, nisi per easdem ecclesias quas ipsi apostoli condiderunt, ipsi eis praedicando tum viva, quod aiunt, voce, quam per epistolas postea. Si haec ita sunt, constat perinde omnem doctrinam quae cum illis ecclesiis apostolicis matricibus et originalibus fidei conspiret veritati deputandam . . . omnem vero doctrinam de mendacio praejudicandam quae sapiat contra veritatem ecclesiarum et apostolorum Christi et Dei. . . . Si haec ita se habent, ut veritas nobis adjudicetur, quicunque in ea regula incedimus, quam ecclesia ab apostolis, apostoli a Christo, Christus a Deo tradidit, constat ratio propositi nostri, definientis non esse admittendos haereticos ad ineundam de Scripturis provocationem, quos sine Scripturis probamus ad Scripturas non pertinere. Si enim haeretici sunt Christiani esse non possunt. . . . Ita non Christiani nullum jus capiunt Christianarum literarum, ad quos merito dicendum est: Qui estis? quid in meo agitis, non mei? quo denique, Marcion, jure silvam meam caedis? qua licentia, Valentine, fontes meos transvertis? qua potestate, Apelles, limites meos commores? Mea est possessio. Quid hic ceteri?'—TERT. *De Praescript. Haeret.* c. xv.–xxxvii.

NOTE C.—PAGE 10.

Quae supra sunt non verbo docentur sed spiritu revelantur. Verum quod sermo non explicat, consideratio quaerat, oratio expetat, mercatur vita, puritas assequatur.—BERNARD, *De Considerat.* v. 3. Fides ambiguum non habet; aut si habet, fides non est, sed opinio. Quid igitur distat ab intellectu? Nempe quod etsi non habet incertum non magis quam intellectus, habet tamen involucrum, quod non intellectus. Denique quod intellexisti, non est de eo quod ultra quaeras; aut si est non intellexisti. Nil autem malumus scire, quam quae fide jam scimus.—*Ibid.* Magister Petrus in libris suis profanas vocum novitates inducit et sensuum, disputans de fide contra fidem, verbis legis legem impugnat. Nihil videt per speculum et in aenigmate, sed facie ad faciem omnia intuetur, ambulans in magnis et mirabilibus super se.—*Ep.* cxcii.

Note D.—Page 11.

For the arrangements in the matter of theological study, reference may be made to Tholuck, *Academ. Leben des siebzehnten Jahrhunderts*, i. p. 104. It seems needless to occupy space with citations from the writings of the Reformers in illustration of the statement made in the text.

'Fidei symbolum in scriptis potius quam animis esse coepit, et tot pene erant fides, quot homines ; creverunt articuli sed decrevit sinceritas, efferbuit contentio, refrixit caritas. Doctrina Christi quae prius nesciebat λογομαχίαν, coepit a philosophiae praesidiis pendere. Hic primus erat gradus ecclesiae ad deteriora prolabentis. Tandem res deducta est ad sophisticas contentiones, articulorum myriades proruperunt.' —Erasm. *Praefat. in Hilar.*

Note E.—Page 17.

In the *Theologica Dogmata*, vol. ii. (where he takes up the topic *De Trinitate*), Petavius gave a very frank account of the sentiment of the Ante-Nicene Fathers on some points connected with the doctrine of the Trinity, characterizing the teaching of a considerable number of them as 'de Trinitate sententiae ab catholica regula, saltem loquendi usu, discrepantes.' The implication appeared to be, that even in the doctrine of the Trinity points were not at first *de fide*, which afterwards became such by the decision of the Church. Nor was it easy to see how, according to the representation of Petavius, this decision could be based on an express unambiguous tradition. Rather it would seem to be a decision of a point on which tradition varied. This would be substantially a development in Newman's sense. Petavius was strenuously attacked by Bull and other members of Protestant churches, as having betrayed a fundamental doctrine by this (as they maintained) uncalled-for concession ; and the motive imputed was a desire to exalt the authority of the Church, even at the expense of the orthodoxy of the Fathers. Besides this, serious dissatisfaction was felt by many members of his own Church, who conceived it to be a dangerous thing to disintegrate and break down the historical tradition in behalf of so fundamental an article. Nor could it add to his comfort that the latitudinarian Arminians (as Curcellaeus) gladly laid hold of his admission, and pleaded it as proof of the latitude which obtained in the early Church. Petavius accordingly felt himself constrained to modify his representation, and for that purpose prefixed an explanatory preface to the Treatise *De Trinitate*, in which he assuages the impression his former statement had produced, and argues that those same Fathers, on a broad view of their whole teaching, sustain the Church's doctrine on the important head in question.

Newman, in his earlier writings, followed Bull in referring with grave censure to the statement of Petavius. When he published his work on Development, he altered his view, and maintained that a divergence ought to be recognised, at least on one point. See Note I to Lecture V.

Note F.—Page 18.

Was ist also Tradition? 'Der Eigenthümliche in der Kirche vorhandene und durch die kirchliche Erziehung sich fortpflanzende christliche *Sinn*, der jedoch nicht ohne seinen Inhalt zu denken ist, der sich vielmehr an seine und durch seinen Inhalt gebildet hat, so dass er ein erfüllter Sinn zu nennen ist. Die Tradition ist das fortwährend in den Herzen der Gläubigen lebendes Wort. Diesem Sinne, als Gesammtsinne ist die Auslegung der heiligen Schrift anvertraut: die durch denselben ausgesprochene erklärung in den bestrittenen Gegenstände ist das urtheil der Kirche, und die Kirche darum Richterin in den Angelegenheiten des Glaubens (judex controversiarum). Die Tradition im objectiven Sinne ist in der in ausserlichen historischen Zeugnissen vorliegende Gesammtglaube der Kirche durch all Jahrhunderte hindurch. In diesem sinne wird gewöhnlich die Tradition die Norm, die Richtschnur der Schrifterklärung, die Glaubensregel genannt.'—MOEHLER, *Symbolik*, p. 357, 6th ed., Mainz 1843.

Evidently here the real fountain of decisions is the 'Sinn,' which interprets and decides as by a sacred instinct, and which therefore can from time to time evolve that which was never expressly delivered to it by any tradition, but which is now discerned to pertain to the completeness or security of the Christian faith. Accordingly, in another passage, p. 369 :—

'Nachdem nun aber das göttliche Wort menschlicher Glaube geworden war, musste es auch in alle rein menschlichen Schicksale eingehen. Es musste fortwährend von den menschlichen Geisteskräften auf und mit denselben angenommen werden: das Bewahren und Wiedergeben desselben war gleichfalls an menschliche Weise gebunden.' This is said to be visible enough in the Scriptures, in the Gospels, and still more in the Epistles, with the effect of varying greatly the form of the original truth. 'Es blieb immerhin noch das ursprungliche, und doch auch nicht: es war sich selbst gleich dem Wesen nach, von sich verschieden rücksichtlich der Form.'

'Anders konnte es nie werden, auch nach dem Tode der Apostel. . . . In dem die Kirche die ursprungliche Glaubenslehre in der eben entwickelten weise, Entstellungen gegenüber, erklärt und sicherstellt, geht nothwendig auch der apostolische Ausdruck in einen Anderen über, welcher gerade am geeignetsten ist den bestimmten zeitlichen Irrthum recht kenntlich dar zu stellen und zugleich abzuweisen. . . . Die Entstehung der nicänischen Formel gibt hierüber den besten Aufschuss. Diese Form ist das Menschliche, Zeitliche, an sich Vergängliche, und konnte wohl gegen hundert andere ausgetauscht werden. So überbringt demnach die Tradition das Ursprüngliche den späteren Geschlechtern oft in anderer Form, weil dasselbe Menschen anvertraut wurde, die sich nach den Umständen in welchen sie sich befinden, benehmen muss.' . . . 'In der Kirchenlehre kommt uns die Schriftlehre in stets fortschreitendem Verhältnisse entgegen. So geistloss es demnach ist, einen anderen als formellen Unterschied zwischen der Lehre Jesu und der der Apostel zu finden, eben so gedankenlos ist es, wenn zwischen der Spätern und ursprünglichen Tradition ein anderer Gegensatz erkannt wird.' In general statements like these the difference can easily be represented as purely formal. But in applying them to cases like that of the Immaculate Conception, and the Personal Infallibility, this 'formal' difference between the original deposit and the developed doctrine would be found to amount to a good deal. But Möhler refrains from examples in this context. Nothing more clearly evinces the confidence of Newman in his own theory, than the frankness with which he applies it to all sorts of arduous cases.

NOTE G.—PAGE 19.

Essay on the Development of Christian Doctrine, by John Henry Newman, second edition, London 1846. The theory is completely stated in the first two chapters. The tests of true Development, pp. 57–93, are particularly worthy of consideration, as illustrating the vagueness of the process, and the loose connection postulated between the original *datum* and the ultimate *quaesitum* or *inventum*.

Besides the numerous English publications called forth by the appearance of this work, some discussions in Germany were more or less occasioned or influenced by it. Schröder, *Die Idee der Entwickelung, und deren Bedeutung für die protestantische Kirche*, 8vo, Hamburg and Gotha 1848.

NOTE H.—PAGE 19.

Perrone, in the *Tractatus de Ecclesia*, P. I. c. iv. (vol. viii. 1, p. 263 of the Roman ed.), cites at large from Möhler the passage quoted in Note F, with emphatic approbation. Yet for himself he keeps commonly the track of the older way of it, *e.g.* in *Tractatus de locis Theologicis*, Pars II. sec. ii. The truth is, however, that the older view of tradition, when completed by the assertion of the power claimed for the Church to decide, infallibly, emergent questions, slides necessarily on toward the later view of development. The power in question is practically a power to add articles of faith. It must prove so, unless it had been exercised with a sobriety, the bounds of which Rome long ago transgressed. All that remains is to adjust the theory of it, and that varies as the exigencies of controversy may suggest.

Note I.—Page 21.

Specimens are plentiful, *e.g.* John Owen:
'Cum vero Deo placuerit initio reformationis seculo superiori tentatae, lumen et veritatem suam in simplicitatis evangelicae praedicatione emittere, nihil fere erat in tota Ecclesia apostolica quod aeque piis et bonis viris odio erat et abominationi, ac theologica ista scientia quae tum temporis in scholis et academiis dominabatur. An in ipsis ecclesiarum reformatarum scholis, atque inter omne genus viros doctos illa ipsa theologia philosophica denuo locum suum recuperaverit, necne, penes alios judicium esto. Addam, quae habet vir doctissimus Johannes Drusius. "Canis ad vomitum redit," inquit, "qui redit ad id, quod primi reformatores evomuerunt. Ea est theologia scholastica, quam qui sectantur, veram negligunt, hoc est, verbum Dei ; unde omnis veritas Christiana, et ea ipsa quam scholasticam appellant, mixta fermento humano, sic est tam pura et sincera non sit quam esse debeat. Quando tandem haec reformabuntur? nam ante non erit pax in ecclesia." '—*De natura verae Theologiae*, vi. cap. 8.

Or Amesius: 'Nostri autem theologi praeclare se instructos esse putant ad omnes officii sui partes, si dogmata tantum intelligant, et utinam intelligerent. Neque tamen omnia dogmata scrutantur, sed illa sola quae praecipuè solent agitari, et in controversiam vocari. Scripturae idcirco illas tantum particulas inspicere curant, quae ad locum aliquem communem aut controversiam definiendam ab aliis vident citari. . . . Sit igitur haec prima et unica vestra cura, ut scripturas distinctè perceptas habeatis quasi familiares, ex quibus et stamen et trama theologiae constat. Ex aliis authoribus, illi praecipuè eligendi et lectitandi qui succum et sanguinem Scripturae sapiunt, qui ad praxin pietatis deducunt.

Controversiarum scientiam necessariam nobis fecerunt haeretici : sed studium pietatis ut absolute necessarium Deus ipse mandavit. Si igitur sic insaniamus circa quaestionum pugnas, ut pietatis doctrinam negligamus, nescio sane an haereses multae non aeque fere noceant impugnantibus, quos abstrahunt a tanto bono, ac recipientibus ipsis nocent, quos attrahant tamen in magna mala.'—*Paraenesis ad Studiosos Theologiae*, appended to *De Conscientia*.

These have been selected, because no one who knows the writings of these authors will accuse either of them of indifference to orthodoxy, or of an indisposedness to doctrinal distinction and debate.

NOTE J.—PAGE 21.

It would be easy to adduce specimens in illustration of the statement in the text from the literature of any of the leading churches. Perhaps, however, there is not a more striking example anywhere, than is furnished by the controversy concerning grace in the Church of Rome, including both the dispute technically known as De auxiliis, and also a large part, the greater part, of the Jansenistic controversy. Matters were discussed in these controversies of very considerable moment, and men took part in the conflict who were of undoubted eminence. And yet little indeed is left to reward the student, in those hundreds of volumes of controversy, which still forsake the true sources of certainty, and still decline the true issues.

The unprofitableness, speaking generally, of this body of controversy, was occasioned partly by the mere proclivity of the disputants to raise and discuss questions of a kind, and in a form, which precluded sure footing and sure progress. But besides, there were particular difficulties attaching to the position of each party, which kept each of them beating the air. It is worth while to mention what these were, because they present an instructive instance of the ways in which theological discussions, intensely interesting and animated at the time when they are undertaken, may be well-nigh wholly bereaved of fruit for those who come after.

Several parties have here to be considered. First, there were the Jesuits or Molinists, and those who in the main concurred with them. They held views which were really semi-Pelagian; and had they frankly taken up the responsibilities of that position, they would have contributed their share to make the discussion real and instructive. Molina himself may be said to have been explicit and candid in his statements, unless his peculiar modification of the doctrine of Predestination may be regarded (which is not my own opinion) as an attempt to mystify his position. But the party, as a whole, desired to be semi-Pelagian in effect, without being quite semi-Pelagian in show; they desired to differ from Augustine on every head of the doctrine of grace, and yet to avoid too sharp a collision with the great reputation and authority of that Father. A certain amount of complication arose from this cause. Still more, probably, arose from the fact, that their object was not so much to make good their own theory on the field of argument, but to get their opponents condemned as heretics. But they had to condemn them, without at the same time manifestly condemning Augustine. Hence their strength is largely spent on laborious and insincere distinctions, with a view to be able to qualify as heretical, modes of teaching which in all their substantial features were Augustinian, and yet to leave Augustine in honour.

The Dominicans again, or the new Thomists, had it for their point of honour to maintain the doctrine of sufficient grace, and yet to maintain the distinction between sufficient grace and efficacious grace. The former they maintained because it was the general Church doctrine, also because the denial of it would have exposed them to be regarded as heretical Jansenists. Moreover, it agreed with the view they took of the conditions of human responsibility. They taught, therefore, that ordinarily a sufficient grace is given, of which the definition is, that by it a man *can* repent, and *can* turn to God. But then, as followers of Augustine and Thomas, they felt it to be their mission to maintain that another kind of grace, efficacious grace, is necessary, must be present, in order to any truly good will or work, and that without it, by the mere sufficient grace, no man ever did or shall turn to God. Their opponents (on either hand) at once fastened on this inconsistency, and charged them with either contradiction or equivocation. Their business, therefore, came to be to explain that it was an intelligible and consistent position, to hold a grace truly and completely sufficient, and yet to hold that, unless efficacious grace were added, the former did not suffice. On arguing this point, a great part of their labour was spent. There was, however, another complication in their position. As followers of Augustine and Thomas, they held not only the necessity of efficacious grace, but also the certain operation of the grace that deserves that name. It secures and operates the consent of the will. But it happens that the Council of Trent, rather to the displeasure of the Dominicans at the Council, had defined the operation of justifying grace to be such, that the will is able to dissent if it chooses. The will is free in such a sense, that it retains throughout the power of arresting the process, which grace is carrying on, by dissent. The Thomists had courage enough to face this difficulty. It would have been simple, but not satisfactory, to decline the decision of the Council of Trent; it would have been simple also to renounce the teaching of Augustine and Thomas. But the Thomists adhered to both. They professed to be ready to say, with the Council, that the justified man ' posse dissentire si velit ;' and yet to maintain, in the line of their hereditary doctrine, that 'haec duo sint *incompossibilia*, quod scilicet gratia efficax ponatur in homine, et homo actu dissentiat.' Here was another paradox, in the defence of which another great part of their strength was spent.

The Jansenists maintained a doctrine regarding man's original state, its responsibilities, and the principles on which sin is to be measured and the guilt of it assigned, which was of high importance, capable of thorough defence from Scripture, and supported by the authority of Augustine, if his teaching is fairly understood and expounded. The illustration and defence of it did not necessarily involve anything petty or unworthy. But then it came into conflict with Papal bulls issued in the case of Baius of Louvain. Hence it became necessary, or was thought to be necessary, to state the tenet not so much in its natural terms as in an equivocal manner, and so as to distinguish it artificially from the doctrine condemned in Baius. Again, the Jansenists, like the Dominicans, held high doctrine on the necessity and the certain operation of efficacious grace. They differed from the Dominicans in refusing to involve themselves in the contradiction of asserting a sufficient grace which is not efficacious. But then they also, as much as the Dominicans, had to reckon with the decrees of the Council of Trent, and to furnish, if they could, some decent sense, in consistency with their principles, for the 'posse dissentire si velit.' Their battle too, therefore, revolved round these fixed points. They had to be ever busy fitting their expressions as best they could to the conditions here referred to. Lastly, the Church of Rome, guided by a sure instinct, meant to condemn the Jansenists. This would have been a clear and intelligible business, had that Church proceeded on semi-Pelagian or Arminian principles, enacted these into law, and passed sentence accordingly. In that case, the propositions condemned might have been made unequivocal in their turns, and the discussion might have been worthy of the subject. As it was, the condemnation was really animated by a semi-Pelagian feeling, yet Augustine and the Thomists were not to be openly attacked. Therefore the propositions condemned are vague and equivocal, and the discussion about them soon resolved into elaborate hair-splitting about the senses in which they might be taken, and the shades of distinction which separated the Calvinistic, the Jansenistic, and the Thomist sense. A church that makes room equally for the Thomist and the Molinist doctrines of grace, may, if she chooses, condemn the Calvinistic and the Jansenistic; but her reasons for doing so cannot be of much interest or importance to anybody.

All round and all through this elaborate controversy, therefore, we find all the parties engaged in a highly refined and artificial kind of fencing, or, to vary the figure, balancing themselves on tightropes in a dexterous, unstable manner. Considering the solemnity of the topics, the impression made is saddening; and, for the student, a great part of the discussion proves wearisome and unfruitful. This may be regarded as a capital instance of the fatal manner in which considerations foreign to the real doctrinal issue, as a mere question of Christian truth, may operate to divert and waste the energies of generations of earnest men, and to annul the benefit which discussion, when it must be undertaken, ought to leave behind it.

NOTE K.—PAGE 22.

For example, Semler: 'Wenn es nun aber weiter auch wahr ist, dass Theologie, wie alle sogenante Wissenschaft und dazu gehörige Lehrbücher, unter der allgemeinen Ordnung aller menschlichen Arbeiten und Beschaftigungen, stehet; ich meine der Succession und Veränderlichkeit, selbst nach Gottes Ordnung, unterworfen ist; welches die Vergleichung solcher Bücher mit sich bringt, wenn jemand sie von irgend Einem Jahrhundert mit einander und mit nachherigen zusammen hält: so war ja auf meiner Seite weder Vorsatz noch Sünde daran Schuld, das ich dieses immer mehr deutlich und gewis einsahe! Es war ferner gewis, dass kein Theologus über den andern ein Gebiet hat, weil es unmöglich ist, der Einschränkung und Localität sich zu entziehen: so war es also keine Frechheit wenn ich solche Lehrbücher, gegen jetzige Localität, nun als mangelhaft und unrichtige erkennte; und theologische, stets veränderliche Meinungen, nicht für die ewigen christlichen Wahrheiten ansahe. Und wenn ich den Begriffen oder Vorstellungen zusahe, die ich nach und nach aus Osten und Westen, aus allerley Zeiten, zusammen sammelte und verglich so war es ja wol eine unschuldige, gar nicht grosse Entdeckung, dass diese Begriffe niemalen ihre ganze Vollkommenheit und genannte Bestimmung schon halten; dass also das Wesen der christlichen eigenen Religion nicht in Unveränderlichkeit der Begriffe, über irgend einen Gegenstand, zu setzen sei; sondern gerade in das Gegentheil, in eigene freie Erkenntnis und ihre locale Anwendung.'—*Lebensbeschreibung*, 2ter

Theil, Vorrede. More suggestive is Lessing, in his *Erziehung des Menschengeschlecht*. I regret that, at the moment of preparing this note for the press, I have not the book at hand. He regards Christianity as a great *providential* element in the training of the race, and so far recognises a capital movement of human history, not without a significant divine intention. But it is clear that, to his mode of thinking, a supernatural revelation, especially if it embodies authoritative teaching, must be a superfluous and unwelcome conception. Accordingly, he regards the Old Testament as a lesson-book which man has long outgrown; and the New Testament, also, as a better and more advanced specimen of the same thing, which in turn must and will be outgrown in various respects, both intellectual and moral.

It is perhaps superfluous to make citations on a point so notorious. One more specimen may be given, from a representative of a quite different school :—

'Daher konnte sich das begriffliche Bewusstsein vom Christenthum nicht auf einmal darstellen, sondern man musste zuerst dasselbe in die innere Erfahrung annehmen, und dann entwickelte sich allmälig das Bewusstsein, was man in dieses Lehre habe. Die Art wie diess geschah war bedingt durch den dermaligen Standpunkt der geistigen Bildung. Das Christenthum fand, so bald es in das innere Leben der Menschheit eintrat, eine fremde Richtung des Menschlichen Denkens vor, ein Missverhältniss, was allmälig überwunden werden musste. Daher nehmen wir in den ersten Jahrhunderten eine grosse Differenz der dogmatischen Begriffe, und noch manche inadäquate Formen wahr, und doch konnte dabei die Continuität des christlichen Lebens und Bewusstseins bestehen. Die Dogmengeschichte zeigt nun den genetischen Entwickelungs-prozess der christlichen Lehre, zeigt, in welchen Formen die einige christliche Wahrheit als Lehre entwickelt ward, und wie sie sich zu einander verhalten, und zu dem Wesen des Christenthums selbst.'—NEANDER, *Dogmengeschichte*, i. p. 4.

Note L.—Page 26.

The way in which this is done is to treat all views of the atonement, preceding Anselm's, in so far as they involve the vicarious element, as manifestly unreasonable, and now forgotten or superseded, and to take Anselm's as the point of departure from which all modern developments must be derived. So in *Essays and Reviews;* also in *Tracts for Priests and People,* 1861, No. III.

A fair account of the mind of the Church on this matter, as revealed along the whole course of early literature, would show that the idea which constantly reappears, amid all variations and fluctuations, is the idea of substitution. The recognition of this is essential to any true account of the history of the doctrine. It is, in this view, a serious defect on Ritschl's part, that in his late work he dismisses so unceremoniously the earlier indications of the Church's faith concerning the Lord's death.

Note M.—Page 33.

The course of treatment indicated here, and pursued in succeeding Lectures, is, I am aware, in some respects peculiar; and I hardly hope that the conception of it will be regarded as very satisfactory. The obvious objection to it is the abstract character which it assumes, in consequence of which I am exposed to the double imputation of indifference and presumption: of indifference, inasmuch as I discuss questions of form, and not of matter; I forego the animation which the attack of error or the defence of truth might often have imparted to the treatment; and I touch the borders of a hundred interesting and momentous questions, and yet decline to treat them on their merits;—and of presumption, since it is hard to avoid an air of pretension in speaking of matters of so wide a range of application; not to say that, in the second and third Lectures, things are rapidly touched and disposed of, which belong in a peculiar manner to the unsearchable wisdom of God.

I am not disposed to overrate the importance of the subject, treated from the point of view from which I regard it. It is, in my judgment, of sufficient importance to warrant its being looked at by itself.—The existing course of theological discussion is pervaded pretty thoroughly by assumptions of various kinds about the place, use, warrants, and nature of doctrine or dogma. Those assumptions are influential pretty much in proportion as they are vague. Incoherent and contradictory assumptions are often operative in the same mind or in the same work. A power is manifestly exerted by habits of thought formed on such assumptions, which few would regard as legitimate if they were fairly looked at. It seems desirable, therefore, that men should give account of the views on this subject by which they abide. In proportion as this is done, we shall know better where we are : extravagant theories will vanish of themselves ; the controversial responsibilities of all parties will become more apparent. But if it is desirable thus to disentangle the topic from the material merits of the mass of concrete questions into which it enters as an element, then abstinence from meddling with those material merits becomes a condition of the treatment. For this reason, in the present course I have been sparing of illustrations; and have drawn them rather from controversies which are not particularly active, than from those which are. Neither have I made it my business to collect and discuss all the various theories on the subject which are demonstrably or presumably entertained. It would be found hardly possible to do so, without implicating the discussion in the concrete questions through which the theories appear or are presented. I have therefore referred to the known views of most writers only in the measure in which it appeared desirable to do so for the purpose of making clear the drift of those here advocated. I have said, in the text, that I speak from the position of the Reformed Theology. But I mainly postulate two things, viz.: 1. That Scripture conveys to us a real Revelation ; and, 2. That it constitutes a sufficient rule of faith. Those who discard either postulate will organize their theory of Christian doctrine differently ; but to them it is maintained that the theory which those two postulates supply, is at least a consistent, credible, and worthy one, exposed to none of the incoherences and subject to none of the weaknesses which are occasionally imputed to it. To those who accept the postulates referred to the statement here made is submitted, as a contribution towards the adjustment of thought in one department.

LECTURE II.

Note A.—Page 34.

It may be expected that the attitude maintained in these Lectures towards the question of Inspiration should be stated. I do not know that anything is assumed which is likely to be disputed by any who hold the Scriptures to be the record of a real Revelation, who accept as reliable the account it gives of the history of God's ways with men, and who regard its teaching as the authoritative guide for human faith and practice, however they may differ on some subordinate questions regarding the conception to be formed of inspiration. On those subordinate questions, however, the writer himself, while admitting the existence of difficulties that have not been solved, sees no sufficient reason for departing from the view that Scripture claims for itself plenary authority,—a claim which the existence of a certain number of difficulties should not avail to weaken. Once the existence of an agency such as inspiration has been established or admitted, one is entitled to proceed to apply the fact with the expectation that some difficulties will be met with, and without being greatly moved by their occurrence. The objections made, from more than one point of view, to the assertion of the superhuman character of the Bible ought to be met on the merits on suitable occasions; and sometimes, and for some purposes, it may be well to treat questions into which Scripture authority enters on the footing of a scrupulous regard to the objections taken, and a careful adduction of evidence for everything objected to. Here anything of this kind is out of the question; it would require me to write, not one volume, but many. I shall only say that I consider the position which expresses the common faith of the Church to be in itself far more reasonable, and far more defensible, not only than the extreme one which reduces the Bible to the level of other mythologies, but also than the various intermediate positions, in which theorists hover in so uncertain and dubious a manner. There is a 'supranaturalism ashamed of itself,' as a lively German writer describes it, which tries to escape from difficulties by bleaching all its assertions. This course fails in the object for the sake of which it is embraced, and has nothing to recommend it otherwise.

Note B.—Page 36.

No one doubts the fact of a development exhibited in the Hebrew Scriptures. How it is to be conceived, and how explained, is the question. If not due to divine revelation, it must be traced to ordinary causes. Much has been written to make the latter alternative credible. The Hebrew nation and the Old Testament, as we are told, are to be explained by a double development along two distinct but connected lines. First, in the race itself you have a stock destined, and tending, to unfold a powerful and elevated religious consciousness. Such a nation may be expected to produce—does produce, from time to time—men who exhibit in an exceptional degree the characteristic tendency of their race. Such a nation passes through experiences, often remarkable, but yet essentially as earthly in character and origin as those of any other nation. There is here nothing divine, except as all providence is divine. But yet, conformably to their prevalent tendency, the race wed their lofty religious impressions to their history. Those national experiences are singled out by the national mind as the memorable and decisive ones, which fall in with its religious cravings, or which are capable of being regarded as providential expressions of divine thoughts and principles. The usual fancies of superstition, and exaggerations of tradition, obey the same influences,—they assume a religious character; and thus the vast distortions of fact which these causes import into all early history, and have plentifully imported here, serve in this case to render more pronounced the religious character of the whole. The tradition sets in a definite religious mould, and reacts on the national temperament in the way of confirming and strengthening the tendencies from which originally it received its own type. The people, or the more characteristic representatives of it, are more and more disposed to see in the present the continuation of the past, which they have learned to represent to themselves in the manner thus suggested. They are more and more disposed to take all their experiences as containing and developing the same significant history—to understand them *prophetically.*

Then the accounts of the primeval history of the world (as distinguished from that of the race) are to be understood simply as the remodelling, under the more modern influences and impressions, of the mythology which the fathers of the race handed down. It is an improved version, conformed to the type of thought and feeling which gradually grew up and became confirmed.

In a similar way, the literature is to be conceived as growing gradually into form, moulded by that spirit of the race (which age by age grew into strength and precision) within which each individual mind worked. The earlier portions of it attained the measure of congruity and consistency of tone which they possess, in consequence of a process which is to be assumed to have taken place, viz. that the most important parts were substantially worked over again, and again, and again, so that what was or might have been anomalous and refractory gradually disappeared. How many times (according to this account of it) Genesis passed through the fire of brooding minds, intent on conceiving harmoniously and fittingly the rise and progress of the race! Or, to change the figure, by as slow a process, as incapable of being described in all its details, as that of a stream working on the rocks, the history was gradually water-worn—chiselled into shapes which, however various, have a consistency, and impress the mind with the sense of pervading analogies, and of one informing spirit.

Not, however, that the process by which the literature

gradually took its final shape was wholly unconscious. A pretty free operation of design has to be asserted. Thus, some one very greatly possessed by the spirit of the chosen people in its most energetic operation, produces, later in the day, the book of Deuteronomy. *He* knows, of course, that his book is not authentic history : it is only a modern divination of what the last words of Moses might have been. But to him, and those who are acquainted with the source of his work, this is a very insignificant circumstance. Being a version in harmony with the national ἦθος, it ought to be treated *as if it were* historically true ; and presently it is so treated, and continues to bear faith thenceforward.

On our side of the Channel, views like these are apt to be associated with a rather emphatic rejection of what has proved to be thus unreliable—at all events, a rejection of it in the character of a religious guide. I will not assert that this must be so. A man like Ewald, persuaded that this spirit which grew in Israel was in the main, and in its choicer instances, a truly divine breath in the world's history, and that its growth and operation were one of the greatest blessings the world could receive from the supreme Lord of providence, will contrive to preserve in honour and influence in his mind the spiritual aroma of the history, when all the facts become fluid, and transform themselves under the operations of criticism. According to him, indeed, the history becomes tenfold more precious and edifying, more fruitful of faith towards God and service toward men, when considered as arising from this process, than if we had to take it in the comparatively vulgar and unspiritual character of a report of facts which fell out as they are told. But the landing-place to which the theory will conduct its adherents is obvious ; and few of them will be at so much pains as Ewald, or will possess the qualities which enable him, to conceal the character of it from their own minds.

On the discussion of the critical questions I do not pretend to enter. But a remark may be made on the general conception of the process which is supposed to have made the Hebrew people and the Hebrew Scriptures.

In the first place, it proceeds on a false conception of the people, and of the national genius. There is not the least reason to ascribe to the Jewish people the elevation or purity of sentiment which the theory requires, nor yet the genius for spiritual thought. It is reasonable to ascribe to them a great susceptibility for what may be called religious intensity. But that susceptibility will not secure worthy religious developments. It may ally itself to the baser as well as to the loftier modes of religious thought and feeling, and in the case of the Jews it was quite ready to do so. As regards spiritual thought, the character of the race suggests rather retentiveness than originality and initiative. The whole history suggests the idea of a race raised above itself by thoughts and institutions to which it proved unequal.

Secondly, and more particularly, the moral and religious consistency of the Old Testament Scriptures never can be accounted for in this way. There is a great deal of variety in some respects in the Old Testament: very different stages of progress are represented, and different points of view suggest different modes of view as you pass from one age to another. With this, however, is combined a most remarkable unity,—the unity characterizing the fundamental elements, moral and religious; and it is not of the nature of a dead monotony, as if, after the fashion was set, people ceased to care about the matter, and merely repeated the old patterns of things: it is a unity realized in an intense and living way. It attaches to such conceptions as those of God, sin, morals, the destiny of Israel, and so forth; although, in connection with each of those topics, there is growth and progress, the fundamental key-note is never forsaken, and the harmony grows richer. Now let it be considered what is in evidence of the contrarieties of thought and feeling realized among the people—the inveterate idolatries, the resolute rebellions, the impression of being in a minority so often expressed by those who upheld the good cause. Nobody doubts, probably, no one certainly need doubt, that, amid the various impulses which swayed the people to and fro, there were many that could ally themselves with strong religious enthusiasm, and could rise in that way to heights of wild, or gloomy, or eudæmonistic heathenism. Why are not these influences represented in the literature—why do we not find the incoherence and inconsistency reproduced there,—if the literature sprang from the national genius stimulated by the national experiences? It may be said that a virtual expurgation may have been effected, and the heterogeneous elements expelled, by the predominance of one particular school of religious thought at the particular time or times when the canonical writings were selected, and had their text settled. But a cause of that kind could only have operated superficially: it could never have fused and recast the whole literature, and brought its deepest thoughts into harmony.

There are various characteristics of the Old Testament Scriptures to which similar consideration may be applied. For example, the argument of Warburton in the *Divine Legation*, though overpressed, has a basis in fact, and is capable of being extended. There are clear evidences, though remarkably scattered and occasional, of a hope after death cherished by Hebrew saints; but, in a degree that is extremely striking, the territory of the present life is directly and immediately in view (in terms at all events) in this record of divine intercourse with a chosen race. There is a most wonderful abstinence from directly bringing into view what might transpire in a life after death, even on occasions when one would think it most natural and fitting. Evidently it belongs to the scheme of intercourse and of revelation here carried out, to be thus sparing. But how came it, that through such a succession of time the writings keep so true to this characteristic of the scheme? How was it, that intensely religious men, and intensely religious periods, did not, as it were, break into the unseen world, to find there far the most effective leverage and machinery with which to operate on human motive and human conduct? For although, in the later books, indications of an eye turned to the life after death may be more frequent, still in the latest book, the general strain, the prevailing method, is the same as in the earlier. Is this to be accounted for by supposing that the idea of another world had hardly dawned on the Jews, or that they regarded it as too unreal to be a source of influence? Surely what the Egyptians had imagined of judgment after death is proof that there were not wanting hints and suggestions, had they been needed, for the religious fervour of the Jews to work on. The abstinence, I believe, can well be accounted for by considerations connected with the due order and method of divine revelation to the human race, which now from our standpoint may be discerned. But if we are here dealing not with divine revelation, but with religious vision, aspiration, and imagination, how is it to be accounted for? Certainly Ewald gives a very lame explanation, *Geschichte des Volkes Israel*, ii. p. 121 (Göttingen, 1845).

It ought to be acknowledged, at the same time, that the rationalistic writers have done service in showing how large a part in the whole history has been played by the forces which are native to man and society, and which from one stage to another carry on the history of nations. There is no reason whatever why the divine scheme should not embody, and, so to say, avail itself of these in the fullest and most habitual manner. Rather, there is every reason to expect that it should. But the tendency of the theologian as such is to contemplate the divine intention, and the divine action in carrying it out, and so to ascribe everything or many things to God in a more direct and immediate manner than the history warrants: in so immediate and direct a manner, as to make too little of that in the sacred history, which is perfectly analogous to the process of all history.

NOTE C.—PAGE 40.

The theory of many persons, proceeded on sometimes where not proclaimed, is, that even if you let the miracles fall, as mythic elements which wove themselves into the history, or at any rate as doubtful elements, incapable of being satisfactorily established, you lose nothing. Whatever is permanently excellent and great in Christianity, *e.g.* in its representation of the relations of man to God, to duty, to his fellows, and so forth, will still remain. They are great thoughts, that can never fail out of the mind of the race, now that they have been suggested; and whatever power they have to evidence themselves to the mind and heart as worthy of God, and congruous to the constitution and wants of man, is in themselves. It is an internal evidence, not an adventitious; and whether the cogency of it is more or less, it will operate according to what it is worth. For example, if there be moral or spiritual force in the idea of resurrection to spiritual life in fellowship with Christ's rising, the mere suggestion has put us in possession of it. We have it, whether Christ actually rose or not. Meanwhile, in their opinion, you gain by disembarrassing religion of a set of assertions of miraculous events, which are not acceptable nor credible to the *Zeitgeist*, to employ the convenient abbreviation which Mr. Arnold sanctions by his usage. No one can desire that those who have ceased to believe in the miracles should be deprived of any benefit which they conceive themselves still to derive from the great Christian thoughts. But they must, of course, cease to be believers in the central Christian facts of the Incarnation and the Resurrection. And even as regards the Christian ideas which they retain, their position is wholly different from that occupied by the ordinary Christian. They retain certain views, but only as suggestions or impressions which human minds have entertained, and which appear acceptable to their own minds. It is quite another thing to receive the same views in the character of truths proposed by God Himself, and with a corroboration of their divine origin. To believe in the miracles, is to take the attitude of receiving a communication. Moreover, when the miracles are dismissed, the whole structure of sacred history falls to pieces; and all the purposes which, as explained in the Lecture, it serves in connection with the development of principle embodied in it vanish.

The *soi-disant* philosophic argument against miracles, *i.e.* against the admissibility of such an idea, or such an assertion, deserves only to be characterized as despicable. The argument against the sufficiency of the evidence, on the contrary, grounded as it mainly is on the proved proclivity of human nature to make baseless assumptions and assertions of the miraculous, in connection with religious movements, must always deserve careful attention. At the same time, it is to be remembered that complete proof for each separate miracle as a distinct fact is not at all required. What is required is proof that a miraculous administration, or an administration which involved the element of the miraculous, was going on. Many different kinds of proof conspire to establish that position; for example, whatever is fitted to establish in our minds the belief of a *revealing interposition* on the part of God. Then, once that is established or made credible, the order of things to which miracles belong is given; and the occurrence of miraculous events as part of it, requires no more special support than any other part of the narrative.

On the subject of the place and ends of miracles, I may here reprint some passages of a lecture delivered long ago, and now out of print:—

'What God will do, or the style of operation which He will adopt, depends on the ends He has in view, and which, by His working, He designs to bring to pass. Now the experience of the world, as observed and analyzed by scientific investigators, shows us God's way of working for the unfolding of the physical world from age to age, and for enabling man to develope his ordinary history in the scene so constituted. God's way of working here, and for these ends, appears to be by upholding constant forces, which operate according to fixed laws. And this result of observation may be taken as yielding a presumption that, in general, that will be His manner in this sphere and for these ends. Yet it can never be more than a presumption; and even as a presumption cannot be stretched very far. We do not know where or when reasons may exist, which shall make it fit for God to interpose some altered mode of working, some form of energy that cannot be reduced to the formula I have referred to. Still we see how stedfastly, for ages, the order of the universe abides, all things being set in number, and measure, and weight. We see how fitted this is to promote the education of the race, and to give us the opportunity of penetrating one depth after another of creative wisdom, power, and glory. We see how impressively such a mode of working, by its very stedfastness, is fitted to train us in the knowledge of some divine attributes. We see how the conceptions which this order supplies, meeting us and shining out on us from every domain of science, furnish the mind of man for steady and growing mastery over nature. And so we may well gather that this is to be the ordinary character of our experience, as it regards God's ways of working in this sphere and for these ends.

'But there are other ends which God may and does design, for the attainment of which miracles seem to be the appropriate and most admirable means: not miracles scattered without an apparent reason through the workings of nature, but occurring as marked exceptions to the general order, and in marked connection with the object for which they are designed.

'For miracles accompany revelation. They present themselves as fit works of God when He reveals. This, I may say, furnishes us with the reason why we have seen no miracles for so many ages (the fact on which the doubt is based). If God has closed His revelation, it is no wonder that He has ceased for the present to add those signs. Objectors love to reason as though miracles, if possible at all, might be expected to turn up occasionally in the midst of our experiments as pure anomalies, that come from nothing and go to nothing. We assert, and are bound to assert, no such thing. We believe in no miracles but such as are the birth of God's stedfast purposes, and are ordered to ends. And believing the ends of miracles to be connected with the process of revelation, the fact that they do not occur during this period in which revelation has bid us wait for our Lord's return, is precisely what we should be prepared to count upon.

'I repeat, then, miracles present themselves as fit works of God Revealing. They come to us, then, as part of this general allegation, that God has been pleased to deal with the minds and wills of men by something additional to the works of nature, viz. by revelation. So that it is with reference to the end thus assigned, and with reference to that only, that the question ought to be raised: Is the natural order of things, with its constant course, the only revelation of Himself which God has made to man? or is there a further dealing with the minds and wills of men by revelation? For if so, then here, where God passes forth beyond nature to speak, it may be very fit that He should pass beyond nature to do.

'Now through natural things God does deal with our minds. They supply to our minds a noble field of exercise; they disclose to us depths and reaches of beauty and order that are inexhaustible, for still the boundaries retreat as we pass onward over the field. Nor is it only with the creatures that our minds become conversant in this discourse. That which may be known of God also, is here. His being and perfections are in these things displayed to us. And there is that within us which teaches us to refer those works to a personal and righteous God, and suggests to us the law under which He has placed us, and which we cannot doubt to be the expression to us of His eternal will. He does reach our minds through the things that are made; and the minds which He reaches are so constituted, that, being put in play, they do or may gather true thoughts of God,—they may discern something of His nature, and something of His will. But then this is not enough for man. We have the best reason for believing it was not enough even in the unfallen state; certainly it is not enough now that man is fallen.

'God speaks to us by His works; yet there remains a distance; yes, and there is a silence too. The voice *is* gone through all the earth, the words to the ends of the world; yet there is no speech, there is no language, their voice is not heard. For this great nature stands and utters herself from age to age in her play of laws, unbending, equal to herself; so that the more she is searched, though the chorus deepens, widens, swells immeasurably, yet the sum of meaning is found only the more certainly to be the same, one unvarying sameness from age to age—one tranquil and majestic testimony to every man and every race—uttered still as fully and persistently if there is no man to hear, no mind to be filled by it. Here indeed God is revealed, yet so that He remains veiled. There is not enough here for man. Bearing God's own image, he needs more. He was made for fellowship, for intercourse, for friendship, not only with his fellows, but with his Maker. And that implies the disclosure of personal meanings, mind apprehended bending to my mind, and heart moving to meet my heart. Moreover, that element in man, in virtue of which he can choose and take his course as a moral being, finds no sympathy in the stedfast and equal sequences of nature. Man feels, indeed, that God must be one who has a moral character. But he finds no adequate *utterance* addressed by this God to the capital capacity of his nature.

'Even conscience, the monitor within, which, as life unfolds, suggests to us what the character of the great Creator is, does not speak the adequate utterance of man's Maker to such a being as man; rather it moves man to a listening earnestness—to say, Speak, be not silent unto me. If there be no answer but that which nature gives, then God remains veiled and distant. For, let it be remembered, it is the nature of man, and the very meaning of his place in this scene of things, that he should be dealt *with from without*. The conscience and capacities within fit him to hearken to voices from without. And if the constitution and course of nature be the only divine utterance so addressed to him, then as to the highest wants and capabilities of man God remains veiled. Wise, indeed, He is, and benevolent, in general arrangements, but remote and immovable — disclosing only purposes and meanings that are equal to themselves from age to age. He never, nowhere, comes down to walk, step for step, beside my path, and to make me feel that, as my life of changes passes on, He has a purpose and a meaning for every change, and an individual purpose and meaning for the result to which every change shall bring me.

'That God, therefore, should reveal Himself, in some way that is additional to the revelation in nature, should deal with our minds and wills in a way more personal and special, is surely an *admissible* idea. It is so in any view; but it is more evidently so when we view man fallen. If God has any purpose of mercy towards man fallen, it must be revealed to him and made good to him in a way proportioned to his actual state. But man's actual state is that of having fallen out of harmony with himself, and with God's works around him. He is plainly prone to miss and lose even those teachings which nature might afford to a purer mind. And he plainly needs information and direction which a purer mind would not need to seek from nature, or from any other quarter.

'The sum is, that on all accounts we may judge it fit that to His creature man God shall have *meanings* to declare,—meanings which nature does not disclose, of which her whole course seems calmly ignorant,—meanings which she was not fitted to embody or attain.

'Now, the method which God will take in this special dealing with the minds of men may be easily assigned. For we see how He has done it; and we may at all events maintain to our opponents that so He *might* do it. There is nothing unworthy or unlikely about it. God can convey His meaning by a direct and most inward impression on His creature's mind, accompanying it with an assuring evidence as to the source from which, and the authority with which, it comes. He *might* do that in the case of every man. But as I have already said, so I now repeat, it is the nature of man, and the explanation of his whole place and constitution, that he was meant to be dealt with *from without*. He is dealt with through persons, and through *things without him*, in all of which he finds the materials of his history, and the objects upon which his capacities are exercised. God, therefore, has chosen to deal with man, by making His inward impression on His servant's mind to be a message and a meaning concerning things and events transacted in the world. To these things and events the divine meaning is attached, or in these it is embodied and realized. And this being declared by God's servant, God is seen and found entering into a special course of dealings with men; setting them forth into a history of transactions with God, at every turn of which they may be conscious of His nearness to them, of that regard and bent of His thoughts, His judgments, and

His mercies, which mere nature never could disclose. So He did before man fell. So He has done ever since. And thus man's nearest and most momentous relations to his God, in those matters in which man is above nature—in which man is not measured by mere mechanical forces—*those* relations are ascertained, unfolded, exercised, so as to produce the effects that are embraced in God's design. This is the kind of professed revelation to which the alleged miracles are attached. No one can show that such a revelation is unsuitable to man or unworthy of God. Now I say that such a revelation, unfolding meanings of God which nature cannot disclose, of which from age to age she takes no note and makes no sign, might most fitly be accompanied by works of God that are no part of the order of nature, are no birth of the forces that are governed by her laws. Are not such works a fit token that those divine meanings, which man is now to apprehend and deal with, and keep in view as he looks out on the scenery of his life, are sure objective realities? Do they not fitly assure him, that though nature does not echo them to his inner man, as she does some other truths, yet he need not doubt nor fear, as though this persistent silence of nature were a silence of God? Do they not fitly assure him, that this *added meaning* with which he is called to deal is no fancy of some erring brother passing into his own fancy, but is indeed the unfolded mind of God?

'So then, in general, the miracles come to serve for attestation of the authority of the messenger; they are the work of divine power, here and now accompanying the man, and going forth at his word. He that is able to announce a present work of God, of the nature of immediate interposition, apart from the ordinary forces of nature, may well be thought commissioned to declare God's mind on those other matters in respect to which He announces a message from on high. This, in general, is the leading function of miracles. But there are several additional considerations which are fitted to show you how fitly miracles occupy this place, and in how many ways they are adapted to produce on the human mind the precise effects intended.

'For, first, they are striking in their own nature; they attract and secure attention by their very unlikeness to the ordinary course of things. They call into the liveliest exercise that sense of awe to which immense and strange power wielded by the will of one unseen, disturbing the ordinary course of affairs, always gives birth in human minds. This effect, indeed, is produced primarily in the witnesses and the contemporaries; but it is not confined to them. For every one who receives the message, down to the latest generations, may receive it as a message *so* from God, that when it came, God laid claim to human attention and human submission by these emphatic and exceptional signs. To us, who are hardened and confused by sin, this admonitory emphasis of communication serves a most important purpose. For who does not feel that, as a race, we are in a condition of bondage to the creature, "serving the creature more than the Creator?" This is our sin, that we have regard to the creatures, the order of things around us, as a seat of power, and a source of good, independent of God, and considered apart from Him. On the other hand, that Divine Being, whom we do not altogether deny, we are skilful to place far away; and we think of His will, so far as it is His, as no such august matter, just because all things continue as they were. On these accounts the appeal to our attention is made in a way precisely adapted to the evils of our state, when along with the message (which, even if we believed it, we might be disposed to treat so idly) we have presented the idea of God's power in movement—in movement along a line of sudden energy that is strange to nature. This presents to us a person who sets forth his will in deeds. It suggests to us how much we need to have our relations to that Power, and the results it brings about, and to the principles which it is pledged to enforce, adjusted and set right.

'But again, in another respect, the miracle is precisely adapted to be the proper and convincing pledge of the truth of revelation. For observe what it is that revelation is concerned to set forth. It sets forth or reveals God; yet not merely, nor mainly, God in the internal glory of His immanent perfections, but rather God contemplated in that *which He is doing and will do.* The communion or fellowship of God with man always proceeds by a manifestation of that which God will do. Special dealings and ways of procedure on God's part, on which nature is silent, are announced; things which God pledges Himself to effect are declared. And man is to order and conform his ways answerably to those pledged proceedings of God. For man, as a historical being, is not called to stand with God, but to walk with Him.

'What the revelation therefore declares to man is this, how the power of God will go forth in action, in justice, faithfulness, and love; and this egress of God's power man is thenceforth to expect, and in the expectation of it, dealing with God as pledged to it, he is to go. This, I repeat, is the general character of divine revelations. Now, on account of this general character which attaches to them, the fit evidences are miracles and prophecy. Of prophecy, which is itself a miracle, I will not speak now. But the miracle is an exhibition here and now of divine action going forth in a manner and along a line strange to the action of constant causes and ordinary laws, singling out an effect which is not contained in the order of nature, and bringing it to pass. So it stands for a token that the agency of God shall not fail to be there and to do its work, when the times of the promise come round; it stands for a token that the likelihood based on the appearances of things, on that certain order which seems to look so impassive on all our hopes and fears, is not to measure or bound our faith. It justifies us in resolving that our faith shall measure its confidence only by the word, from which shall not be parted the power, of the Infinite One.

'Still more impressively, however, do such considerations present and press themselves when we come nearer to the practical exigencies of man, and consider what God undertakes and calls us to expect in a revelation of mercy. The revelation comes to sinners, and it sets forth a scheme of restitution. It finds us not only darkened and perplexed, which we have stated already, but undone.

'It finds us fallen, and so fallen, that neither nature nor conscience, in virtue of any power in either or both of them, shall enable us to emerge again on the platform of a state of solid well-being. The object, therefore, of the divine word and deed is not merely to unfold the possibilities and impossibilities of our actual state, but to make a new beginning of our highest life, from which beginning there shall go forward a career of deliverance and glory. This indeed may be denied; men may assert that the fall was not so deep, and that the remedial dispensation does not import anything so extraordinary. But it is enough for my argument, that the case may be in this respect as I have stated it. This may be the actual fact and the Scripture doctrine: the fall *may* be so deep, the remedy so wonderful and decisive. When we are maintaining the fitness of the miracle to be appended to the doctrine, we must be allowed to bring forward our own persuasion of what the doctrine is, and to allege the congruities discernible from our own point of view. At all events, whether granted or not, it must be asserted and maintained against all who deny it or explain it away, that the case is even so, that the fall is so ruinous, that the redemption must be so decisive. But if the case be so, or be anything like this, then manifestly the question which is raised, and may be addressed to every teacher inspired or not, about every doctrine revealed or imagined, is not a question of truth merely, but a question of *power*. Let true things be said bearing on the case, and on the relations both of God and man to it—true things, never so true and never so clearly truths, which God only could reveal,—that is not enough: the question is, whether they are truths that set forth an assurance of power, actually coming forth to do the work required; and whether they are accompanied with tokens and pledges that may certify and sustain the faith of so great a thing as the actual egress and exercise of this power. Is this truth wedded to a power and declarative of a power fit to deal with such a case as ours? Is it allied to power, in whose going forth a divine hand shall be laid on the ruin of the fall, a new life breathed, a new beginning made; power that shall clear away the difficulties that obstruct our return, and open a pathway for us, and bring us thereby back to God? Are we left to the order of nature, and to the resources that are contained in and measured by her laws? Are we left to those forces, doomed to labour in contrivances that still break down, seeking to make nature serve a purpose for us, for which her powers were never destined? Or, ceasing from the toil, are we left to stand in the world, amid its many-ordered harmonies, and feel how sadly they look on the creature that has fallen and gone astray? Is that our case? Or is there power, and does there come to us the assurance of a power, which has entered into history, and can enter into our hearts,—a power *above* any or all the powers that are contained in the order of nature—*above* them all; power, which, however gently it entered into history, however secretly it may work within the heart, is a power of that order which wrought in the beginning, and made the beginnings,—a power that can lay, has laid, a new foundation, and can wake the pulses of a new heart? That is the question of *Redemption*—a question not of truth only, but of power. God means us to feel it to be *the* question. When we say so, we neither deny nor disgrace the natural order, which is good, and worthy to abide stedfast for its ends. Nor do we forget that that redeeming power has also its order, doubtless a glorious order, which we partly apprehend. Nor do we forget that usually that redeeming virtue is so co-ordinated to the natural order, or takes up that into its working, as to make no jar. But yet, in the end, that question still returns. Is there such a power pledged and working—power measureless? Are we assured that it comes, able to exceed and bear rule over all the forces of the natural order? Are we assured that there is no fate in that order that can stay its blessed course? Is there a power that can bid any waves be still, make any diseases whole, awaken out of the most real death? We need a revelation that shall deal with us so as to make this manifest and plain to us,—a revelation that shall mark it as a most experimental matter of fact. For this is the condition and the only ground of true faith in *redemption;* not otherwise shall there be born and reared a faith that, in the presence of the evils of our state, shall expect and embrace redemption. There are times, decisive times, in the lives of men, when this order of nature that girds us about, with its sure recurrences, its unhalting processes, its onward march, in which it seems to say, " The sum of power is mine, and I am the highest law," presses upon men very sore. There are times when, doubting if there be anything beyond this that they can practically deal with, men begin to realize what the order of nature means for a transgressor ; for this is the order of nature, that the past determines and shapes the future. And the question rises,—He that came, asking for our faith, did He come like so many others, bringing words only, very good words, but oh how feeble! or did He come with word and deed, words wedded to power, as one able to reverse the past, and make all new? Surely miracles were one direct, fit, most reasonable way to make this clear. Marvellously it sustains and leads on the mind, when we are passing in to deal with Christ about the inward mysteries of the heart of man, and the life of God, that we see those mighty works of His; that we see how the magnificent and ancient order, which claims silently to sum in itself all the possible, retreated before His word to make way for new possibilities, for divine effects ; so that what was most wayward and what was most stable in nature put a new demeanour on when He came near, and waves and storms were quieted, and death awoke to life.'

NOTE D.—PAGE 41.

The hypothesis of a sinless state, not lost but maintained, is not to be excluded in considering the possible roads which lay open before our race in the beginning. In following out that idea, there is no necessity to assume extraordinary degrees of knowledge or attainment as the starting-point. All that need be assumed are those simple elementary conditions which Genesis suggests. Those might have been the beginning of a noble career of progress. As man went forward in earthly works, as new relations unfolded, as the spiritual nature of man was exercised in the changing scene, and as successive revelations, when it pleased God, attached themselves to the facts and duties of life, those earthly things would no doubt have turned out to be the elements from which the loftiest lessons as to divine and spiritual things would have been evolved, and by means of which noble attainments in fellowship with God would have been achieved. The history, in point of fact, has taken another course; but it is still well to remember, that to be trained in this historical method is proper to us, not merely as sinful (and therefore dark and ignorant), but as men.

No doubt, if we argue from effect to cause, applying the principle that ordinary experience is a sufficient specimen of *all* experience, we shall be led to the conclusion that the first man (*if there was a first man*) originally was, like ourselves, disposed to do those things which are called sinful, and therefore, like us, did them. That is as much as to say, that there was no fall from a sinless state. According to this view, the Bible narrative only brings out strikingly the principles of evil, that may be held to be involved in every sin. So the rationalizing theologians generally. It is the same principle which leads Schleiermacher to maintain that, along with the perfection which, as he acknowledges, must be conceived to have belonged to man at his creation, a sinfulness must be conceived also to have existed. As he explains it, it seems to amount to (1) a liability to temptation, and (2) an incapacity to resist temptation with success for any considerable time. (*Glaubenslehre*, § 72, compare § 94.)

But the sentence of conscience judging sin is an affirmation that in some way it pertains to man's nature to be sinless, and that to be sinful is a fallen state. On the ground of that affirmation, it will, at the very least, always occur as an *alternative*, and indeed as the *preferable* alternative, that man has existed as one not yet sinful. This is the alternative that is conformable to the *faith* of conscience. The Scripture account has on its side an inward sentence which predisposes us to embrace it.

At the same time, it is to be observed that Genesis simply gives us, in historic form, the fact of a primeval sinlessness. The subsequent representations, on to the end of the Bible, thoroughly harmonize with this view, and strongly presuppose it. No pictures, however, are drawn of the state of man, ascribing to him attainments and virtues such as can only be the result of experience and development. On the contrary, the simplicity of the narrative strongly suggests the opposite view. It is to be observed that, in framing to oneself a conception of the method and order of the divine dealings with man, it becomes indispensable to form some conception of his primitive state, and of the relations in which he then stood. Theologians can hardly escape the necessity of taking some ground about that, either provisionally or definitively. Yet it must be admitted that, beyond the fact of a yet unfallen state, Scripture does not give us much material bearing directly on the primitive condition of man. Therefore the view taken of that condition of its various elements, and of the amount of change wrought by the fall, is regulated in each system to a considerable extent by the ground taken up on the general topics of Anthropology and Soteriology. Scripture materials bearing on man's present state, and on the nature and means of his salvation, are supposed to establish a general connection of truth; and this is held to imply, because it presupposes, such and such a doctrine of the unfallen state. This is a department, therefore, in which the peculiar genius of the different theological systems reveals itself in an interesting and instructive way.[1] When considerations extrinsic to the proper merits make it inconvenient for contending parties to reveal frankly the real amount and ground of their differences regarding the doctrine of sin and the doctrine of grace, the fight has not unfrequently been carried over to the theology of the unfallen state, as to a ground on which greater liberty could be taken. The disputes regarding grace which have taken place in the Church of Rome are full of illustrations of this remark.

In these circumstances, it is not very wonderful that theologians have been led to over-press their text.

It was not unusual for the orthodox systematic writers to depict the unfallen state in an exaggerated manner, by way of bringing out more forcibly the ruin of the fall.[2] Exaggeration naturally creates recoil, and a strong disposition to distrust the theology of 'original righteousness' pro-

---

[1] See Cunningham, *Hist. Theol.* i. 516.
[2] See *e.g.* quotation from Hyperius in Note F, *infra*.

bably exists very generally. Where the opening chapters of Genesis are regarded as containing not a historical but a purely ideal representation, or where they are set down as simply Jewish myth, this tendency is of course very thoroughly confirmed; for although those chapters may not in themselves supply the materials for the whole Church doctrine of original righteousness, they do supply the basis which it needs, and it can hardly stand when they are swept away. In so far as the theory of natural development of animal species has been accepted as a complete account of the origin of man, it works in the same direction.

But the detail or filling up, which theologians may think capable of being supported by grounds more or less strong, must not be confounded with the doctrine or assertion of an unfallen or sinless state as the original state of man. The detailed theological explanations, or some of them, may be inferential and precarious: the general doctrine or assertion cannot be dismissed without transforming the scheme of man's relations and obligations from end to end.

NOTE E.—PAGE 42.

From the point of view of the Christian student, the history resolves itself, perhaps, most naturally into three lines of development. It is useful to distinguish them, though they are never separated, and cannot usually be completely disentangled even in thought.

First, there is the historical development of human nature into its earthly destiny, proceeding according to its actual capacities and powers. What was in the capacities of human nature and human society had to be unfolded. Those capacities were injured; man was fallen; but he was spared still in the enjoyment of many natural gifts. Much, therefore, could be done in the way of subduing the earth, combining and applying the resources it offered, organizing and developing human society, so as to exhibit a notable history of earthly achievement. This might be done variously, as various tendencies prevailed. It might in particular cases be blighted by untoward circumstances, or by failure of the vigour of races. Looking to moral causes, it might be, on the one hand, marred or made to retrograde by the destructive influence of moral evil; or, on the other hand, way might be made for its development to great degrees of splendour, if counteracting influences prevented sin from bringing forth and ripening all its ruinous fruits. Secondly, there is the history of human sin and ungodliness, working onward from the first fall. It is variously modified by many causes—by outward circumstances; by the view men took of their own interests; by the wholesome and beneficent influence of the providential structure of society, family relations, civil government, aiding and sustaining the operation of conscience; or, lastly, by the counteracting influence of grace. Thirdly, there is the history of redemption, *i.e.* of the way in which God taught and trained men, or some of them, and the measure in which His grace made the teaching effectual. This third head might subdivide into two branches: 1. The history of divine revelation, or of the system under which God placed man; and, 2. The history of the experience and attainments of men under the successive stages of divine revelation. The second branch involves an inquiry full of interest; but the materials, for obvious reasons, are by no means so full and adequate as they are in the case of the first branch, and one must content oneself with somewhat vague and general approximations.

Note F.—Page 43.

The view asserted in the text does not rest on specific evidence, but on the general impression that Scripture, in recording for us the ways of God with men, has so recorded as to give, if not all that was revealed, at least a just impression of the progress and gradations of the revelation, and the style and measure of it at each successive epoch. Unless it be so, it is difficult to conceive on what principle the Scriptures are constructed.

It is possible, of course, to maintain that matters with

which we have now no concern, the interest of which was wholly for the men of a past age, may have formed the occasion of quite peculiar and remarkable revelations; and yet, because the matters are no concern of ours, no record of the revelations has been preserved. It would be sufficient to reply that this ought not to be assumed without evidence. But besides, if the hypothesis were granted, it would make no practical difference. Revelations wholly aside from those which we possess, and belonging to some quite different series, could not affect our impression of the connection and gradation of those which we possess. If made known to us, they would stand apart in our minds, and those which we possess would present themselves precisely as they do now.

It was not any idea so far-fetched as that just supposed which called out the remark in the text. It has been supposed sometimes, that revelations bearing on the great central verities, and more clear than those which are recorded in at least the early part of the Old Testament, more fully anticipative of evangelical grace, may have been given to the men of those early days, though no record of them remains. The object of this suggestion is to facilitate explanations as to the possibility of the same evangelical faith and experience having been entertained and realized in the world's youth as now. But a theological object such as this is, rather exposes the suggestion to suspicion than lends it strength. The unity of the faith, in whatever sense asserted, must be made out from the material we possess, not based on mere assumptions.

However, there must be strong inducements to entertain the idea in question, for it is met with in thoughtful theological writings at all periods down to our own days. How it used to be put, it may be worth while to illustrate from a very estimable theologian of the Reformation period—Andreas Hyperius, in his *Methodus Theologiae* (posthumous ed., Basiliae 1574), p. 103: 'Certum est Adamum ante lapsum perfectissimam cognitionem de Trinitate habuit: a lapsu vero, tametsi ea cognitio fuerit aliquo modo obscurata, minime tamen fuit adempta: imo vero multo adhuc clarius ille universum hoc mysterium perspexit, quam id in principio geneseos describitur, quàm illi unquam ex posteris doctoribus explanarunt. Et quomodo posset fieri ut permissionem de semine benedicto, id est, de filio Dei mittendo, rectius quisquam intelligeret quam ille ad quem ipsius Dei viventes voce primum facta est? Qui autem Patrem et Filium novit, Spiritum sanctum pariter ut novit necesse est. Idem vero Adam fidelissimè omnem eam doctri nam inculcavit apud suam ecclesiam tradiditque eam filio suo et ministro ecclesiae, Seth,' etc.

Note G.—Page 43.

In a more detailed statement many points would require to be made prominent which in the text are assumed or are passed by. I may specify the doctrine of the divine unity, or the sole and universal majesty of the one God; the energetic conception of the divine nature as the living God, in connection with which may be taken the Old Testament doctrines of creation and providence, both of them delivered and sustained with extraordinary power; and the attribute of the divine holiness, 'in virtue of its pregnancy, one of the hardest to expound of biblical ideas,' as a recent writer says. The attempts of the naturalistic schools, either to convict the Old Testament of inconsistency on these points, or to account (on their principles) for the remarkable teaching which it presents, are signal failures. This remark applies to each of the points specified taken separately. When the doctrine on all these points is combined, the result is still more impressive. The directness and force with which the Divine Being is presented, first of all, in the form of personal agency; then, in connection with that, the relation which He is represented as holding to the creatures universally, as the spring of all their manifold life and force—both in the more ordered and recurrent forms and in the more singular and startling; lastly, in connection with both of these, the view given of this God, implicated though He is with all kinds of being and action, as the Holy One, with the intense self-assertion and self-separation which that implies;—all this is a most extraordinary combination. It appears in these Scriptures presented with perfect simplicity and ease; and it comes to light in those concrete exemplifications, in which a mere speculative theory runs the utmost hazard of shipwreck.

K. O. Müller, in one of his works, speaking of the vacillation in classic mythology between inconsistent views of the highest God, which simply contradict one another, has made the remark that there is only one book in which the difficulty is solved,— in which the absolute and self-existent One appears without effort and without incongruity at the door of Abraham's tent.

Note H.—Page 44.

The view of sin presented in the New Testament, *e.g.* in the writings of the Apostle Paul, is stern and dark, and has always been resented as exaggerated by a certain class of thinkers. It is anticipated, however, and the rudiments of it clearly furnished, in the biblical representation of the early world. Sin appears as, first of all, a free decision, beginning with unbelief and disregard of God's word and will. It causes a fall, and thenceforth the race appears in an exiled and perverted state. From time to time special instances of sin in particular men and races rise into portentous prominence, and an intense energy of divine displeasure is seen breaking through the patience and goodness of God, so as to write out His sentence on sin, in large letters, for the world to read. But the whole Old Testament history is of such a character as to bring into special prominence this aspect of all sin, that it is a forsaking of God, and imply that it is to be judged with special reference to that aspect of it.

So, also, the hold which sin has upon man in his present state, its power over him, the strength with which it tends to its results, are everywhere made visible. This appears, not more from the dominion it exerts over evil men, than from the energy with which it rises up in men who are, on the whole, servants of God. In this connection it is interesting to notice how the significant word flesh begins as early as

Gen. vi. to be charged with its peculiar weight of meaning. Notice how the word is harped upon and recurred to throughout that chapter. It is not maintained that the full sense of it is here already presupposed; but some sad divorce of 'flesh' and 'spirit,'—at the least, some mysterious weakening of the previous connection between them,—is implied throughout.

If no doctrine is here dogmatically set forth, a mode of view and a mode of feeling are formed which are perfectly definite, and which were fitted to operate in receptive minds with an energy and a precision not a whit inferior to any that can be ascribed to dogmatic statements.

NOTE I.—PAGE 44.

The interpretation of this great foundation promise—this 'beginning of the gospel of Jesus Christ'—has of course exercised the theological mind, and gathered around itself a copious literature. The essential fulfilment in Jesus Christ is not doubted by any believing theologian. The question however remains, as to the range of meaning which the words were fitted and designed to convey into the minds of those to whom they were addressed; or, to put it otherwise, what sense, put upon the promise by those to whom it was addressed, would have been as much as they were warranted to believe on the strength of it, neither more nor less. It may be said that there are three alternatives as to the literal reference of the words: first, that they refer to Christ alone, directly and exclusively; second, that they refer primarily to the Church, or to Christ, so that the Church is included with Him in the promise; third, that they refer primarily to the race, and apply to Christ as the hope of the world and the desire of all nations. The first may be said to be the old Lutheran view; the second more especially Calvinistic; the third probably finds more favour among modern writers, and is susceptible of various forms, more believing, or more rationalizing. For the first, reference may be made to an excursus appended to Glassius' *Philologia Sacra*, in which his censure on Calvin is worth observing; also J. F. Buddeus, *Historia Ecclesiastica*, p. 125. For the second, see Witsius, *Œc. Fœd.* lib. iv. 1, § xxiv. For the third, among many others, reference may be made to Hofmann's *Schriftbeweis*, i. p. 438. The passage is fitted to suggest various other forms of the theory besides that which Hofmann himself advocates. See Note K, *infra*.

Delitzsch, adopting a principle often appealed to by Hofmann, finds a proof that not merely the general contents or drift of the promise, but the very form of it, is divinely given in this, that every word of it takes emphatic and pregnant fulfilment in the Messiah; the mode of phrasing, which might seem indifferent and accidental, so far as holding forth the hope of good to the race in general was concerned, proving to be precisely adapted to the ultimate fulfilment. (*Die Genesis*, 1853, p. 75.)

NOTE J.—PAGE 48.

In connection with the Abrahamic covenant, a remark may be made. Attention has already been directed to the significance of the fact that, according to the Scriptures, the God of nature enters into historical relations with man, and continues to evolve them. Now let it be observed how the condescension implied in entering into covenants—such as that with Abraham—brought a new element in, and constituted a step towards the great condescension which crowns the ways of God. God not only reveals what He has fully resolved to do, but He binds Himself in a covenant. He assumes a position in relation to Abraham in which reciprocal obligations are recognised; He has made an agreement which must be fulfilled; He has conferred on Abraham an interest in His own future procedure—a right, which may be pleaded, to claim the benefits engaged for. Now the early Scriptures speak, and theologians have reasoned much, of the 'Angel of the Lord,' the 'Angel of the Covenant.' Very considerable difficulties attach to the complete explanation of all the passages, and gather about the question,

How much the old believers attained to think about this Angel, and what impressions they cherished in connection with Him. But let it be observed, at all events, that in the very fact of entering into covenant, Jehovah does silently assume to Himself the character of an angel—one sent. He takes office.: He binds Himself to ministries which must be certainly and punctually discharged. He takes on obligations which He is henceforth to be seen fulfilling. God is the sender forth of all angels. But here, if it may be reverently so expressed, we see Him becoming at the same time the Sent—sending Himself along a prescribed path of long-suffering divine dealings. In that path He is thereafter seen proceeding, year after year, age after age, not only with the majesty of divine decrees, but with the patient faithfulness of one who—shall I say?—executes the commission which He has taken on Him in behalf of Abraham, His friend. It does not seem wonderful that henceforth, in the faith of the Church, along with the impression of the mighty and gracious One, who sends out all powers and agencies that work in all the world, there is an impression also of One who follows His people in a holy unfailing attendance, in the attitude of one who executes a charge. It does not seem unreasonable to read the remarkable texts concerning the Angel of the Lord, in the light of this general impression. 'The God before whom my fathers Abraham and Isaac did walk, . . . the Angel which redeemed me from all evil, bless the lads.'

A good statement of the opinions regarding the Angel of the Lord may be found in the late G. F. Oehler's *Theologie des Alten Testament*, vol. i. § 60, p. 199.[1]

NOTE K.—PAGE 50.

In a previous Note, the promise of the woman's seed was referred to. The promise of blessing to Abraham's seed has a peculiar interest, because of the references made to it in the New Testament, and particularly on account of the

[1] 8vo, Tübingen, 1873. (In course of translation for Clark's Foreign Theological Library.)

construction put upon it in a well-known passage of the Epistle to the Galatians (iii. 16). Such passages illustrate the principle that revelations, once made, may become more luminous and significant to succeeding ages. Along with the disclosure of divine purposes, they may have at first something of a secret or riddle in them; and the secret unfolds itself long after.

It can scarcely be doubted that these promises, like many others, were not only intended to have, as Bacon phrased it, a springing and germinating fulfilment, but also a growingly precise and significant interpretation. That is to say, while the bare words of a promise, taken in connection with the circumstances in which they were first uttered, might be in some respects vague,—fitted only to indicate in general a certain kind of good, and the quarter in which it was to be expected,—a progressive commentary followed, which determined the sense more and more precisely, and made the believing expectations converge more closely on the intended fulfilment. This commentary consisted not merely in subsequent revelations and promises of a more specific character. It consisted also of a course of providences and divine dispensations. These practically shut men up to certain lines of expectation, and rendered the hope more intense as they made it more definite. If one may use so plain an image, at the delivery of the promise it might be impossible to tell in what direction, within many points of the compass, the promise would seek its fulfilment; but after a while, one can see that it is marching towards it by given roads and in a definite direction. The New Testament references to Old Testament oracles commonly take for granted that this help to interpretation is made use of. They do not rest on the bare words of the passage referred to, but presuppose that the organic connection of those words with the series of the divine history is observed.

Those who find Christ in the first promise are accused of turning a perfectly general augury regarding the race, into a specific prophecy applicable to one single person. And just so the apostle is accused of having yielded so far to the suggestions of a baseless habit of accommodation, as to turn a promise regarding Abraham's descendants into a specific promise of the single individual Messiah. He is also accused of having supported his argument by a demonstrably false exposition of the word 'seed,'—an exposition intended to exclude the only true and legitimate sense of it.[1] But let us suppose that the apostle had in view not only the promise, but the manner in which it was commented on by the series of recorded dispensations which carried it out. The word 'seed' is vague and large. But from the very beginning, a significant principle of limitation began to operate. Not all Abraham's children, but Isaac only, not both of Isaac's, but Jacob only, fall within it. Then the family begins to multiply — all Jacob's sons are dealt with as pertaining to the covenant. And yet, within this family, expectation is by and by concentrated on certain given lines. Not only so; all through their history there is a sort of hidden kernel in this people, which is the central thing perpetually dealt with. This is the unity amid this multitude all too loosely joined to God in covenant; this is that which abides and persists amid all the siftings and scatterings. A tenth, a holy seed, is the substance of the people (Isa. vi. 13). Until, as time goes on, the Messianic expectation becomes more luminous and definite, and when Christ at last is given it becomes clear as day, that this was THE seed whose coming gave life and meaning to everything else. The result is, that the whole history of the seed, from Abraham onwards, *had* to be managed, and *was* managed, so as to make the lines tend towards Christ. Looked at in this light, the apostle's criticism is full of significance. If the promise had *not* intended Christ as its proper birth; if it had not been a promise requiring to be fulfilled that way; if it had been a promise of indiscriminate good, to be imparted (conditionally or unconditionally) to all Jacob's, to all Isaac's, to all Abraham's posterity, as they went scattering down the diverging lines of their histories, then the word *ought* to have been σπέρμασι. For the promise in that case would

---

[1] 'He saith not, And to seeds, as of many; but as of one, And to thy seed, which is Christ.'

not have been to one fellowship, made one, and interested in the promise, by the seed which is Christ. It would have been a promise to a miscellany of diverging fellowships and races. It was not that, simply because it aimed at Christ.

Similarly, the first promise was compatible enough, in its bare terms, with the idea of diffused blessing in the race. But apart from subsequent revelations, the mere course of providence immediately began to comment upon it: the first step being the emergence of two tendencies, and two fellowships within the race, representing different and hostile principles.

NOTE L.—PAGE 55.

A remarkable contrast obtains between the manifestations of God to Abraham, Isaac, and Jacob, and those which are made to Israel in connection with the giving of the law; a friendly and gracious character prevailing in the former, as a stern and peremptory tone appears in the latter. It is worth observing how delicately this is proportioned to the historical conditions existing in either case. During the former period a process of selection takes place at each generation. Abraham is a selected man; of Abraham's sons, Isaac is set aside; of Isaac's sons, Jacob: and thus at each stage a man is dealt with who is specially influenced and trained. He is head of the family, exerts influence upon it, stands forth in his representative character (as head of it) as a believing man. So long, it is a congruous thing that the same evangelical friendliness, so to say, which sheds such a peculiar light over the history of Abraham, should continue on the whole to mark the dealings and communications of God with his great successors, though varied somewhat with reference to the very distinct characters of each of them.

But it was not intended always to conduct the history of the family on this principle, which indeed would not have been consistent with the promise of the multitudinous seed. Accordingly, with Jacob the process of selection ceases. The family becomes a nation. Any one can see, apart from further designs, that the mode of dealing which was fit and becoming, when Abraham, Isaac, and Jacob walked before God, when the little society might be regarded as characteristically believing and obedient, could not continue to be employed without modification when a mixed multitude like a nation was to be dealt with. A change is made accordingly. Yet God does not draw back from His promised goodness. He interposes in a way more wonderful than ever. He brings them out of Egypt with a mighty hand; and He opens His testimony at the mount with the assurance, ' I am the Lord thy God, which have brought thee out of the land of Egypt, out of the house of bondage.' He laid claim to Israel, and privileged them, as His own peculiar people. But He did so in connection with a certain terrible majesty in His manifestations. Near as He is, a certain distance and separation are expressed in His ways of dealing with them. And now, moreover, He is ever proving them with laws—specific, stringent, detailed requirements of service. Apart from more special reasons connected with the order of the divine dispensations, there is an obvious fitness in some such method being employed in dealing with a nation. Indeed, the change or transition from the one system to the other keeps pace precisely with the change of conditions. When all Jacob's sons are grown up, begin to act for themselves, and to impress the character of their own choice and action on the family life, the new state of things may be said to be already manifesting itself in its beginnings. And, contemporaneously, a certain distance and self-withdrawment on God's part becomes observable. All the latter part of the history in Genesis betrays this feature. It is the preparation for the new attitude, so to speak, which is to meet us in Exodus.

I may remark that all this, which is very intelligible if, as these books say, God was dealing with the race in these successive stages, becomes very unaccountable if the Hebrew history and books have taken shape under the influence of natural causes, and if, therefore, it is a myth that is here before us. If the genius of the nation as formed and developed led them to present such a view of God's attitude towards their race as is implied in the giving of the law, with the subsequent enforcement of it by the prophets, how comes it that the same genius gave such a very different view of the previous attitude of God to the patriarchs? How came it to shape the conception of the two stages of its mythology so diversely?

Leaving that point, however, I may add that the contrast, conceived in the manner indicated above, falls in well with the Pauline representation of the law, or at least of one great aspect and function of the law. The apostle was willing to let the observance of it linger on in the case of those who had a national reason for keeping it. For them it might be 'nothing'—do neither good nor harm. But he counted it perfectly intolerable that it should be selected as the form in which a man of another nation, called merely to be a personal believer in Christ, should express or embody his relation to God. It was a departure from God to do so—a renunciation of Christ. When we consider that this same law-keeping had been the mould of true religion for ages, the divinely ordained form within which it grew, and that Paul himself, as a Jew, exercised a Christian discretion as to conforming to it or not, and circumcised Timothy because of the Jews that were in those quarters, it becomes a striking thing to find him fasten upon it the character of being so fatally opposite to the truth of the gospel. But, with all its evangelical elements and references, it had essentially a fitness to set forth and bring out the attitude which it befits God to take towards a mixed multitude. That is to say, it was essentially fitted to express the relation to God which is common to men, not that which is peculiar to the believer. While doing that, it also did more; but that character inhered in it essentially as the Law of the Lawgiver to Israel.

NOTE M.—PAGE 59.

In the early Church, the question regarding the view to be taken of the law, and generally of the Old Testament economy, was naturally felt to be a pressing one. The

Tübingen school, along with other scholars, have turned history into romance by their theories as to the controversy between Petrine and Pauline Christianity, and the influence exerted by it. But they have done service in turning attention to the subject, and producing a more lively impression of the difficulties and misunderstandings between different sections of early Christians, which must certainly have perplexed the Church. Besides this, there was the necessity of giving to the heathen and the Jews a consistent account of God's ways with men. And lastly, every thoughtful Christian had to give some account of the matter to himself. The Church held on to two positions: First, that the whole ceremonial of the ancient economy was done away in Christ. Here they were opposed to Jews and Judaizing sects. Secondly, that in all the steps and arrangements of that economy, God, the God and Father of our Lord Jesus, was preparing the way for revelation of grace and truth— that the same verity which was open in the New Testament was present throughout the Old. Here they were opposed to most Gnostics; and the method of explication by which the point was to be made good was allegory. But the way of reasoning from these two positions, and applying them, was often exceedingly crude. The pseudo-Barnabas, for instance, sometimes reasons as if he believed it to have been a mere blunder of the Jews that they supposed the law was ever binding in the letter of it. Indeed, a careful reading of the Epistle of Barnabas will more vividly suggest the way in which the Gnostic sects arrived at a part of their conclusions, than much study of Irenaeus and Epiphanius.

NOTE N.—PAGE 64.

I have endeavoured to state this point with studious moderation. Important as it is, it is desirable not to build on doubtful grounds. Passages which some interpret as properly Messianic prophecies, others prefer to regard as prophecies of certain kinds of blessing, *known to us, in our day*, to be Messianic, *i.e.* to be connected with the appearing and mediation of our Lord, but which are not contemplated in the prophecy under that notion, but simply as benefits coming. More particularly, the question in various cases is whether the prophet spoke, and the people were warranted to understand him, of *the* Messiah 'which was for to come,' or only of *some* bearer and instrument of good to be raised up in coming days. Was it clear in those days that all such passages pointed to one all-sufficient and perfect Messiah? Or was it indeterminate, whether some of the prophecies might not take fulfilment, one in one coming person, and another in another? The latter view may be held as to some passages, while the former or more explicitly Messianic view is regarded as alone sufficient to explain others. The statement in the text is consistent with the admission that a difference of judgment on this point, with reference to some passages especially, exists among those who believe equally in Messianic prophecy as one great feature of Old Testament Scripture.

However, I may be permitted to make this remark: It is unquestionable that the personal faith, the religious exercise and aspiration—in short, the experience—of the prophets, entered largely into their preparation for their function. The impressions made upon their minds by the whole scenery of that dispensation, past and present, formed great part of the material employed by the inspiring Spirit in the oracles which they uttered. They had their point of view, their natural and providential preparation; and that point of view, that preparation, were made use of: they spoke from the one, they spoke with the other. A much fuller and clearer recognition of the large place which this element fills in the prophetic utterance is one of the characteristics of modern interpretation. To consider the prophet as a holy man thus and thus circumstanced, and in these circumstances enabled to great exercises of faith, is no doubt indispensable in order to a sympathetic and appreciative understanding of these writings. *How* far this will carry us, *how* much it will explain, can only be ascertained by trying. The tendency therefore is, and has been for some time, to make as much as possible of this method, to try how much can be done with it. Probably, after this necessary experiment comes to be reviewed, it will turn out, as usual, that it has been carried too far. When this method is made to explain everything, the whole prophetic writings are interpreted so as to *need* no other explanation. That is to say, they are made to be merely compositions of able and devout men surveying things around them, under the influence of earnest faith and enthusiastic religious fervour. The men may still be regarded as invested with divine authority. But the thoughts which they are authorized to reveal, are supposed to have been all naturally attainable, along lines of suggestion which can be traced. When the same method is made to explain, not everything, but yet too much, then some of the things in the prophetic writings which ought to be set down to an influence that lifted men beyond themselves, are explained so as to require no such extraordinary elevation. Now, commonly, the assumption proceeded on is, that everything ought to be explained by this natural method that possibly can be. If afterwards something remains which *cannot* be so accounted for, let it be explained otherwise; but the latter element is jealously restricted within the narrowest bounds. This would be a fair assumption, if it were doubtful whether an influence existed carrying prophecy more decidedly out of sight of natural tracks and suggestions. But I speak to those to whom this is not doubtful. I have those in view who cordially admit a range of prophetic vision not to be measured by any such line. If so, then there is no obligation to force passages of prophetic writing down to the level of what might be naturally suggested. We must assume the free play (according to the objects divinely intended) of all the forms and modes of impulse, and the free occurrence in prophecy of all the kinds of effect which any of those modes of impulse might produce. And we are under no necessity or obligation to *presume* the presence of one only, as if the other must never be contemplated unless it is absolutely forced upon us by sheer inability to interpret it away.

However, the interpreter's tendency is to make the most he can of the line of natural suggestion; because that is a track which human investigation is competent to travel, and to make discoveries in. When we get beyond that, we may recognise and confess something, but we can explain nothing.

I repeat, then, that we shall probably find, on a review of things, that the tendency even of believing interpretation has been to resolve too much by this one key.

Now, starting and proceeding on the method of natural suggestion, it is natural to qualify and disintegrate Messianic prophecy. That is, it is natural to assume that the prophet, looking around him, and seeing certain forms of evil, and exercising faith in God as the God of covenant, was divinely set on to give assurance to the people of the reality of conceptions which arose *in this line*—conceptions of good that was to replace the evil, glorious kings instead of base and foolish, a mighty and effectual priesthood instead of a dubious and unsatisfactory, and so forth. To suppose that all these anticipations were connected with the hope of one single, sublime, all-glorious person, and knit up into the hope of him, is more supra-rational, in the sense of being more beyond the line of attainment towards which we can discern natural tracks and pathways leading up. But if we must own such inexplicable attainment in the prophets,—if, in particular, we must own true Messianic prophecy, *i.e.* prophecy that was such in the prophetic consciousness,—then a counter presumption arises in favour of at least a possible direct Messianic reference in all prophecy that points to Messianic blessing.

NOTE O.—PAGE 64.

The Psalms in which divine judgments are denounced against opponents with intense severity, have been felt to occasion difficulty. Much depends on appreciating the point of view from which such compositions must be held to proceed. The whole course of things was fitted to form men's minds to the conception of God's kingdom as a cause, sustained under difficulties, against opposition. All those who took an interest in the promises and calling of Israel, necessarily had their minds much occupied with the sense of contrast and conflict hence arising. Two forms of contrast came prominently into view. First, that between Israel and the surrounding nations. If Israel had been perfectly true to her calling, it would have been more apparent. Often she seemed to be doing her best to become even as all the nations. But that could never be; the contrast always remained. It was attended with dislike and opposition. A sense of something irreconcilable obtained. The feeling of the nations was, on the whole, a desire to cut Israel off from being a nation, and to make it plain that their resources in divine promises would not prove able to maintain their cause. And the view which believers in Israel cherished, the faith which it was their duty to maintain, was that these adversaries should never work all their will; that in seeking to do it, they were attacking Jehovah, and ensuring their own overthrow; that the cause which sets itself against Jehovah's cause ought to go down, and shall go down. This they were taught most earnestly to long for, and most stedfastly to believe. Therefore also they express it in many a psalm.

But there was another contrast, and a nearer one. There were many ungodly within Israel. These brought down upon her judgment instead of blessing. They paved the way for the success of foreign enemies; and they were at the same time the obstructors of goodness, and the persecutors of good men who strove to uphold God's cause. Which of the prophets did they not slay and persecute? These were the true, and far the most deadly, enemies of the great cause. How easily would invaders have been repelled, but for the fatal weakness introduced into Israel by those who brought on her God's judgment! Thus the work of those who feared the Lord grew to be very much the assertion of His cause by faithful testimony, and (in the days of pious kings) by due execution of judgment against those who fought against God. In this conflict, far too often, their experience was such as to suggest the idea of sin prevailing. The good cause had to be borne up against depressing disadvantages.

In these circumstances, they were to believe that the cause of God would triumph after all. In particular, they were to believe that those who withstood God should meet with assured and tremendous overthrow. The two causes were impersonated in the two parties. One cause or other should go down, in the persons of those who adhered to it. And it was a capital and essential exercise of the spiritual life of all who feared God, stedfastly to believe and earnestly to pray that the cause and party which are against God's cause should be irretrievably overthrown. God was to assert His cause in a way of judgment. However the wicked might seem to triumph, this was to be counted on as sure, that the cause and party of sin should go down at last in a conclusive overthrow, which should make an end at last of the conflict, so sorrowful, trying, and weary. Then, at length, when 'the righteous should wash his feet in the blood of the wicked, and rejoice seeing the vengeance, men should say, Verily there is a reward for the wicked; verily there is a God that judgeth in the earth.' This was waited for with inexpressible longing. It was fit it should be. It is true that the cause of sin shall go down, in the persons of those who maintain it, in such a manner as to throw back on them all the evil they have sought to do. This is not the only truth bearing on the point; but it is truth; and it was then the present truth. To cherish the faith of it was a principal duty during many dark and weary days. The questions of God's being, God's dominion, the Church's hope in God, were wrapped up in this. Believers contended for this, as for their all, that the other side, with its pride and falsehood, with its numbers and its seeming security, should not prevail, but should in due time have conclusive right done upon it by God. This is the point of view from which those psalms are to be understood.

Note P.—Page 69.

The methods of representing the origin of the Old Testament, and the relation in which it stood to the series of the world's religious history, which prevailed among the Gnostics, are a very interesting study, and afford curious cross-lights. Practically they held the same views, at bottom, as the more advanced schools of modern criticism. They found in Judaism, or imputed to it, a thorough dependence on the seen and the material, an external method of goodness, and a Deistic relation to God. Therefore they regarded it as radically foreign to Christianity. They confessed points of connection between the two systems, which they accounted for, partly on the ground that Judaism, more than some other religions, developed the better capacities of the style of religion which is natural to psychic men; partly on the ground that a higher power, working in a manner and for ends of which the author of Judaism was unconscious, inserted into it some anticipative germs belonging to another order of things. All this led them to impute Judaism to the Demiurge, as his peculiar and not very successful contrivance. Here, of course, they diverged wholly from our critics, who must account for the whole development from human and historical sources. But this is a difference in deducing the rise of the phenomenon; the similarity of view in estimating the character of it remains.

However, this is hardly the place for following out the subject.

LECTURE III.

Note A.—Page 78.

On the assumption that the Scriptures embody a divine revelation, adapted to the peculiarities of the condition of man, which has been completed in the New Testament, one might expect a certain character to manifest itself. The revelation, in its completed form, is supposed to be left to operate, without further change or addition, among men, in all the conditions into which they successively pass. The conditions of human minds vary indefinitely with the progress of history; yet the supposition is, that the sealed and unalterable record is divinely adapted to do its work at each stage, through all these variations. If so, we may expect it to prove flexible and fertile, capable of copious applications, many of them not foreseen until the necessity for them arose. And this must be combined with the explicitness and clearness befitting a divine revelation. Now, in point of fact, it will hardly be denied that the Christian records have exhibited this capability in a remarkable degree. Many systems built upon them, as well as phases of feeling and modes of conduct professedly based upon them, have passed away; they had their time, and were superseded. But the Scriptures, and the message of the Scriptures, have proved able to enter as a most powerful force into the life and combinations of the present, as of past ages. No writings laying claim to the character of a revelation have exhibited this capability in anything like the same degree.

Hence also it is, that so many various mental tendencies find something to lay hold of, or something that lays hold of them, in the Scriptures. For these were designed to claim affinity with human life in all its states. No wonder that many various minds, powerfully attracted by some aspect of Scripture teaching or sentiment, have striven to make themselves its interpreters and representatives; to interpret out of Scripture whatever they felt to be unwelcome; and to give further their peculiar version of the drift of Scripture, and the lessons which it is designed to teach. This does not prove that there is no definite meaning or message in the Scripture; but only that the contents of Scripture lay hold of various phases of mind with great power, and that hence a strong temptation arises in the case of each to endeavour to gain the verdict of this book on its side. Each school sets in the foreground what it seems to understand and appreciate, and throws into the shade what it dislikes and misunderstands. And the Bible *does* lend itself to the process in so far as this goes, that whatever each school possesses of sound method and sound instinct, finds something congenial in the Bible; whereupon it claims to have found corroboration there. This is the foundation, in so far as it has any foundation, for the implied taunt in the well-known lines:

> 'Hic liber est in quo quærit sua dogmata quisque
> Invenit et pariter dogmata quisque sua.'[1]

And so viewed, there is no ground for a taunt, but rather for the recognition of one necessary quality (not the less necessary because capable of being abused) which a genuine revelation, designed for use under existing conditions, ought to possess.

NOTE B.— PAGE 80.

According to the views maintained by the 'advanced' schools, the New Testament writings are due to a great religious impulse operating in the minds of men as a consequence of the appearance of Jesus Christ. This impulse, operating according to the ordinary laws of human nature,

---

[1] The lines quoted, which are from the pen of Samuel Werenfels, were not of course intended by him to direct a taunt against the Bible, but only to convey a sneer at the doctrinal divines of all schools. They are often quoted with an application to the book rather than to the readers.

but under various conditions which altered as time advanced, elicited from various men the writings now admitted into the canon, and also some, due to precisely similar causes, which have not been so received. The writers are to be venerated as men of high sincerity (though in many cases it was of a kind compatible with the palming of their own works upon the world under the names of other men of greater authority than themselves), and of high moral enthusiasm. Some of them, besides,—one or two at any rate,—were men of remarkable genius. Such works, whatever defects attach to them, must ever occupy a great and venerable place in the minds of men, and can never be antiquated or superseded. In religion, as in art, the works of remarkable men, especially the works of great men, produced under elevating and stimulating conditions which have never since returned, possess a power, and a truth also, peculiar to themselves; and therefore they have a value which time and criticism cannot alter. We cannot, indeed, accept their mere authority, nor receive their teaching, except in so far as it commends itself to our own sense of truth and duty. But as certainly as good taste will prize the works of Greek art, so will sound religious instincts set store by the New Testament writings, will find in them a fountain of welcome suggestions, and will look up to the writers as to men who in *some* respects stood nearer to the central Light than we do.

One of the conclusions which follows, by steps needless to be reproduced here, from this mode of view, is that the Apostle Paul is to be regarded as the true originator of far the greater part of Christian doctrine. Not that he gave to it the full measure even of its New Testament development; but where he came short, disciples trained in his school worked out his hints as the necessities of the times required, and embodied the results in writings which pass under the names of Paul, or of other apostles. The only important contribution independent of the Pauline influence,—but certainly a contribution that was most important,—is that embodied in the Gospel and Epistles ascribed to the Apostle John.

The evidences produced in support of this theory, in so

far as they consist in critical details, shall not be adverted to in this place. The *ex facie* improbabilities which attach to it have not perhaps, even yet, been sufficiently considered. An essential part of all these theories is to transfer the authorship of many New Testament writings from the men whose name they bear, to unknown or conjectural persons of later date. Otherwise the development cannot be put plausibly into shape. With reference to this, it has been argued by the defenders of historical Christianity, that to palm off a writing of one's own, as that of another man, is an act which implies a low moral tone; and that it is inconceivable that writings such as those in question, remarkable for their moral elevation and their moral heat, should have been produced by minds in that condition. The reply made to this obvious and very weighty argument is contained in the assertion, that the giving forth of a book under the name of some one, the general drift of whose views it was thought to represent advantageously, was not, in the second century, felt to be an injurious or objectionable deception; it did not therefore imply the moral obtuseness which we are apt to associate with such an act; and so the moral elevation of these writings does not preclude their composition by some one who assumed an apostle's name. This reply comes far short of what the case requires. All that it really goes to show, is that the conscious perversity of the process supposed might be somewhat less than appears at first sight; not that the process is compatible with such a moral and spiritual tone as we find in the Scriptures. But even if it were conceded that the whole difficulty, so far as it is merely moral, were removed, other difficulties remain.

A writer who assumes a name and character not his own, in the circumstances and for the ends supposed, is first of all a person anxious to bring authority to bear in behalf of some development, or mode, or variety of Christianity, and some way of explaining and defending it which he prefers; he wishes to place this safe under the shelter of a great name. In the next place, he is necessarily imitative, according to his lights,—more or less trying to compose what the great man might have written, more or less trying to keep out anything that would decisively indicate the true writer. On both accounts,—on account of the man's general attitude and design, and on account of the plan he takes to make it effectual,—mediocrity necessarily attaches to the performance. It turns out superficial, because the strenuous application of one's own whole strength to the mental problem is not the leading and guiding thought. It turns out artificial, because the performance is wrought out under constraint, and in an attitudinizing manner. Now look at the disputed Pauline Epistles. This rapid, sudden reasoning, this speaking from the vision of a whole of truth which underlies the particular utterances, this fire of moral energy which keeps conscience and intellect balanced and connected,—these are not the tokens of an anonymous partisan, who under cover of a borrowed name is trying to break down a dreaded or a detested theory. The attempt is indicated by anxious detail, careful arguing out of the external and superficial elements of the case; and, in short, flatness and littleness are stamped on the performance.

Compare, for instance, the Epistle to the Colossians with such pseudonymous works as the Epistle of Barnabas and the Clementines.

Note C.—Page 83.

These lectures keep in view doctrine. But it is worth while to note how the morality also, as to its great characteristic movements and tendencies, is *first* in the history, and *then* becomes a didactic lesson. As, for example, the peculiar spirit of Christian morality is love in meekness, forgetfulness of self, and fidelity to truth and right. But this is first *embodied* in the great fact of the Incarnation—the συγκατάβασις, or condescension, as it was well called of old; it is continually exemplified afresh in all steps of our Lord's history; and lastly, it becomes a Christian lesson and a Christian attainment. There is much material of Christian evidence in such considerations. For if the Christian narrative had been planned by men to make a

LECT. III.] NOTE F. 355

foundation for their moral doctrine in this respect, the artificial character of it would have been too plain. The motive would have shown through the whole story, and would have appeared with awkward earnestness at every step of it.

NOTE D.—PAGE 85.

On the growth of knowledge and discernment in the mind of the apostles, and generally on the development of doctrine *within* the New Testament, see Bernard's Bampton Lecture, *On the Progress of Doctrine*,[1]—a book full of striking and suggestive matter, and eminently deserving to be read by Biblical students.

NOTE E.—PAGE 90.

Hence Duns Scotus argues for his own conception of Theology :— Non est inventa ad fugam ignorantiae, quia multo plura scibilia possent poni vel tradi in tanta quantitate doctrinae quam his tradita sint. Sed haec eadem replicantur frequenter, ut efficacius inducatur auditor ad operationem eorum quae ibi persuadentur.—In *Sent. Prol.* qu. iv. 42.

NOTE F.—PAGE 93.

It is an inquiry very interesting in its own place, and not without a practical bearing on expository purposes, how far the sacred writers are to be conceived as handling, while they write, resources of which they had conscious possession, and applying these to purposes of instruction and impression which they clearly discerned,—wielding means as adapted to ends, and proceeding on a perception of the adaptation of the one to the other ; and how far, in addition to this, they might be conceived as led out into statements which rose in their minds, wider than their previous thought, and having bear-

[1] Macmillan & Co., 1864.

ings and applications beyond the horizon of their designs. Both conceptions are consistent with the belief in the supreme and certain guidance of the inspiring Spirit. The former of the two must at any rate have place; the only question is, whether it accounts for everything, and whether the latter is to be wholly excluded and disregarded. What is said in the text is, that questions of this kind, however interesting, do not concern my present purpose. For if it be once admitted or established that the Divine Spirit is securing and regulating the communication, then His wisdom is the source from which the supply required is provided, whatever the economy may be which arranges the channels and measures the flow of the stream.

There may, on various accounts, be difficulty in applying a theory of Inspiration to all the passages of the New Testament, or to all the phenomena which it presents. Such difficulties are to be expected. They might in all reason be reckoned on beforehand. But the efforts made to show that the New Testament is not inspired,—*i.e.*, which is the same thing, that the writings it contains are due merely to the influences which operate in the minds of religious men at any great crisis of religious history,—all such efforts may be set down as labour thrown away. On the mind of each generation of Christians these writings impress their claims with an evidence which outlives all objections.

NOTE G.—PAGE 98.

The characteristic of Scripture teaching, and of the materials which it applies, here referred to, goes a long way towards explaining the strong feeling always cherished in the Church of an explicit consent and unity in the teaching, notwithstanding the fact that in some respects very considerable changes unquestionably took place. See, for fuller remarks, Note K to Lecture V.

Note H.—Page 99.

Looking to the unsystematic character of the Scriptures, and noting how little its method seems fitted to the exigencies of school discipline or doctrinal drill, it has been maintained that in the earliest age, in the days of the apostles themselves, there must have been in use catechetical formularies, designed to lay the foundations of Christian knowledge. We are to conceive of these as quite different in structure from any of the Biblical writings; rather as analogous to our summaries, catechisms, or brief systems. It has been argued that such statements of doctrine were indispensable for the purpose of describing the faith compendiously to inquirers, and for the purpose of instructing the young. And we must suppose them to have represented the essential and fundamental Christian instruction, to which the New Testament writings were related, as on the one hand a repertory of more minute and lively historical detail, on the other hand of more free and various discussions, doctrinal or ethical, such as were suggested by the occasional exigencies of the nascent Church.

On the assumed existence of these compendiums, compact but complete, of which the New Testament gives us no hint (or at most only allusions which are obscurely capable of being interpreted in this reference), but which must be supposed to have accompanied or even preceded it, different conclusions have been based. It has been argued, for instance, that this early, this more definite and connected teaching, presupposed and proceeded on in the somewhat fortuitous collection of writings which we call the New Testament, must be conceived to be the starting-point of Ecclesiastical Tradition. Some such tradition ought therefore to be regarded as having legitimate independent authority. The very fact that these catechetical formulas, forming so important an element of early teaching, were providentially left to the Church to constitute and to authenticate, serves, it is said, as a proof that the Church was intended to be reverenced as an authoritative teacher. The vague and manifold traditions of Rome may comprehend much spurious accretion. But a tradition in the Church, not dependent on the Scriptures, although in harmony with them, should be sought for and reverenced.¹

On the other hand, starting from the same assumption, it has been ingeniously argued that no one formulary of the nature of Catechism or Creed was intended to be permanently imposed, or to attain unconditional authority. Had this been intended, some of these early forms of sound words would have received apostolic sanction, and would have been received into the canon. But no one Catechism and no one Creed would suffice for all ages. The Church was intended to produce such documents, using as best she could the lights which she possessed, in the measure and in the form which each age required.²

But, in truth, there is no reason to suppose that any such summaries existed, exhibiting a form of teaching contradistinguished from the method of the Scriptures, in the way which these writers would have us believe. It is, indeed, quite true that the office of the Church has from the first been required, and been discharged. There never was a period in which God has not made use of tradition (*i.e.* of Christian intelligence and feeling, existing in believing minds, and coming out in all the natural forms of manifestation) for the purpose of influencing neophytes, and helping them to discern both the general scope of Christianity, and the elements in it which claim primary regard by reason of their primary importance. In particular, Christian teaching must have been summarized, of course, as often as, for any reason, it was briefly exhibited; and so, whether there were any written summaries intended for that especial purpose or not, many a spoken summary must have been uttered. But these summaries may well have been perfectly conformable to the manner of presentation which the Scriptures on the

---

[1] Hawkins' Bampton Lecture, Lond. 1841. Dr. Hawkins made application of his postulate cautiously and temperately. In particular, he denied this tradition to be authoritative in any strict or complete sense. The whole book, indeed, is written in a considerate and circumspect manner. Readers of Newman's *Apologia* will remember how Dr. Hawkins taught him the office of the Church one day during 'a walk round Christ Church meadows.' Transplanted to such fertile soil, the seed grew rapidly.

[2] Whately, *Peculiarities of the Christian Religion*, Essay VI.

whole exhibit. The apostles taught, no doubt, as they wrote, and those who followed them kept their steps as nearly as they could. In particular, we have good reason to think that any early summarizings would be threaded on a historical rather than on a doctrinal string. They would briefly recapitulate the history of redemption, past and future, with brief indications of the bearing and results of its several steps, and with a statement of the obligations of repentance, faith, and Christian obedience. And if they went into detail at all, it was probably in the way of dilating either, on the one hand, on the history of Christ, or, on the other hand, on the practical duties of redeemed men. Then as time went on, and heresies arose, this point and that would receive a sharpening and an emphasizing, to guard the catechumen against the erroneous teaching. A certain amplification of statement, and a certain increase of precision and of definition, might thus take place. But it would take place then, as it takes place still, by drawing on the materials of the apostolic teaching, such as we have them, and applying them to the exigency as we apply them. There is no reason to suppose, far less to assume as certain, that any form of teaching existed in the apostolic Church which was of divine authority, which constituted a divinely instituted discipline for some classes of minds, and which is yet unrepresented in the New Testament writings. What is thus maintained may be objected to as conjectural; but it is sufficient to meet the conjectural assumption on the other side. And it is the more probable conjecture. It agrees with all that we can gather from the New Testament, and from subsequent writings.

It agrees with the impression made on our minds by such passages as 1 Cor. xv. 1–11, and Heb. vi. 1, 2, in reference to the way in which it was, at that date, natural and suitable to state summarily the evangelical teaching.

It agrees with the character and structure of the so-called Apostles' Creed, which may be taken as a specimen, not greatly altered, of the early forms of baptismal confession. Answerably to the words of institution (Matt. xxviii. 19), it is a confession of the name of the Father, Son, and Holy Ghost.

But this confession is made very suitably to fall into the track of the history of redemption. The life, death, resurrection, and ascension of our Lord lead on to a confession of the Holy Ghost (which manifestly has respect to the manifestation at Pentecost), the calling and upbuilding of the Church, and the preaching of the forgiveness of sins.

It agrees also with what is suggested by the post-apostolic literature. This is a wide field to enter on in a note, but what seems to be of moment may be stated as follows:—

1. The earliest writings in which one might expect to see traces of the influence of the supposed form of Christian teaching, if it then existed, show no trace of it; such are the writings of Clement and Polycarp, and, I may add, the treatise ascribed to Barnabas. Still more to the point, perhaps, is the Epistle to Diognetus, inasmuch as it contains an animated account of Christianity, intended for an intelligent person who was not a Christian. There is nothing in these writings but what might naturally be suggested by the New Testament writings, or by a current κήρυγμα, which kept as near as it could to the same type. I will refer to Ignatius separately.

2. After the Gnostic heresies were full-blown, and when the Monarchian heresies were appearing, it becomes customary to refer to the *regula fidei*, the *ecclesiasticæ prædicatio*. We have, as is well known, statements of what it was, from Irenæus, Tertullian, and Origen,[1] not to speak of Novatian, and references by Clemens Alexandrinus and others. From their accounts, nothing is more evident than this, that it was not, in any of the churches, a written or settled formula. They give, in different ways, their conception of what might fairly be regarded as accepted and prevailing teaching in the churches. Each gives to it a development suited to the occasion for which he adduces it, sharpening the statements on the points in reference to which heresy was to be encountered. It is far from unlikely that in the churches generally such more precise and definite statements had been brought out and rendered current in the teaching by the progress of

---

[1] Iren. *Adv. Hæret.* i. 10. 1 and 2; c. iii. 4. 1 and 2. Tert. *De Velandis Virginibus*, c. i.; *De Præser. Hær.* 13 and 14. Orig. *De Princ.* I., *Præf.*

heresy. But there is nothing whatever to suggest that they are drawn from primitive catechetical sources, rather than from Christian meditation guided by apostolic teaching *such as the New Testament presents*, and quickened by collision with antichristian error.

If there was any very early catechetical summary which assumed a tolerably set form, besides the confession of Father, Son, and Holy Ghost, one might be tempted to find traces of it in a context which refers not to dogma, but to Christian morals. I refer to the description of the two ὁδοί, Barn. Ep. xviii. xx. It has been observed that the style alters, and becomes simpler and clearer in the latter part of the Epistle. This cannot, for known reasons, be accounted for on the ground of that portion being spurious; but it may be accounted for, if the author at that point begins to work over ground that had been cleared before. The same context in substance reappears, a good deal amplified, in the *Apostolic Constitutions*, vii. 1 sq.[1] Probably the author of the Epistle, if he found anything of this kind pre-existing, wrought upon it as freely as the author of the seventh book of the *Constitutions* did afterwards. However this may be, the performance is a cento of maxims from the apostolic teaching and the earlier Scriptures, with amplifications by the collector. It proves nothing as to *independent* summaries.

With respect to Ignatius, the difficulty as to the authenticity of his writings, and the text to be preferred, has first to be encountered. I confess to feeling a great deal of difficulty as to all the three texts, and am far from feeling positive as to the account to be given of the origin and history of any of them. The shorter Greek still retains the majority of suffrages, and may therefore be referred to. The point in hand at present is its doctrinal teaching. There is an interesting article on this subject by Dr. Newman, originally written in 1838, reprinted in the first volume of *Essays Critical and Historical*.[2] He there picks out and argues from the precise dogmatic statements which the Epistles

---

[1] And in the Coptic Canons, Book I.
[2] London, Pickering, 1871.

contain, and compares them with those which occur in writings of the fourth century. I confess that the effect on my mind is only to increase the feeling of the absolute singularity of these epistles, if they are to be accepted as a literary phenomenon of the opening graces of the second century. It is a very suspicious singularity.

Waiving the critical difficulty, and assuming the shorter Greek text as authoritative, we find in it a good deal of interesting and precise dogmatic statement especially regarding the person of our Lord. But it does not naturally suggest the idea of having originated in any catechetic summary. It suggests rather the disquisitions of lively and devout minds in Christian discourse and preaching, and in controversy, leading to various forms of emphatic and illustrative exhibition of the great fact of the Incarnation.

LECTURE IV.

NOTE A.—PAGE 108.

IT may be as well to make a distinction, sufficient for practical purposes, between Truth of Doctrine and Truth of Fact. Sometimes those who desire to diminish the *quantum* of doctrine to be recognised in the Scriptures, lay it down that the Scriptures give us facts, while we spin doctrines for ourselves; and to make this out, they give the name of 'Facts' to whatever the Scripture affirms as truth concerning God, man, and so forth. But this is to make unjustifiable confusion. Although doctrine and fact run into one another,—the incarnation, *e.g.*, being both fact and doctrine,—it remains true that a great deal in the Scripture has the nature and attributes of doctrine, and for human minds must rank in that category. Probably the distinction may be most conveniently taken, by ranking as mere facts all those things entering into revealed religion which might have become known to us through ordinary historical channels. In reality, many of them are known to us through Scripture only, and the accounts come to us authoritatively. But in so far as they might conceivably have been known in human experience and recorded by human testimony, they may rank as mere facts. That, on the other hand, which could be made known to us only by divine testimony, goes beyond fact, and becomes doctrine. Thus, that a certain child was born at Bethlehem, grew to manhood, performed such and such remarkable works, is fact; that He was the Son of God (which no doubt is a fact) is also doctrine. That He died upon a cross is fact; that that death was for our sins is doctrine. If the distinction is thought not well taken, I should not take the trouble of defending it. It is enough to have indicated that the two distinguishable and distinct provinces meet there or thereabouts.

Note B.—Page 133.

Christian feeling, or what is postulated by Christian experience,—this has constituted a great force in the whole history of Christian doctrine, and has powerfully moulded the form of many a system. It has, an excellent right to operate in this way,—in so far, namely, as it is one of the conditions on which a true intelligence of the Scriptures depends; and it must enter as an element into all real contemplation of Christian verities. Yet no task would be more difficult than to assign the measure of the influence which it ought to exert, or of that which in given instances it has exerted. It is one of the interesting peculiarities of Schleiermacher's *Glaubenslehre*, that he consecrates this element to be the foundation and the principle of his whole system. The Christian consciousness, according to him, spins its dogmatic out of its resources; or rather, it is necessitated to postulate it by its own connatural cravings. Exaggerated as this is, and lamentably defective also both in principle and result, it is in the highest degree suggestive. In systems quite remote from Schleiermacher's, the active force which sustains many a dogma is not so much the texts and arguments appealed to on its behalf, but rather the congruity in which it is apprehended to stand to modes of Christian disposition and devotion, which have, or are thought to have, their witness in themselves. It is a tact or taste, a sense rather than a perception, that is the organ practically applied to discriminate false and true by many who suppose themselves to proceed on strict and definite principle. And probably they judge much more soundly on the former method than they would on the latter.

Note C.—Page 138.

In asserting the sufficiency and perfection (for its designed end) of Scripture, there has sometimes been a tendency on the part of Protestants to give forth representations in which the office of the Church, *i.e.* of the Christian community, in perpetuating and reproducing Christian sentiment and belief, is not taken account of. This opens the door to Romanists, who at once rejoin with an appeal to the undeniable fact that men are very greatly dependent on their fellows for instruction and impression, and who assume that the necessities of the Protestant argument require these facts to be overlooked. Dr. Hawkins, in his Bampton Lecture, has criticised such controversialists as Stillingfleet and Tillotson on this ground. In Note H to Lecture III., *supra*, reference was made to some views of Dr. Hawkins in this connection, from which I dissent. But he (along with many others—Whately may be named) has very well pointed out that the office of the Church is a great providential force, which was of course contemplated in the divine arrangements, and which ought to be taken account of in any theory we form of the process by which His truth reaches and influences our minds. There ought to be no difficulty, on Protestant principles, in recognising the fact, that while the Scriptures are the infallible rule, we depend on one another in many ways for an acquaintance with its contents and meaning; in particular, that the organized Christian community practically administers the Scripture teaching to its members, and has been fitted to do so advantageously on the whole. Thus every child is dependent on parents and teachers for a report of what the Scripture teaches; and many a grown-up person is in a condition of pupilage with reference to one department or other of his Christian training. He sees largely through other people's eyes. Nevertheless the office of the Church is to manifest what is in the inspired Rule; and so doing, and when she does so, and when those taught refer what they learn ultimately to that standard, then truth, and evidence of the divine original of the truth, will shine into individual minds in the measure needed by each.

NOTE D.—PAGE 152.

On the subject of Analogy as related to the truths and the language of Religion, besides the works of Butler and Bishop

Browne and Archbishop King, see Tatham's *Chart and Scale of Truth*, Davison's *Discourses on Prophecy* (Notes), Grinfield's *Vindiciæ Analogicæ*, Copleston's *Inquiry concerning Predestination*, Whately's Bampton Lecture, and more recently Dr. James Buchanan's *Analogy a Guide to Truth and an Aid to Faith*. In the last-named work, p. 7 sq., will be found a brief sketch of the controversy on the subject of the application of analogical language to God and to God's perfections.

NOTE E.—PAGE 165.

The Monothelete could say, with great plausibility, to the Catholic, 'If, while holding the continued existence of two natures in Christ, you really hold the unity of the person, you must admit the two natures to be so united as to imply only one single will and operation. If there is but one person, then in each act of our Lord's there is but one agent. The person is the agent. But if there is but one agent, you must hold one will, and one entire, undivided, conscious, and voluntary energy of the whole attributes of the person; one operation, as by a single impulse of all the complex capacities and powers which pertain to Him, whether as divine or as human. Otherwise you have two agencies, therefore two agents, therefore two persons. Personality, if it be really one, implies unity of the whole movement, whatever natures, one or more, are drawn into the sphere of it, and lend their capacities or attributes to the result.'

On the principles common to both parties, this was tantamount to an assertion that there is to be recognised in Christ the divine will only, and no other. If His human nature in any way has a faculty or capacity of human willing, it is superseded or drawn into the current of the divine will, so as to have no proper exercise or egress.

NOTE F.—PAGE 167.

The theory of Phlogiston was once a probable theory in chemistry, and conclusions were built on it. But the true view turned out to be a different one. That theory might not be wholly misleading, in practice, in so far as it gathered together some important experimental facts, and held them together by a provisional tie. But treated as a source of inference, it could only breed errors.

NOTE G.—PAGE 169.

I have thought it better to relegate this topic to a Note, rather than load the conclusion of a Lecture, already too long; for such a subject, if introduced, could scarcely be lightly dismissed. It may appear, indeed, that it should have come prominently forward at a much earlier stage, and that a lecture on Doctrine leaves out the part of Hamlet, if it omits to treat expressly of Scientific Theology, its validity and its office. All that shall be said in defence of the course pursued is simply this. Doctrine is maintained to arise not primarily in obedience to the scientific interest or impulse, but out of the necessities of the believing mind. It appeared to be important to contemplate it steadily under that leading consideration, and to inquire simply into the indispensable or the legitimate workings of the believing mind in this department. But, this line once adopted, it became necessary to decline introducing the considerations connected with the other topic, in order that the treatment might not become too complicated. It is admitted, however, that in a full and leisurely treatment, a separate Lecture on the subject of this Note ought to have place.

Christian Doctrines, if they are articles of knowledge, must be objects of science in some way. And if they have any rational connection with one another, that can be discerned, they may properly be the object of a special department of science. Moreover, as soon as Doctrine began to be handled by inquisitive and intelligent minds, a form began to be imparted to it, and processes began to be carried on with respect to it, which were, in their way, contributions to scientific treatment, or a preparation for it. Still more was this done when active controversy began; for controversy on such topics must necessarily lead to sifting of evidence, to exactness of statement, to indication of connections. The efforts put forth were *pro tanto*, in point of fact, efforts to comply with the requirements of science. This is not to assert that they were scientifically successful. They might be, or they might not. Neither is it asserted that these efforts were made with a conscious or deliberate intention to satisfy the scientific interest. On the contrary, that was very often hardly at all in view, or at all events was not kept in view with any seriousness or persistency. Other ends, connected with more profound and pressing wants, were aimed at; viz., to settle what God had given to be believed on leading points, and to guide aright the souls of men. The objects of the early Alexandrian school, indeed, dictated a professed and express regard to scientific principle in conducting their labours. To treat doctrine so as to make it comply, or to show that it complies, with philosophy, so far as philosophy is valid, was their design. Their notions of what scientific treatment ought to be in a subject-matter of this kind were for the most part extremely loose and vague; but, at any rate, they suggested the problem. Speaking generally, however, it is rather remarkable how little tendency appears among the Fathers to be drawn or swayed, in the form of their work, by any exigencies of scientific method. Such exemplifications of scientific method, and specimens of its results, as they furnish, arise merely because vigorous minds, working at high tension in matters which deeply interest them, do comply with those demands for investigation, definition, arrangement, and so forth, which science is supposed to present in a complete and rigorous manner. But the Fathers were thinking mainly of what appeared to them to be the great Christian interests; and any aptitudes for scientific treatment which they possessed, they merely bring in for occasional service, to clear the road to some practical object, or to build an argument in behalf of some point of the faith that is impeached. It may probably be said, that Augustine showed more than most of them of the peculiar style of query and of suggestion which tends to careful correlation of Reason and Faith, and also to awaken a craving for system and internal order in connecting and unfolding theological thought. But it was the internal necessity of the great controversies, rather than any special design on the part of individuals, that introduced into some departments of Theology a considerable degree of minute and careful adjustment. The form of teaching so settled either was scientific, or at least manifestly challenged a verdict with reference to its scientific form, as well as with reference to its agreement with the rule of faith. So we may describe the result reached in the case of the doctrines of the Trinity, and of the Person of Christ, and partly also in the case of the doctrines involved in the Pelagian controversy.

It was the schoolmen who took up in earnest the whole question as to the relations of Reason and Faith, and strove to present theology as a rounded whole of ordered thought. John Damascenus need not to be regarded as an exception to this statement. Anselm was the great forerunner of the scholastic enterprise. And his name may serve to remind us, that whatever failures of spirit or of performance befell the schoolmen, their work in its origin was inspired by a magnanimous and grand thought. The great awakening of the European mind, under the leadership of the Church, suggested to the thinker the idea of a glorious whole, or kingdom of Truth, pervious to the Reason that is prepared by Faith; just as to the practical man it suggested the idea of a kingdom of God in the world, orderly and beneficent, in constituting and perfecting which the Vicar of Christ should be the chief agent. The scholastic enterprise was an attempt to set up that kingdom. It failed, indeed; and the grandeur of the conception turned out to be like the grandeur of a child's thoughts, which take no adequate account of means and possibilities. But ever since then, the idea of Theology as a science has been far more powerfully and constantly present to the contemplations of divines.

It would serve no purpose here to recount the origin and progress of the various subsequent schools; the Romish, as reconstructed on the lines of Trent; the Lutheran and the Reformed Orthodoxies; the Socinian system; and afterwards the Arminian. It may be as well to remark, however, that none of these, as schools, can be said to have taken up the enterprise of achieving a complete speculative system, and none are chargeable with *all* the audacity and extravagance with which that enterprise usually is attended. Individual theologians might make speculative ventures; and each school was charged by the others with a perverse bias in framing its system, and moulding its materials with a view to lend strength to some favourite doctrines. But all, it may be said, that any of these schools proposed to do, was to determine and arrange a body of materials which they accepted as given. The Romanists professed to find their materials in Scripture and Tradition; the other schools in Scripture, admitting Reason, or what went by that name, in different degrees, to act upon the process, either simply as interpretative, or partly also as dominating and limiting. The system-makers of these schools did press into questions on which no satisfactory guidance was furnished by the sources on which they relied. But they commonly did so under the influence, not of a speculative, but rather of a controversial temptation. The differences on leading points were carried over inferentially into metaphysical regions. Doctrines that were defended had to be accommodated to received views of God and of the world; and consistency seemed to require the accommodation to be made in one way for one system, in another way for another. Positions were taken up, therefore, which merely indicated how a man who held the main doctrines of a given system would be apt to extend and connect his thinking. They merely constituted illustrations of the drift and genius of each theology. But controversial exigencies made it desirable to treat them as substantial doctrines, and to contrive some show of separate and independent authority for them, that they might buttress more securely the system to which they were attached.

Subsequently, the chief influence which has affected systematic theology has been the doubt, or more than doubt, with respect to the divine authority of the Scriptures, which has wrought in so many forms during the last hundred and forty years. The first effect was to dispose men to fall back on the elements of the Christian system which seemed most capable of being verified to each individual mind,—in short, to be very cautious as to carrying Christian assertions much beyond the border line of Natural Theology. Then came systems in which Christian Doctrine is treated simply as so much speculative material, which must stand, like other speculation, on its merits, *i.e.* on its probability, as an account of our relations to God. Other systems proposed to regain a Christian position, without relying on authentic divine information. Such was Schleiermacher's; but as he threw Dogmatic into Historical Theology, as a branch of it, he deprived it of independent value. Others still, while asserting a positive value and authority for the teaching contained in the New Testament, make it fall into the compartments of a system radically speculative. It is a philosophy of divine things, in which they find room for their interpretation of New Testament teaching.

From the point of view of these Lectures, no systematizing can be recognised as valid which does not proceed on the assumption of the complete authority of Scripture teaching. That supposed, systematic theology must be recognised as one form of the tribute which human minds owe to truth. No one can deny me the right to analyze the contents of the religious ideas which I am authorized to entertain, to trace their limits, to mark the connections in which they stand to one another. To extend this process over the whole field of revealed truth, is as legitimate as to apply it to any part. The process certainly will take place, in virtue of the constitution of human minds, in a partial way, or in a half-conscious way, *i.e.* without adverting fully to the responsibilities involved in it. It is better that it should be gone about with a deliberate and definite aim, and in full view of the conditions under which the work must proceed. At the same time, while the partial and half-conscious systematizings have their own dangers and temptations, there are others which undoubtedly are attendant on the deliberate aim and effort of the systematic theologian.

His office is to do justice to revealed truths as regards their capabilities for being defined, connected, and presented in an order in which the mutual connection and common reason of the whole shall be as much as possible apparent. And his temptation is to overdo his work.

First, as regards individual truths (which he is to link on to others before and behind), he is apt to assume a precision of knowledge, and to employ a precision of definition, which are not duly warranted. The language of Scripture itself furnishes us on many subjects with information which is, and was designed to be, approximate rather than precise. The language of the Church, expressing her conclusions from Scripture, her well-warranted conclusions, ought notwithstanding to be regarded, in many cases, rather as indicating the line that must be taken in order to escape erroneous tendencies of thought, than as delivering a meaning which the words are adequate to fix and measure. The history of the words employed in the first great controversy, such as οὐσία and ὑπόστασις, illustrates this. In both cases the systematic theologian may be tempted to press upon the words of Scripture, or of received belief, in order to fix on the truths he handles a greater precision of form, with a view to more dexterous and plausible articulation of his system.

Secondly, in exhibiting the connection of truth with truth, there is, of course, a temptation to apply pressure to truths, or to take one-sided views of them, in order to bring out connections which serve the purposes of the system, or to escape difficulties on which the system might be shipwrecked. And in virtue of a like influence, it comes to pass that, when the spirit of system prevails strongly, truths are unconsciously transformed to some extent as to their meaning, and their bearing on men, by being always presented in their systematic and not in their Biblical connections. The significance they have for the system, as contributing to its harmony and unity, is the only significance which they are allowed to reveal. But even in a well-ordered system, if it be a human one,—and all our systems are human,—the significance which the truth has for the system is less than its full and genuine significance.

For example, Dr. Cunningham (*Hist. Theol.* i. 344, 352) remarks that there is a great systematic connection between the topics of original sin, saving grace, and election to life ; which connection, from the Augustinian point of view, is brought out by the assertion of man's entire depravity,— which may be looked on as the link between the doctrine of original sin and that of the necessity of grace,—and by the assertion of the certain efficacy of saving grace, as the link between the doctrine of grace and that of personal election. Those who hold with Calvin, recognise the connection thus asserted ; and those who do not, will at least acknowledge the systematic strength and coherence of the line of positions exhibited. But even those who belong to the former party need not hesitate to acknowledge that the controversial assertion of this system, during and after the Arminian controversy, formed a habit of undue and exclusive regard to the systematic value of each member in this chain of positions, and tended to intercept the full impression of the Biblical connection and setting in which assertions bearing on these subjects come before us in the Scriptures.

Thirdly, it may be said that the ideal goal of the systematist, as such, is completeness ; his enthusiasm would aspire naturally to the perfect order of a perfect knowledge. All the more difficult it is to keep in view what ought to be the practical goal, viz. to trace (so far as evidence enables us) the incompletely discerned order of an imperfect knowledge ; setting forth not less, yet also not more, than God has been pleased to give us. Here incompleteness, *i.e.* the befitting incompleteness which the nature of our knowledge implies, ought to be deliberately aimed at. But the power of halting at the right point is one of the rarest powers even of clear-sighted and truthful minds.

LECTURE V.

NOTE A.—PAGE 175.

See Note D to Lecture III., *supra*.

NOTE B.—PAGE 179.

See, on this subject, the Magdeburg Centuriators, *Praefatio in Historiam Ecclesiasticam*, etc.[1] The assumption is, that the Church started with the Lutheran teaching; then in each succeeding period we have these elements: first, the *doctrina ecclesiae*, or *doctrina sacra*; second, an *inclinatio doctrinae*, or a manifestation of *peculiares et incommodae opiniones, stipulae et errores doctorum*. These, however, are not *haereses;* they are not, indeed, merely *imbecillitates communes*, but worse than that — *turpissimi opinionum et corruptelarum naevi*. Still they affect the views of men who must not be called heretics. Thirdly, we have the *haereses*, proceeding from various quarters.

The whole Protestant churches with one consent recognised in even the most ancient teachers traces of infirmity. Their teaching was not only subject to be tested by that of the Scriptures, but was plainly enough marked one way or other by tokens of human proclivity to error. But these infirmities were conceived either as simply sporadic and occasional,—one man falling into this mistake, and another into that,—or else, more frequently, as the starting-point of the great development of error, which was *the* development that especially exercised the Protestant mind.

NOTE C.—PAGE 180.

Unless room is made in the mind for the idea that the

[1] *Ecclesiastica Historia, etc.* Basil. 1560-74, vol. i.

Church under new circumstances, and under the influence of a progressive discipline, may attain to further insight into the Scriptures, there is great plausibility in maintaining that all Christian doctrine may be gathered from the writings of the first five centuries. If God cared for His Church, and fulfilled the promises to her, it is plausible to say that all that is essential in Christian doctrine, all that is entitled ever to be treated as important, must have been present in the Church, and may be gathered from the writings, of the first five centuries. But the plausibility disappears if we make room in our minds for these positions: first, that fresh views of the Scripture teaching on important points may be attained by the Church under the influence of a progressive discipline; and secondly, that with reference to new questions and new alternatives, pressed on the Church's mind with a stringency not felt in her earlier experience, these views may acquire an importance, *i.e.* the explicit recognition of them may acquire an importance, which the later age of the Church legitimately feels, but which the earlier age could not anticipate.

To this extent it is reasonable, in my opinion, to acknowledge the force of the argument urged by Newman in the *Apologia* and elsewhere, from the successive creeds of the early Church. Adherents of those creeds, who draw the line there, have to answer the question why just those creeds should be thought to comprehend all that the Church ever may confess. Why may not the Church in later times legitimately confess more, for reasons analogous to those on account of which the early Church confessed so much?

NOTE D.—PAGE 181.

'All varieties of real development,[1] so far as this argument is concerned, may probably be reduced to two general heads—*intellectual* developments, and practical developments of Christian doctrine.' The former alone concern us. 'By "intellectual developments" I understand logical inferences

[1] Archer Butler, *Letters on Development.* Dublin, 1850, p. 56.

(and that whether for belief or for practical discipline) from doctrines, or from the comparison of doctrines, which, in virtue of the great dialectical maxim, must be true, if legitimately deduced from what is true. . . . Intellectual developments, it is thus obvious, are in the same sphere with the principles out of which they spring; they are (even when regarded with a view to rite and practice) unmixed doctrine still—they are *propositions*. . . . Let me exemplify. . . . Revealed doctrines may be compared with one another, or with the doctrines of natural religion; or the consequences of revealed doctrines may be compared with other doctrines, or with their consequences, and so on in great variety: the combined ultimate result being what is called a System of Theology. What the first principles of Christian truth really are, or how obtained, is not now the question. But in all cases equally, no doctrine has any claim whatever to be received as obligatory on belief, unless it be either itself some duly authorized principle, or a logical deduction, through whatever number of stages, from some such principle of religion. Such only are legitimate developments of doctrine for the *belief* of man; and such alone can the Church of Christ—the Witness and Conservator of His truth—justly commend to the consciences of her members.

'To take one or two examples that present themselves at the first moment: it is thus that when we have learned, as the infallible authority of inspiration, that the Lord Jesus Christ is Himself very God, and when we have learned from the same authority the tremendous fact of His atoning sacrifice, we could collect (even were Scripture silent) the priceless *value* of the atonement thus made, the wondrous *humiliation* therein involved, the unspeakable *love* it exhibited, the mysteriously awful *guilt* of sin, which would again reflect a gloomy light upon the equally mysterious eternity of *punishment*, and similar deductions of immense practical importance. These would be just and legitimate developments of Christian doctrine. But in truth, as our own liability to error is extreme, especially when immersed in the holy obscurity ("the *cloud* on the mercy-seat") of such mysteries as these, we have reason to thank God that there appear to be few doctrinal developments of any importance which are not from the first drawn out and delivered as divine authority to our acceptance.

'Or, again, to take another instance. . . . When three Beings are, on divine authority, represented as acting with mysterious but real distinctness of operation, yet each possessing the attributes of Supreme Godhead,—that Godhead which is and can be but one,—we can scarcely be said to "develope;" we do little more than express these combined truths, when we acknowledge, and bend in adoration before, the ever blessed Trinity. And we can easily perceive that wherever or whenever there may have been, or is, any difficulty in arriving at this truth, it is *not*, as if in the nature of things this truth could be had only by long processes of conjecture and slow successive contemplation—it is not as if, after it had been revealed in Holy Writ, men *must* err and stumble on the road to receive it, and pass through a discipline of centuries before they can arrive at admitting that Father, Son, and Holy Spirit are one God; but simply from the fact (granting for a moment any such supposed or imputed charge of error) that the numerous and melancholy causes that impede the perception of valuable truth in so many other departments of human knowledge, may be conceived more or less to have operated in this, incomparably the most precious of all.'

As another illustration is adduced, the inference from the fact of our Lord's birth from the Virgin, that she is, and ought to be called, blessed.

'I have thus instanced[1] what may exemplify legitimate "intellectual developments." Such justly carry authority, for such bring with them their own credentials. To make such comparisons and conclusions with accuracy, is doubtless a fruit of divine favour, blessing the just researches of faith (Prov. ii. 4, etc.). To perceive some of them more prominently than others may be the characteristic of different ages or crises in the history of theology, and unquestionably has ever been the object of a very special providence in the divine government of the Church; to receive such conclusions with practical effect on heart, spirit, and life, is, above all, the

[1] Page 59.

peculiar and supernatural gift of God. But as truths of theology, evolved from its revealed principles, such developments are in all cases, since the close of the canon of Scripture, commended to us through the ministry of enlightened and sanctified *reason*.'

It is plain that the developments which Mr. Butler admits are direct logical inferences from known doctrines, and mostly such as are specifically revealed, as are the doctrines from which by inference they may be derived. But no distinction is taken between the Revelation given on the one hand, and the Revelation received, or the degree of perception of the meaning of the revealing word, on the other. Moreover, although it is noted that the Church of different ages may vary in the degree of attention to and perception of some of the possible inferences derivable from doctrine, the idea of an organic growth in perception of revealed truth, and of conditions which promote such growth, is not taken up.

Still, as a learned and thoughtful theologian, Mr. Butler could not avoid the impression that, in point of fact, there had been a good deal of valid development for which his principles hardly accounted ; and hence sometimes he limits his statement to this, that 'no new doctrine, *in itself necessary to salvation*, is anywise to be anticipated' to come of development,—a statement to which Dr. Newman himself could comfortably accede. However, even in the passage where he is led, half unconsciously apparently, to limit his thesis so seriously, he still presents the same conception of what, to his mind, is the whole account of development : 'That the reason of man rightly exerted, under God's blessing, is capable of exhibiting these truths'—those delivered in the New Testament—' under various forms, by comparison and deduction ; all which new forms, standing the usual tests of sound reasoning, become, of course, to those to whom they are made known, as authoritative as the principles from which they are drawn.

'That in this way, though no new doctrine, in itself necessary to salvation, is anywise to be anticipated, yet the general Church of Christ, or particular branches thereof, may in fact possess a fuller light upon different points in different ages ;

even as any *individual* believer by divine grace increases his spiritual knowledge in different points at different times, through social conference or private meditation.'— *Letters*, etc., p. 316.

The last remark, if followed out, might have suggested a more complete treatment of the topic. But there is another passage, p. 240,[1] in which he lays it down that 'theological knowledge is capable of a real movement in time, a true successive history;' and this takes place 'in two principal ways: the first is the process of logical development . . . of primitive truth into its consequences, connections, and applications. . . . The second is—positive discovery.' The latter includes unexpected confirmation and illustration of revealed truths from new sources, new proofs in support of the evidences, and the like. But it is the former only he conceives himself concerned with,—'that operation beginning with the earliest times, . . . by which, under God's high providence, divine truth is arranged, unfolded, and applied by the natural faculties of human intelligence' (p. 243). And thus he reverts, on the whole, to his controversial position, that the later Christian teaching, so far as it is valid, varies from the earlier only as syllogistic manipulation has varied it.

Note E.—Page 200.

A tendency has been evinced by all theological parties to run their teaching up to a tradition, asserted to be primitive. So the Church did, so did various heretics, so did the Alexandrians. In the case of some of these pretenders the plea was groundless enough; but it might not be a deliberate fiction, even in cases where the grounds of the assertion are most slender. There is always *something* precedent which more or less paves the way for each new manifestation, connects it with the past, accounts more or less for its appearance. The impression that this is so is easily transmuted, by the zeal of party adherents, into the imagination of a tradition.

---

[1] See also Wordsworth's *Letters to Gondon*, p. 260, note (3d ed. Lond. 1848).

The Church writers were always disposed to assert a clear tradition against each successive heresy. 'It has been taught so always in the Church.' This was not in all cases strictly accurate; for ancient teaching that applied clearly and precisely to the new question as raised, was by no means always producible, nor had it existed. But those writers were not wholly wrong in their assertion. There had been (in accordance with the suggestion of the text) a common *position* of the Church's mind, which prepared and predisposed it to take a definite line when the question was raised. And the consciousness of this, perfectly well grounded, represented itself, after the discussion had begun, as a pre-existent and articulate tradition. Any one who has had experience of active Church life must have observed analogous instances.

Note F.—Page 205.

It is hardly necessary, probably, to say that nothing is further from the writer's mind than to assume that every age of the Church excels that which went before it in full and exact doctrinal knowledge; the Church may retrograde, and often has done so. What the Church might and ought to attain, is quite a different question from what she does attain.

As regards the early Church, and the manner in which it should be thought of, there have been extremes of praise, and of unfriendly criticism, both alike ungrounded, as Mosheim long ago pointed out (*Inst. Cent. I.* iii. 9). I do not here refer to the specialty of doctrine, but to the vigour of religious life generally. On this subject the following remark may be made. Setting out of sight special divine influences, and looking solely to the ordinary operations of human nature, such an institution as the Christian Church, having a message to the world, might be expected to unfold the contents of it more considerately, and deliberately, by degrees, as time advanced; but, at the same time, it might be expected that the influence of circumstances, and the gradual participation in the common and prevailing elements of the world's thinking, would tend to modify, on the whole, the original peculiarity of the message. Power, peculiarity, energetic originality, would characterize the first thinkers and speakers; in their successors these would be lowered, and a character of compromise and commonplace imparted to the scheme. Now, in point of fact, originality and power concentrate round the cradle of Christianity. Our Lord with His apostles stand apart. Then also we do see the influence of time and of foreign elements exerted with a debasing effect, and exhibited in a thousand forms down to our own day. But, on the other hand, a counteracting influence is supplied by the promise of the Spirit, and by the energy of His gracious operations. Hence it is that succeeding generations do *not* stand hopelessly below the sub-apostolic one. A recuperative force works always, sometimes with extraordinary manifestations of its power; and Christianity is continually rehabilitated, and enters again and again into possession of the originality and enthusiasm of its earliest days.

NOTE G.—PAGE 207.

Some references on this subject will be found in Note F to Lecture VI.

NOTE H.—PAGE 208.

At bottom, ancient thought was moulded on articles or positions which were anti-Christian. These pervaded all the varieties of its manifestation, not always explicitly declared, but virtually present. For instance, the conception of the divine, of that which is to be worshipped, seems to be very different in the popular creed of the polytheists and the purer teaching of the nobler philosophies. Underlying both, however, was the maxim that God is no more and no other than what man discerns in nature: this is His measure, and indeed His life. The various life of nature might be interpreted by the vulgar into polytheism ; its unity might be speculatively represented in the doctrine of one supreme, by the philosophers ; but the method was the same at bottom. So also as to the world, including human nature. In spite of dreams and myths, the fundamental view was, that the existing state is a fair average specimen of what the world has been, and must be. There are endless changes, varied types, which recur and alternate. But these lie on the surface. They do not imply a progress from that which never shall be again to that which never was before. And thus the defect of the average state of things must simply be accepted. A wise man, indeed, may deal more dexterously and successfully with the elements of his state, and so escape out of some of the evils which mar it. That is, on the whole, exceptional. It does not alter the average state of the race, that certain individuals make their fortune.

NOTE I.—PAGE 213.

It will be seen that the illustration given in the text implies dissent on the writer's part from the elaborate argument of Bull (*Def. Fid. Nic.* sec. iii.), with respect to one section of the teaching of many Ante-Nicene Fathers. He has endeavoured to reduce their language, with respect to the pre-existent state of the Son of God, and the relation of it to the Creation and the Incarnation, into harmony with the views ultimately received as sound. Without entering further here into a discussion which is connected only incidentally with my present object, I may refer to Note II. in the Appendix to the last edition of Newman's *Arians* (London, 1871, p. 430), for a brief statement of the grounds on which Bull's reasoning cannot be accepted as satisfactory. See Note E to Lecture I., *supra*.

NOTE J.—PAGE 214.

A well-known example of the influence exerted by

systematic considerations and suggestions, is the development given to the doctrine of the Sacraments by the schoolmen, *e.g.* by Peter Lombard, *Sent.* iv., and especially by Thomas. See Baur, *Vorlesungen über die Christliche Dogmengeschichte*, ii. 460 sq. Among the Lutherans, the doctrines of the ubiquity of our Lord's human nature, and the *communicatio idiomatum*, are corresponding examples. In the Reformed branch of the Protestant Church, considerations connected with systematic consistency operated strongly from the first, through the medium of the clear and powerful mind of Calvin. Among the later movements of the Reformed Theology, an example may be taken from the advance into importance, theologically, of the conception of the covenant of works. Compare, on the one hand, Calvin, *Inst.* ii. cap. 7, 10, 11 ; Musculus, *Loci Comm.* 1567, p. 306 (*De Foed. Dei*); Ursinus, *Explic. Catech.* 1593, vol. i. pp. 52, 194 (*De Miseria; De Foedere Dei*); with such writers as Polanus, *Syntagma* (1624, 2d ed.), p. 1445 ; Cloppenburg, *Opera*, i. p. 489, ii. p. 143 ; and Amesius, *Medulla*, cap. 10, p. 46, and compare his *Chief Heads of Divinity* (publ. 1612), p. 12. The divines of the latter series bring forward this aspect of the divine providence towards man, but with different degrees of prominence.

NOTE K.—PAGE 217.

The statement in the text may be controverted on the ground of the importance notoriously attached to the tradition and consent of the Church in early times. On this subject I shall refer to the third volume of Dr. Goode's *Divine Rule of Faith and Practice*, and content myself with a few remarks on the manner in which the consent of the Church came into consideration.

First, however, it may be observed that there was, of course, a period during which the apostolic teaching was present partly in a traditionary form, and no complete collection of the writings of the New Testament existed, not even an approach to a complete collection of them in any Church. This period was not very long ; but while it lasted, the tradition was a complete historical proof of the main articles of the teaching which it embodied. On points on which it was not conclusive, and after it became more remote and less authoritative in all points, an appeal could always be made to the apostles while they lived, or to their writings when they were gone. There is nothing in this state of the facts to require a modification of the statement in the text.

But in setting the teaching of the Scriptures against the heretics, weight unquestionably was laid on this, that it was not only the teaching of Scripture as presently understood, but as always heretofore understood, in the churches. It was a continual consent (so it was said) as to what from the first had been taught, as authorized by the apostles, and in harmony with their writings. In many cases this was perfectly true, and in the early times it was an argument of great force against the kind of errors then brought forward. For these were essentially subversive: they propounded another gospel, and yet they boldly attempted, on one pretext or other, to lay hold of the Scriptures, and vindicate to themselves scriptural support, to the bewilderment of simple people. It was therefore very natural to say to such a teacher, If yours is the true Christianity—yours, which is so different from ours—it could not possibly have remained hidden from the churches. It is incredible that it should never have been heard of in the great historical churches especially. If it were Christ's, it would have been current among us. Since now for the first time it meets us, it cannot be Christ's, but only an invention of your own. The temptation was strong to urge this argument too far, both as to the principle laid down, and as to the kind of cases to which it might reasonably apply. But on the whole, in those circumstances, it was an argument of real force. Nor did it involve a real departure from the principle that the recorded teaching of the apostles must remain the standard of appeal, and rule the Church's teaching. But it connected that with the other principle, that the churches had not been left to mistake, and ignore the fundamental doctrines of the apostles. Therefore, so far, the authority of Scripture came to be wrapped up, as it were, in the tradition or the consent of the Church.

It was only familiar human nature (compare Note E, *supra*) to plead this tradition or consent (still perhaps on the side of truth) where it could not be so truly and competently pleaded. Scripture teaching was produced against a heresy, and it was said the Scripture has always been understood so. Now that might be only partially true. Partially it was not true; for it was under the influence of the question raised, and the solicitude excited, and the keen vigilance awakened, that passages of Scripture were lighted up into new significance, or disclosed their burden to minds prepared, as they were not prepared before, to mark their bearings. Partially, again, it had this much of truth in it, that the complete doctrine and deliverance were seen growing out of what had always been understood, as part of the same continuous truth, coming only more clearly and minutely into view.

Secondly, the understanding of the Scripture teaching, which was set against the heresies, was determined largely by the common experience of the divine life among Christians. It is the Christian teaching that is the seed of the divine life: but again, that life reacts in the way of forming men's views and impressions; for much of Scripture is interpreted to men through that which they feel to be involved in Christian fellowship with God. A heresy arose, and when tested against the common mind of Christians, especially of exercised and discerning Christians, it was felt to be a form of doctrine that must hinder, or mar, exercises of faith and worship which were familiar and dear to Christians. Instantly those elements of Scripture teaching in which such exercises of Christian life found their nurture, came to aid; and the doctrine was tried and judged, more or less, under the influences thus supplied. And it was natural to say, because it was inevitable to feel, This heresy comes into collision with common principles of the Christian life—as they have always been recognised. This impression was thrown into the argument, without altering its form. It went to increase the currency of the plea about the tradition and the consent of the Church.

In both these cases—both as regards the principles recognised in the Christian understanding, and the experiences cherished in the Christian heart (made the means first of realizing a collision between the heresy and the existing Christianity, and then between the heresy and all previous Christianity)—we have an exemplification of what I have said in p. 199. The Church might not always have a developed doctrine; but she often had, and felt she had, a real position—not now for the first time taken up, but pre-existing. It was this that was expressed by saying it was always so held.

What was really relied on, in all the great controversies, as long as some vitality continued in the Church, was the evidence that could be produced as to the teaching of Scripture. But then it was the teaching of Scripture interpreted and understood from the point of view of the Church's attained principles, and under the influence, more or less, of the Church's Christian consciousness and experience. It was felt that these were not of yesterday: experience, principles, Scripture teaching—all had a continuity and congruity about them, that went back into the past. This was the feeling which sustained the constant allegation that the heretics were condemned by tradition and the consent of the Church. It was represented *higher* than it would bear to be, as an explicit and developed unity of doctrine from first to last; but it rested at first on a very real ground. It was a plea, however, which in its own nature too readily lent itself to serve the purposes of ecclesiastical parties—to embody the arrogance of majorities, or to sustain by an evil conservatism every abuse which became habitual.

NOTE L.—PAGE 222.

The statement in the text admits of various illustrations. The most decisive, probably, may be found in the Reformation doctrine of Justification by Faith only. A good deal of confusion has been allowed to rest on this subject, in consequence of the theological interests involved in the historical question. In connection with the strong sense and the strong assertions of the importance and necessity of this doctrine, it was natural to suppose that there must have been, in every age of the Church, witnesses to the full and explicit doctrine, and very plentiful witnesses in the earlier and purer age. A great deal of citation of testimonies has accordingly gone on, fitted to illustrate the tendency to inaccuracy and irrelevancy which reigns in the department of citation above all others.

The Reformation doctrine of justification by faith only gathers up into a single and simple result the effect of many truths and principles; and it identifies that result with the teaching of the New Testament—of the Apostle Paul, for instance—on the subject of justification. In thus gathering up one result, the Reformers first of all presented to the mind a singularly clear and impressive thought, which they bade men recognise as emphatically declared in many passages of Scripture, and as distinctly present in many others. When a man held this thought or faith, his conception of all the truths and principles, out of which justification by faith springs and effloresces, as their result, became fixed and cleared; his impression of the designed bearing and relation of all those elements of truth became definite. A special conception of the character and ways of God, as embodied in those various truths, was fixed in his mind from the moment when he saw the effect of all those divine arrangements conspiring to reach the sinner in this channel or method of justification by faith. Hence also this same belief gave a peculiar determination not only to his theology, but to his whole religious experience. It imparted to him that consciousness of the mode of his relation towards God, that way of dealing with the elements of the spiritual world, that style of feeling, of religious joy and sorrow, hope and fear, which we call evangelical, using the word in its distinctive and characteristic, not in its general, sense. Here, again, in the department of experience, as well as in that of doctrine, the Protestant affirmed that he found himself in sympathy with the peculiar spirit and with the leadings of the Scriptures. It was just because this doctrine had these effects, in the region of thought and in that of life, that it was so objectionable to the Romanist, and so precious to the Protestant.

Among the topics which the Reformation doctrine of justification by faith presupposes, such as these may be enumerated: the sense of the word justification; the attributes of God, which explain how the word in its forensic sense should be so important, and should be made so prominent, *i.e.* in particular the Divine Righteousness; the inability of man fallen to justify himself; the substitutionary character of our Lord's work; the imputation of sin and righteousness; the office of the Law and Gospel; the benefit of Christ's righteousness, or forgiveness and acceptance promised and given to faith, and not to any other state, exercise, or work; the exclusion of good works done after conversion from the ground of our justification; the forgiveness of sins after conversion, on the same grounds and in the same manner as at conversion. Besides these, the office of the sacraments might be named, as most material to the Romish view of justification, and therefore requiring to be contemplated in the Reformation argument.

Now it is quite reasonable to allege that a Father may be a good witness to the substantial Reformation doctrine of justification by faith, although he does not speak like the Reformers on all those points. For example, a Father might differ from the Reformers about the sense of the word justification, and yet he might hold their doctrine of justification by faith under some other name, and propound it in some distinct but parallel method of explication. Still it is always material to see how much of this complex doctrine is fairly to be ascribed to an early writer, when he is claimed as an authority for justification by faith; for on this it depends whether he decides the main points involved in it, in favour of the Protestants and against the Romanists. It is to be remembered that the Romanists hold many of those underlying positions as well as we, although they give the whole doctrine another turn, partly by what they deny, and partly by new elements which they import.

Now it has been very common to assume, that as the central thoughts of the doctrine of justification are those of free forgiveness received by faith, and entire dependence on the Lord Jesus Christ for acceptance, wherever those thoughts are expressed in early writers, a witness is to be claimed for the Protestant doctrine in its main substance. Nor do I doubt that in many such passages the writers were in harmony with the Protestant mode of thought and feeling, and that this can fairly be made out. Still it is necessary to consider in what sense and under what limits, expressed or understood, those thoughts are expressed. For the Romanists also will express themselves in the same way, on a certain understanding. All Christians trace up their redemption to Christ, all profess dependence on Him, all will in some sense describe it as an absolute dependence. The passage cited from an early writer, in order to be relevant, must at least lean to the Protestant side of the real antithesis between Protestant and Romanist. Looked at from this point of view, the teaching of the Fathers will be found to be extremely inconsistent. It is indeed pervaded by a lively sense of indebtedness to God's mercy, and to the merit of Christ for forgiveness and a title to eternal life. And it does not countenance the later inventions, by which the Church of Rome has imperilled that great foundation element of Christian thought and experience; such as the efficacy ascribed to the sacrament of penance, and the detailed doctrine of merit. But their teaching is far from being clear and consistent; far from suggesting that the Fathers had attained to a doctrinal position which could fairly be described as substantially identical with the Reformation doctrine. It is one thing to assert that all the saved, from the first, have been saved in a way of free forgiveness and acceptance through the merit of Christ imparted to faith only, and that enough appears in the writings of many of the Fathers to satisfy us that in their habitual thoughts and feelings there was nothing to preclude, but much to corroborate, the impression that *they* were saved in that way. This is true, and it is a truth which strengthens our sense of the fellowship of all believers in one Lord and one truth. It is another thing, however, to assert that those same Fathers had attained so much clearness of view as to the principles on which they were saved, as to have held and taught in substance the Protestant doctrine of justification. Most of them speak sometimes in accordance with it, and sometimes not. The only thoroughly satisfactory way of obtaining the verdict of a Father, if that is thought important, would be to break up the Protestant doctrine into the separate theological positions which concur and unite in it, and to take an issue as to his teaching on each of these. Then an estimate might be made of his general tendency—how his face was set. But many of the citations commonly made prove only that the writer was so far on the way towards the Reformation doctrine, not that he had arrived.

For a more specific example of what I mean, let me take that department of the Justification controversy which refers to the forgiveness of sins committed after a man has first received the grace of God. There was no department of the subject with respect to which the Reformation produced a more decisive change than this; none on which the peculiar genius of the Reformation doctrine comes out more energetically; none in which the Reformers stood more characteristically opposed to the Romanists. For the Reformers held that remission was still held out, through Christ, to faith; while the Romanists, owning Christ's sacrifice to lie at the foundation, provided an elaborate system of contrivances, ritual and meritorious, for effecting the requisite cleansing. 'Atque hic praecipuus est nostrae disputationis cardo,' says Calv. *Inst.* iii. 14. 11. 'Nam de principio Justificationis, *nihil inter nos et saniores Scholasticos pugnae est*, quin peccator gratuito a damnatione liberatus, justitiam obtineat, idque per remissionem peccatorum, nisi quod illi sub vocabulo justificationis renovationem comprehendunt. . . . Justitiam vero hominis regenerati sic describunt, quod homo per Christi fidem Deo semel reconciliatus bonis operibus justus censeatur apud Deum et eorum merito sit acceptus. . . . Verum Dominus contra, se fidem imputasse Abrahae in justitiam pronuntiat, non eo tempore quo idolis adhuc serviebat, sed quum multis jam annis vitae sanctitate excelleret. . . . Manet enim perpetuo mediator Christus, qui patrem nobis reconciliet, ac perpetua est mortis ejus efficacia. Nempe ablutio sanctificatio expiatio, perfecta denique obedientia, qua iniquitates omnes nostrae conteguntur.' Now it is true, certainly, that the Fathers cannot be made responsible for the Romish theory on this subject; but who that remembers the statements regarding post-baptismal sin from Cyprian downwards, if not from an earlier date, can doubt that it is stretching benevolent construction beyond all bounds, to ascribe to most of them the Reformation doctrine on this particular point?

However true it be that the sense of redemption by Christ, or dependence on Him and owing all to Him, is the common faith of the Church, in which all believers are at one, yet the giving effect to this in the Protestant doctrine of justification by faith, therein opening up the mind of the inspired writers on this subject, was a great Reformation development, very memorable, and most fruitful.

NOTE M.—PAGE 229.

I have ventured to speak so positively of the date of this Epistle, although I am aware of the authorities which incline to a considerably later date. I cannot persuade myself, that if, when the Epistle was written, the Gnostic theories had already become matter of general discussion, the Epistle could have avoided more explicit and polemical reference to them. The subject treated laid the writer under obligation to make such reference, if they were already prominent in the Church.

LECTURE VI.

NOTE A.—PAGE 224.

THERE has been a good deal of discussion as to the reasonableness of supposing the early heresies to be in view in the Apostles' Creed, as we have it. All competently learned men have long ago given up the idea that this creed could have been composed and delivered by the apostles. But, holding that it represents in substance what the apostles sanctioned as the baptismal confession of Christians, and what therefore existed with variations of form in the different churches from the earliest times, some have been unwilling to admit any influence of the heresies in determining what it delivers. So Bishop Bull, Grabe, and Bingham. The Arminians had taken the other side, in the interest of their view, that the primitive Church was thoroughly latitudinarian, and became stringent only by degrees. In a more considerate tone, the influence of the heresies in determining the wording of the creed, as we have it, was maintained by Basnage and by King (*Crit. Hist.* Lond. 1702).

If it be granted, as it can hardly be denied, that the baptismal confession, with a substantial harmony of contents, remained somewhat various and indeterminate in form for a considerable period, it would, as it appears to me, have been a very remarkable thing if the wording of it had *not* formed itself more or less with a consciousness of the value of given words and phrases as fitted to exclude those heresies, which came into view and had their character recognised in the earlier ages.

NOTE B.—PAGE 245.

The most convenient collections of the Reformation confessions are probably those of Hase or Tittmann for the Lutherans, and Niemeyer's for the churches distinctively called Reformed. The *Sylloge Confessionum* is less complete.

NOTE C.—PAGE 251.

It has recently been stated (in connection with the disruption forced on during the present year by the action of the cantonal authorities), that the Church of Neufchatel has existed since the Reformation without any confession, at least without any in connection with which the clergy were required to undertake obligations. This fact is the more interesting, because it is understood that a type of doctrine substantially evangelical has been all along maintained in that Church. This cannot be meant in such a sense as to exclude fluctuations, of the kind which all churches experience, in reference to time and tendency. It is hardly conceivable that the Neufchatel Church, after the days of Ostervald, should not have partaken in the tendency to reduce the amount and the precision of doctrinal statement, which then prevailed in Protestant churches, and the progress of which can be traced with great exactness in the neighbouring cantons. In any view of it, however, the statement is interesting; for the Church of Neufchatel, though not large, — perhaps forty or fifty congregations, — is still large enough to give room for a genuine development of the genius and the necessities of Presbyterianism. I am not aware what the circumstances were which brought it to pass that the Church of Farel should occupy so peculiar a position in reference to confessions.

NOTE D.—PAGE 251.

The objection mentioned in the text to the practice of dispensing with written creeds will not have any weight with

Congregationalists, but it is fitted to have weight with Presbyterians. The ground of it is simply this. In a congregation all things can be settled by a vote; no one is concerned but those who are or may be present; every one acts on his own responsibility, and there is no appeal. On that system, every one may consult his own impressions regarding Bible teaching, and may act on them for himself. Whatever cause of complaint may exist, on the score of mistake, prejudice, or narrowness, every one feels that the case is remediless. But in a Church system where responsible rulers administer, and a representative principle exists, the disposal of cases cannot be left to the mere impressions of those who are charged with judicial functions. There are serious divisions in the world as to the sense which may be drawn from, or given to, Scripture teaching. The whole body of office-bearers, and the general membership of the Church, have a right to be assured that those who deal with a case on their behalf, undertake to do it on a distinct understanding as to the side to be taken on these points. Such an understanding is, in principle, a creed.

Note E.—Page 257.

Whether it ought to be held that there are Christian doctrines to be distinguished as fundamental; how the Biblical teaching on the one hand, and the duty of the Church on the other, stand related to this distinction,—these are questions which gave rise to much discussion after the Reformation. The cause of argument led the Protestants to lay some weight on the distinction, and hence it came to be their duty to explain, illustrate, and defend it. See, among the Reformed, Franc. Turretin. *Inst. Theol.* Elenet. Loc. i. Q. 14; Fred. Spanheim (the younger), *Opera*, iii. p. 2; De Moor upon Marckius, i. pp. 469–485; Stapfer, *Theol. Polem.* i. pp. 513, 550. The latter gives a valuable list of authorities at p. 516, winding up with, 'Plures non addo, cum dies me deficeret, si omnes qui de hâc re scripserunt allegare vellem, quicunque enim aut de mutua religionum tolerantia, aut de Protestantium unione quidquam ediderunt, hanc materiam simul tractarunt.' Among the Lutherans may be cited Hunnius, διάσκεψις de fundamentali dissensu, etc., 1626 (written to prove the Calvinists to err fundamentally), and Quenstedt, *Theologia didactica polemica*, cited by Hase. See article on Union by Twesten in Herzog's *Encyclopædie*, xvi. p. 665, and an article by Kling on *Glaubensartikel*, v. 176. There is also an article by Tholuck, *Luth. Lehre von der Fundamental-artikeln*, in the *Deutsche Zeitschrift für christl. Wissenschaft*, 1851, Nos. 9 and 12; and a characteristically compact summary of the old Lutheran teaching on the point in Hase's *Hutterus Redivivus* (10th ed. 1862), p. 23.

The tendency of the Arminians, as well as of other latitudinarian schools of later origin, was to reduce as much as possible the amount of what should be considered fundamental. On the other hand, in order to maintain a due sense of the importance of the doctrines commonly taught, the orthodox Protestants were often tempted to multiply fundamentals unduly. This tendency, indeed, appeared very early among the Lutherans.

In the Church of Rome the distinction has not attracted much attention. Their distinction between points decided by the Church, which are *de fide*, and those which are matters of school opinion, may be said to replace for some purposes the Protestant distinction, though the two are not to be confounded.

NOTE F.—PAGE 264.

It will presently appear that I do not overlook the distinction between the case of those who are members only of the Church, and those who, in addition, are charged with official responsibilities. In the case of the latter, *e.g.* of those who are authorized to teach, there is reason for requiring more full satisfaction both as to personal character, and as to fitness to instruct, than it would be reasonable to require universally in the case of all members. But I do not think it necessary to introduce the distinction here. It is, however, the case of office-bearers principally that I have in view.

Note G.—Page 272.

Venio itaque ad illum articulum quem et nostri praetendunt ad ineundam curiositatem, et haeretici inculcant ad importandam scrupulositatem. Scriptum est, inquiunt, Quaerite, et invenietis. . . . Omnibus dictum sit, Quaerite, et invenietis; tamen et hic expetit sensus certare cum interpretationis gubernaculo. Nulla vox divina ita dissoluta est et diffusa, ut verba tantum defendantur, et ratio verborum non constituatur. Sed in primis hoc propono, unum itaque et certum aliquid institutum esse a Christo, quod credere omni modo debeant nationes, et idcirco quaerere, ut possint, cum invenerint, credere. Unius, porro, et certi instituti infinita inquisitio non potest esse. Quaerendum est donec invenias, et credendum ubi inveneris, et nihil amplius, nisi custodiendum quod credidisti, donec hoc insuper credas, aliud non esse credendum, ideoque nec requirendum, cum id inveneris et credideris quod ab eo institutum est, qui non aliud tibi mandat inquirendum, quam quod instituit. De hoc quidem si qui dubitat, constabit penes nos esse id quod a Christo institutum est. Interim, ex fiducia probationis, praevenio, admonens quosdam nihil esse quaerendum ultra quae crediderunt id esse quod credere debuerunt, ne, Quaerite et invenietis, sine disciplina rationis interpretentur.—TERT. *De Praescr. Haereticorum*, cap. viii. ix.

Note H.—Page 274.

'The inspired teaching is before the Church.' For the Church is called out by the word, and takes birth, growth, and life in the faith of it. The mode of expression is adopted to avoid dispute which might arise if the phrase had been, '*The Scriptures* are before the Church.' That is true for every practical purpose; but it is also true, of course, that the Church existed before the revealed truth was committed to writing by inspired men. On this ground, Romanists and others maintain that the Scriptures embody only a portion of revelation, and that another substantial part was handed down, outside of the Scriptures, by tradition. They have thus a distinct interest in keeping the assertion to the front, that the Church is before the Scriptures ; for so they convey the idea of a plenitude of knowledge in the Church, and a capacity to decide for herself on the boundaries of revealed truth, existing antecedently to the Scriptures, and not superseded by the Scriptures. This view has already been rejected in these Lectures, in consistency with the familiar position, that 'it has pleased God to commit' His revealed will '*wholly* unto writing, which maketh Holy Scripture to be most necessary.' Still it is accurately true, that the Church existed before the Scriptures. And so our Confession may be understood when it says, that 'to the catholic visible Church Christ hath given the . . . oracles of God.' Cap. xxv. § 3.

Note I.—Page 278.

It is characteristic of all confessions, taking birth at times when the mind and heart of the Church are deeply stirred, that they speak with assurance. A strong feeling of confidence in the unity of the faith through all ages manifestly pervades them. Yet it is just as true that they are uttered as the expression, in the manner *then* natural and *then* called for, of the existing faith, and without the least idea that the perfect expression has now been reached, or that nothing can be mended. It was not the Council of Nice, but a later council, that forbade adding anything to that creed : it was not the Lutheran Reformers, but a later generation, that exalted the Lutheran symbols to so sacred a supremacy. The truly great Church guides uttered the faith for themselves and for their own generation, in the manner suited to the present time, with no thought of forestalling and prejudging succeeding generations.

The appeal prefixed to the Scottish Confession has been often quoted : 'Protesting that gif any man will note in this oure Confessioun any article or sentence repugning to God's holy word, that it wald pleis him, of his gentilnes, and for Christiane cherities saik, to admoneis us of the samyn in writt ; and We of our honour and fidelitie do promeis unto him satisfactioun fra the mouth of God, (that is, fra His holy Scriptures,) or ellis reformatioun of that quhilk he sall prove to be amyss.' This openness to correction as fallible men was combined with undoubting assurance as to the substantial faith, as appears by the last sentence: 'Thairfoir be the assistance of the mychtie Spreitt of the same oure Lord Jesus, we firmlie purpoise to abyde to the end in the confessioun of this oure Faithe.'

A recent writer in the *British Quarterly Review* (No. cxiv. p. 434) reminds us that in the French Protestant Church, in the Synod of Tonneins (A.D. 1614), a regular provision was made with reference to amendments of the Confession: 'At the request of divers provinces, it was ordained that our National Synods should not only not innovate anything in the Confession of Faith, Catechism, Liturgy, and Discipline of our Churches, unless the matter has been first proposed by one or more, but also unless it were a thing of very great importance; nor should that be resolved on till such time as all the provinces, being duly informed of it, had first debated it at home in their respective Synods.' (From Quick's *Synodicon*, p. 410.)

It is quite plain that, if a confession is of any length and fulness, then (setting aside the possibility of erroneous determinations, and presuming it to express the true faith in substance) it will in many of its features exhibit what was natural and appropriate with reference to the existing circumstances of the time, and the existing form and stage of men's thoughts,—features which render it not so natural and appropriate as the direct expression of the faith in altered circumstances and under new mental conditions.

One might be tempted on this ground to start the theory that each generation should frame its confession wholly *de novo;* but besides the reasons given in the Lecture for cherishing the consciousness of consent with the preceding generations of the Church, so far as truth and honesty enable us to do so, it is also to be remembered that not every generation is qualified for confession-making. There are great epochs which throw out great creeds. It would be to affect an independence which is unreal, to disregard that fact. It ought to be fully recognised in practice. But, at the same time, recognising the Protestant principle of the sole and direct authority of Scripture, and also the fact that the historical confession was most appropriate to its own age, and less adequately so to ours (*e.g.* in what it expresses, in what it omits, in fulness of expression, in proportioning of topics, and the like), there ought to be no unreadiness to give effect to the Church's actual persuasion of what the Scripture teaches, whenever a substantial call of duty in that direction appears.

It is always worth remembering, that as no confession drawn up by men claims to be wholly wise or absolutely perfect, extreme susceptibility or restlessness about mere shades and *apices*, is symptomatic not of a strong and independent mind, but of a weak and feverish one. When, however, a substantial case for some modification does arise, that does not always imply the necessity of patching weighty historical documents by interpolations, or mutilating them by omissions and alterations. An appended explanatory statement may be sufficient.

Note J.—Page 279.

'In its office toward those within its pale, it is the duty of the Church, as *holding* the truth of Scripture as the basis of its union, by some formal and public declaration of its own faith, to give assurance to its members of the soundness of its profession, and to receive assurance of theirs. . . .

'In its office to those within its pale, it is the duty of the Church, as the authoritative *teacher* of divine truth, by some formal and public summary of the doctrine it holds, to give assurance that it teaches what is in accordance with the word of God. . . .

'In its office to those that are without its pale, it is the duty of the Church, as the witness and protest for truth against the error or unbelief of the world, to frame and exhibit a public confession of its faith.' . . . —BANNERMAN, *Church of Christ*, Edin. 1868, vol. i. pp. 296, 299, 301.   See also Note K.

NOTE K.—PAGE 280.

'The distinction . . . to which I have already referred between a confession of faith regarded as a declaration of, or testimony to, divine truth, and a confession of faith regarded as a test of membership and office, has not always been sufficiently kept in view in the Reformed churches. Owing to this especially, the multiplication of articles, true in themselves, but non-fundamental, and of comparatively subordinate importance, has been in some cases unquestionably a practical evil.'

'It is perfectly clear, for example, that the Westminster Confession is not fitted to be a test of Church membership. Accordingly we do not use it as such, and our Church has never appointed it to be so used. Even as regards some of the office-bearers of the Church, it may fairly be questioned whether it is altogether adapted to be employed as a test of their fitness for office. The general principle to be laid down with respect to this matter seems to be this: *Whatever truths it is necessary for a man to believe in order that he may rightly discharge his duty in the Church, these it is lawful in the Church to embody in a confession, and require his subscription as a condition of office;* and, vice versa, *Whatever truths it is not necessary for a man to hold in order to the right discharge of the duties of his office, these it is not lawful to demand his subscription to as a term of office.* What these precise truths may be to which we are warranted in requiring an express personal adhesion in the case of the different ranks of office-bearers, is another and, it may be, a more difficult question; but of the soundness of the general principle now enunciated, there can, I think, be little doubt. Take the case of deacons, for example. They have not, generally speaking, the theological training necessary to enable them fully to understand the Confession of Faith in all its parts; and if they had, they do not need to understand it all, in order to perform efficiently the work of their office in the Church. And so even in the higher office of ruling elder. The amount of truth which an elder requires intelligently to hold, in order rightly to do the duty of ruling in the Church, to which he is specially set apart at his ordination, is much less than that which is needed by the minister, who is publicly to teach as well as to exercise government in the Christian Society.'—BANNERMAN, *The Church of Christ*, vol. i. p. 320. The discussion of the whole subject of the power of the Church in reference to doctrine, including the question of creeds, which this work contains, is exceedingly full, clear, and instructive. It occupies upwards of fifty pages, and thoroughly deserves the attention of students.

NOTE L.—PAGE 284.

It may be proper to explain why I have kept in view only the extent of doctrine which office-bearers may be called upon to adopt as consistent with their own personal belief. Other methods of taking security for doctrine have been suggested and employed; and these, it may be thought, ought to have been considered. For example, the Church may retain a pretty minute and extensive creed, but may not pledge her office-bearers to all its teaching, but only require a general acquiescence or approbation. Or the Church may simply make the confession a law, to be enforced like other laws. Her ministers may be simply notified, that if they teach otherwise, they do it at their peril. I have not forgotten these methods, the first of which, at any rate, is in use in some great churches, while instances of the second may also be produced from past and present times.[1] But it has seemed to me, that whatever may be done in these methods, the Church can never dispense with some testimony from those who enter the ministry as to their personal faith. That testimony may vary, from the simple statement that they receive the teaching of the Scriptures, or the teaching of Christ, to any degree of complexity and minuteness. But some assurance as to their personal belief is the natural basis for any obligations as to teaching others;

---

[1] A discussion of these methods, admirable in tone and in ability, by my colleague Dr. Blaikie, will be found in the number for January 1873 of the *British and Foreign Evangelical Review*.

and it is hardly conceivable that a Church should dispense with this in some form or other,—more or less brief, more or less precise,—however the mode of obligation connected with existing confessional documents might be altered, varied, or relaxed. Now the question, what assurance of personal belief the Church may legitimately or profitably require, appears to me to be the main question; and I cannot imagine it to be less than a disclaimer of the heretical alternatives in regard to what the Church believes to be fundamental points. Usually I think it must involve something more, unless great changes should supervene upon the practical conditions under which the branches of the Christian Church exist at present.

I had intended, however, to introduce into this Lecture a statement of reasons for thinking that it is a wholesome thing for churches to have articles of declared persuasion or testimony, additional to those which they think it needful to have confessed, by office-bearers, as matter of personal belief. Of these, various applications might be made, according to providential circumstances. What was designed on these points, by some fatality has been omitted, and the printing is too far advanced to rectify the oversight.

NOTE M.—PAGE 286.

The Lutheran creeds constitute a volume of several hundred pages. The collection of the Reformed confessions is a body of documents, of which one applied to one branch of the Church, and another to another. But the Lutheran collection was cumulatively imposed (not indeed on all, but) on most of the Lutheran churches. Nothing could be more preposterous. The system could be maintained in vigour for a time; then it became palpably hollow and delusive.

The case of Geneva, among the Reformed Churches, is a memorable example of the way in which creed obligations, strained too high and multiplied too much in the hands of a zealous orthodoxy, may be rapidly relaxed and reduced to nothing, under the influences of a new period and new men. The Church of Geneva rested on the second Helvetic Confession. More recently, the Canons of Dort had also been received as authoritative. Troubles and anxieties arose after the middle of the seventeenth century, from the influence exerted by the school of Saumur in France. A tendency to fall in with the views of that school was shown by some influential men, and an increasing measure of it was apprehended. Regarding this as in itself unsatisfactory, and as likely to lead to further and more serious variations from the received Genevan teaching, the defenders of that teaching, led by the elder Turretine (Francis), after various local measures, decided on concerting with the churches of some other cantons a new formula, intended to shut out innovations in doctrine. Zurich, then the seat of a zealous and resolute Calvinistic orthodoxy, took a leading part in the scheme; and the result was the Formula Consensus Helvetici, which was imposed on all pastors in the cantons that adopted it. It was drafted by Heidegger of Zurich, but was of course amended in consultation.

The Formula is an able and interesting theological statement, which represents the general persuasion of the Swiss Calvinists on the points disputed. In one or two instances, the mere progress of thought and investigation has conclusively disposed of the decision it supports. Otherwise, it still well deserves to be studied, as a deliverance on some difficult questions. But it is unquestionably too minute and detailed to be appropriate as a symbolical book, intended for a church or for a body of churches. It is more like the consultative opinion of a faculty of theology on points submitted to them. In point of tone it is unobjectionable. There is studious courtesy and Christian brotherliness towards those whose opinions are disapproved, and a marked moderation in the terms in which the disapprobation is expressed. These features are very likely due to Heidegger himself, who was admirably free from theological bitterness, and indeed in all respects a thoroughly estimable and right-minded man.

It is probably not generally known that Heidegger was run down at Zurich by an extreme orthodox party there, as a man of questionable zeal and doubtful principles, because he did not choose to approve of all the measures they desired. In public sermons and in private talk, he was attacked so as to make his life uncomfortable, and to subject his Christian patience and good feeling to a pretty severe strain. More hasty and decided measures were desired by the extreme party; and they were anxious, also, to introduce into the Formula a condemnation of the views of the Dutch federalist theologians. It is an instructive and interesting thing to observe that there was an orthodoxy beyond Heidegger's, represented by a number of respectable bigots and blockheads, now forgotten, who were able to a large extent to prejudice the minds of the good people of Zurich, and to run down the only man in Zurich who could perform any important service to the cause to which they professed to be attached.

The Formula Consensus was made binding about the year 1678. Francis Turretine died in 1687. The tendency to change had not been materially checked; it was indeed in the air, and appeared everywhere. In 1706, partly in deference to remonstrances from the Kings of Prussia and of England, who conceived the Formula Consensus to be fitted to give umbrage to other churches, partly under the influence of a party in the Genevan Church of which John Alphonse Turretine (son of Francis) was the destined leader, the authority of the Formula Consensus was got rid of, in so far as no promise with respect to it was now demanded. The question addressed to candidates was now arranged so as to present a curious gradation: 'You *believe and confess* whatever is contained in the Old and New Testament; you *promise to teach* nothing that is not conformable to the confession and catechism of our Church, as containing the sum of what is revealed in the Scriptures; further, you are *warned to teach* nothing, in church or college, against the Canons of Dort and the regulations of the venerable company.' This lasted for nineteen years; and then, in 1725, Formula Consensus, Canons of Dort, and Helvetic Confession itself, were all got rid of together, and there remained only this: 'You confess that you hold fast the doctrine of the prophets and apostles, as contained in the books of the Old and New Testament, of which doctrine we have a summary in the Catechism.' A statement in explanation was attached, setting forth that this was not meant to pledge men to all, nor even to recommend all, that the Catechism contained; but only embodied an acknowledgment that the substance of Christian doctrine was contained or comprehended in the Catechism.[1]

It would be a great mistake to suppose that the relaxation of confessional obligations caused the tendency to low and latitudinarian doctrine in Geneva. The relaxation was itself, on the contrary, the effect, an inevitable effect, of a great change then rapidly proceeding in the minds of men, in many of the churches, with reference to the view to be taken of Christianity as a remedial system, and with reference to the principles on which the Church was to be administered. But the recoil was probably rendered more severe by the introduction of the Formula Consensus.

The prevailing spirit, in the earlier stages of this anti-confessional movement, does not appear to have had the character of specific objection to particular doctrines set forth in the Church documents. It was rather a disposition to undervalue definite doctrine altogether, and to regard the previous zeal of the Church in regard to it as misplaced and mischievous. The great thing was to get attention directed to the practical interests. Hence the Church ought to disembarrass herself of those detailed symbols. It was therefore a simplification of confessions and of formulæ, not proceeding in the spirit of care for doctrine (see pp. 141, 142), but rather in the spirit of deprecating attention to it. Men were concerned in the movement who were personally estimable, and who are not lightly to be accused of having discarded, in their own minds, the fundamental Christian doctrines. J. A. Turretine, Ostervald, and Werenfels all deserve at least that character; and they may all be regarded as having agreed generally in promoting the mode of view and feeling which I have described. Their object was, unquestionably, to promote the efficiency of the Church, and the influence of Christianity in the world; and they believed the line they took to be the warrantable and right

---

[1] Schweizer, *Centraldogmen* (Zurich, 1856), pp. 439 sq., 688 sq.

one with that view. But in promoting and establishing the idea that doctrinal distinctions ought to be regarded as of subordinate importance, they played into the hands of those who were ready to replace Christianity by Deism. Their anti-confessional proceedings were chiefly mischievous as expressing and embodying that general tendency; for here, as in other cases, it is not so much the step taken that is important, as the *animus* which inspires it, and the set of the stream which it indicates.

INDEX.

ABRAHAM, promise to his seed, 337.
Abrahamic covenant, 48, 336.
Amesius, Gul., 299.
Analogical teaching, worth of, 148, 151; works on, 365.
Ancient thought, its basis, 381.
Angel of the Lord, 336.
Apostolic teaching, 85; Constitutions, 361; Fathers, 360.
Apostles' Creed, 243, 392.
Arianism, 212.
Arnold, Mr. M., 150, 316.
Athanasius, 291.
Atonement, 26, 306.

BANNERMAN, Dr. J., 399, 400.
Barnabas, Epistle of, 343, 360, 361, 391.
Bernard of Clairvaux, 294.
Bernard's Bampton Lecture, 355.
Bingham, 392.
Bull, Bishop, 295, 382, 392.
Butler, Professor Archer, 181, 375.

CALVIN, 390.
Children, knowledge of, 157.
Christ in Old Testament, 67.
Church action with reference to creeds, Lecture VI. *passim;* as related to doctrine, 133 sq.; as disciplinary institute, 140; as teaching institute, 140; influence of, on individuals, 136; structure of, in relation to development, 202.
Church, the early, how related to doctrine, 187, 189; estimate of attainments, 196 sq., 204.
Consent of Church, on what grounds assumed, 356, 379, 383.
Creeds, Lecture VI. *passim.*
Criticism, modern, 21.

DE AUXILIIS, controversy in Church of Rome, 300.
Development, theory of, 16, 25; see Lecture V. *passim;* asserted, 183; in Hebrew Scriptures, 310; of human history, 330.
Diversities of judgment among Christians, 235.

Doctrine, competency of, disputed, 5, 22–29, 146 sq.; conception of history of, Romish, 13; Protestant, 13; critical schools, 21–25; effect of differences respecting, 2, 235; and fact, how discriminated, 363; history of, applied to method, 4, 6; is obedience of thought to Scripture, 170; in Scripture, not delivered in school method, 89; in Scripture and in believing mind to be distinguished, 112 sq.; organization of, as science, 3.
Doctrinal statements, human, how arising, 125 sq. See Development.
Dominicans, 301.

ELEMENTS, secondary, in creeds and confessions, 261 sq.
Elements 'of this world,' how used in Old Testament, 45, 89.
Elementary conceptions in early Christian Church, 190.
Epistles, 86; occasional character of, 99.
Erasmus, 295.
Ewald, Dr. H., 312, 315.
Extent of confessions in relation to revision, 278.

FAITH, continuity and unity of, 7, 71; objection to development drawn from, 207; of Christian Church, in collision with pre-existing forms of opinion, 208; in collision with heresies, 211.
Fathers, doctrinal activity, 7; on justification, 387.
Formula Consensus Helvetici, 402.
Formularies, alleged existence of, in apostolic Church, 357.
French Protestant Church and revision, 398.
Fundamentals, 256, 281, 394.

GENEVA, relaxation of Church standards, 402.
Gnostics, 343, 348, 360.
God, manifestation of, vitalizing element in Old Testament history, 37 sq., 49,

65, 66; representation of, in Old Testament, 333.
Goode, Dr., *Divine Rule*, 383.
Gospels, 84.
Gospel, Old Testament manifestation of, 47.

HAWKINS, Dr., 358.
Heidegger, 403.
Heresy, existence of, relation to creeds, 256.
Historical element in Scripture, 35 sq., 80 sq.; how related to doctrinal, 81, 100.
Hope of deliverance in Old Testament, 44.
Hyperius, A., 332.

IGNATIUS, 361.
Ignorance, consciousness of, effect due to it, 165, 173.
Inferential reasoning in theology, 161.
Inherited creeds, 271.
Inspiration, 309, 355.
Irenæus, 8, 291.

JANSENISTS, 301, 302.
Justification, 386.

KINGDOM in Israel, its place and office, 60.
Knowledge, relative, 155; limits of, 153, 160, 164, 173; as God's and as ours, mediated by Christ, 156.

LANGUAGE, freedom of scriptural use of, 97.
Law of Moses, 55; changes accompanying its introduction, 340.
Lessing, 305.
Liberty of Church, as ground of right to form creeds, 252.
Limits of our faculties, 155; of our knowledge, 153, 160, 164, 173.
Lutheran creeds, 402.

MAGDEBURG Centuriators, 374.
Members of Church, creeds in reference to, 247, 253, 267.
Messianic prophecy, 63, 343.
Method of revelation, historical, 35 sq., 80, 129; adapted to man, fallen and unfallen, 40.
Mind, believing, how related to doctrine. See Lecture IV. *passim*, and Contents, p. xi.
Miraculous in Scripture, 40, 315.
Möhler, Dr. J. A., 18, 296.
Molinists, 301.
Monothelites, 366.
Morals in Scripture connected with history, 354.

Mosaic legislation, 55.
Mosheim, 380.

NATURAL Religion in relation to the world, 37.
Neander, 305.
Neufchatel, Church of, 393.
New Testament. See Lecture III. *passim*, and Contents, p. x.
Newman, Dr. J. H., 18, 177, 296, 298, 375, 382.
New Testament, view of modern critical school, 351.
New Thomists, 301.
Nicene Creed, 243.

OBJECTIONS to creeds, 248, 255.
Oehler, G. F., 337.
Office-bearers, application of creeds to, 247, 253; different classes of, in relation to creeds, 282.
Old Testament—see Lecture II. *passim*, and Contents, p. ix; believers under, their attainments, 34; contrast with New Testament, 76 sq.; progress of Church's thoughts about, 229; view of its origin according to some critical schools, 310; view of early Church regarding, 343.
Open questions in relation to creeds, 261.
Original righteousness, 327 sq.
Ostervald, 405.
Owen, John, 299.

PAST, proper attitude towards, 231.
Perrone, Professor J., 298.
Petavius, 17, 295.
Practice, Christian, relation to doctrine, 102, 131.
Principles, explicit revelation of, characteristic of New Testament, 79, 87.
Prophetic ministry under Old Testament, 62.
Protestant conception of history of doctrine, 13, 178; dogmatists, 21; orthodoxies, 21; view of creeds, 239.
Protevangelion, 335.
Psalms, 64, 346.
Pseudonymous writing, difficulties in the way of assuming it in New Testament, 354.

QUESTIONS rise successively, 215.

RATIONALISTS, their theory of development, 176.
Reformation confessions, 245, 392.
Reformation, a doctrinal development, 222, 386; theology, 11.
Resource, sense of, in Church, 198.
Revelation, course of it, how far completely recorded, 42, 331.

Revision, liability of creeds to, 274, 276, 397; difficulties of, 275; in relation to extent of confessions, 278.
Romish conception of development, 177; view of creeds, 239.

SCHLEIERMACHER, 328, 364.
Schoolmen, 9, 369.
Schröder, 298.
Scottish Confession, 397.
Scotus, Duns, 335.
Scripture, relation of development to, 195, 223; rule and guide of development, 217; structure of, renders development possible, 201; alleged tendency of creeds to limit influence of, 254; adaptation to successive stages of human mind, 350.
Semi-Pelagianism in Church of Rome, 303.
Semler, 304.
Sin, one great theme of Old Testament, 43, 334.
Starting-point of development, 183.

System in theology, not a powerful influence at first, 213; examples of influence, 382; its place, 169, 367; its dangers, 371.

TERMS and meaning, relation between, 112 sq., 164.
Tertullian, 8, 293, 395.
Tholuck, 295.
Topics of the course stated, 31.
Tradition, 15, 178, 296.
Trent, Council of, 302.
Trinity, doctrine of, 171.
Tübingen school, 343.
Turretine, Francis, 403; J. A., 404.

VINCENTIUS of Lerius, 8.

WARBURTON, *Divine Legation*, 314.
Werenfels, S., 351, 405.
Whately, Archbishop, 157, 358.
Wordsworth, Dr. C., 379.

ZURICH, parties in, 404.

THE END.

MURRAY AND GIBB, EDINBURGH,
PRINTERS TO HER MAJESTY'S STATIONERY OFFICE.

T. and T. Clark's Publications.

THE SECOND SERIES OF THE 'CUNNINGHAM LECTURES.'

In demy 8vo, price 10s. 6d.,

THE DOCTRINE OF JUSTIFICATION:

AN OUTLINE OF ITS HISTORY IN THE CHURCH, AND OF ITS EXPOSITION FROM SCRIPTURE, WITH SPECIAL REFERENCE TO RECENT ATTACKS ON THE THEOLOGY OF THE REFORMATION.

BY JAMES BUCHANAN, D.D.,
PROFESSOR OF DIVINITY, NEW COLLEGE, EDINBURGH.

'This is a work of no ordinary ability and importance. Quite apart from the opinions of the author, it has a high value, as fairly exhibiting the history of the doctrine of justification at large, but especially in the early Church, the mediæval period, and the era of the Reformation. It gives us a most favourable opinion of the Scotch Theological Colleges, that works of such breadth of view, and exhibiting such solid learning, are produced by their professors, among whom Dr. Buchanan has long been distinguished.' —*Clerical Journal*.

'On two subjects this volume is highly valuable, and may be read with great advantage by the theological student, and by all who take an interest in questions of this kind. These subjects are, the history of the doctrine of justification, and of the true nature of justification itself. He has given the history of the doctrine as it is taught in the Old Testament; as it was held in the apostolic age; in the times of the fathers and scholastic divines; at the period of the Reformation; in the Romish Church after the Reformation; as a subject of controversy among Protestants; and as it is held in the Church of England.' —*Wesleyan Methodist Magazine*.

'After a careful perusal of the volume before us, we are bound to say that our expectations, high as they were, have not been disappointed. We have here the old doctrine about justification expounded with a fulness of learning, and a masterly grasp of all its principles and details, that would have gladdened the heart of a Turretine or a Davenant; while, at the same time, the exposition is suited in all respects to the wants and requirements, intellectual and spiritual, of the present nineteenth century. . . . We would suggest, as eminently desirable, that some wealthy members of our Churches would confer a lasting boon on their future ministry by presenting a copy of it to all the students attending their theological halls.'—*Daily Review*.

'Dr. Buchanan has published a volume of lectures (one set of a series), delivered at Edinburgh, chiefly to professional hearers, on the history of the doctrine of justification, followed by an exposition of the doctrine as held by the author. A belief so important, and assailed now from such different quarters, demands from the learning of these days full consideration and elaborate defence; and therefore we welcome this as a seasonable work.'—*Nonconformist*.

'Our readers will find in them an able, clear, and comprehensive statement of the truth which forms the subject, clothed in language "suitable alike to an academic and to a popular audience." We only add, that the copious notes and references, after the manner of the Bampton and Hulsean Lectures, beside which it is worthy to stand, greatly enhance the value of the volume, and constitute it a capital handbook of the doctrine of justification.'—*Weekly Review*.

'In selecting a subject for his "Cunningham Lectures," he might have chosen a rarer and perhaps more popular theme. No one who knows the vigour of his disciplined intellect, his power of profound and luminous thinking, his large and ripe learning, and uncommon familiarity with the phases of modern thought, will imagine he has chosen this great commonplace in theology from want of ability to deal with a less familiar topic.'—*Original Secession Magazine*.

EDINBURGH: T. & T. CLARK.

T. and T. Clark's Publications.

THE THIRD SERIES OF THE 'CUNNINGHAM LECTURES.'

In demy 8vo, price 10s. 6d.,

THE REVELATION OF LAW IN SCRIPTURE:

CONSIDERED WITH RESPECT BOTH TO ITS OWN NATURE AND TO ITS RELATIVE PLACE IN SUCCESSIVE DISPENSATIONS.

BY PATRICK FAIRBAIRN, D.D.,
PRINCIPAL AND PROFESSOR OF THEOLOGY IN FREE CHURCH COLLEGE, GLASGOW.

'It is an eminently clear, judicious, and very vigorous statement of principles. The whole tone of the book is calm and dispassionate; it is entirely free from anything like sectarian narrowness. . . . One will search in vain for the hairsplitting distinctions and quibbling to which the mere sciolist in theory is so fond of resorting. The author is at once liberal and orthodox, candid and courteous. Nothing indeed has more impressed us in reading these lectures than the most admirable spirit of fairness to his opponents manifested by the author. One consequence of this calm, judicious, and candid treatment of the subject will be that the opinions of the author will carry great weight, and that most readers who entertain anything like orthodox views on the subject of law will close the book with the conviction that they cannot recollect a single finding from which they are inclined to dissent. This is a rare triumph, and it is a great one. . . . We have no doubt that this work will sustain and extend Dr. Fairbairn's well-earned reputation as a theologian.'—*Daily Review*.

'Dr. Fairbairn is well known as a learned and painstaking writer, and these lectures bear out his reputation. . . . They are the writing of a man who is a laborious student of the Bible, and patient readers will find that they can learn something from him.'—*Guardian*.

'This is eminently a book for the times. In no work of the kind will the reader find a more satisfactory and a fresher discussion of the great questions relating to the moral law, or a more complete exposure of the false doctrines respecting it that now prevail. . . . The theme is one of the grandest that can engage the attention of the most exalted intelligences; and few of our readers, we presume, will be satisfied without reading for themselves this masterly and eloquent contribution to our theological literature, which will not only sustain, but augment, the reputation the author has acquired as an eminent theologian.'—*British and Foreign Evangelical Review*.

'This is one of the most important theological works which have appeared in recent times, and should find a place at once in all college libraries. We can scarcely imagine a greater blessing to our theological students than that they should be well drilled in the contents of these lectures. . . . We are thankful that the discussion of the theme of this volume has fallen into the hands of one so capable of doing it justice.'—*Christian Witness*.

'The tone and spirit of this volume are admirable. The lectures are carefully elaborated, the arguments and scriptural illustrations seem to have passed each one under the author's scrutiny; so that, besides unity of purpose in the lectures as a whole, we mark the conscientiousness that has sought to verify each separate statement. . . . It is an excellent book.'—*Nonconformist*.

'It is most profoundly suggestive and satisfactory; worthy of the high scholarship and sagacious mind of the well-known writer.'—*Freeman*.

'The subject of "Revelation of Law in Scripture" opened up new ground, and it has been taken up in a most able manner. We believe that Dr. Fairbairn's volume will become a standard work in theological science. The nine lectures, together with the Supplementary Dissertations and Exposition of Passages from Paul's writings on the Law, make a volume which is invaluable to the biblical student.'—*Sword and Trowel*.

'One of the most scientific productions of Scottish theology.'—*Academy*.

T. and T. Clark's Publications.

The Works of St. Augustine.
EDITED BY MARCUS DODS, D.D.

SUBSCRIPTION:
Four Volumes for a Guinea, *payable in advance* (24s. when not paid in advance).

FIRST YEAR.

THE 'CITY OF GOD.' Two Volumes.

WRITINGS IN CONNECTION WITH the Donatist Controversy. In One Volume.

THE ANTI-PELAGIAN WORKS OF St. Augustine. Vol. I.

SECOND YEAR.

'LETTERS.' Vol. I.

TREATISES AGAINST FAUSTUS the Manichæan. One Volume.

THE HARMONY OF THE EVANgelists, and the Sermon on the Mount. One Volume.

ON THE TRINITY. One Volume.

THIRD YEAR.

COMMENTARY ON JOHN. Two Volumes. [*Vol. II. shortly.*

ON CHRISTIAN DOCTRINE, ENchiridion, etc. One Volume.

THE ANTI-PELAGIAN WORKS OF St. Augustine. [*Vol. II. shortly.*

Messrs. CLARK believe this will prove not the least valuable of their various Series, and no pains will be spared to make it so. The Editor has secured a most competent staff of Translators, and every care is being taken to secure not only accuracy, but elegance.

The Works of ST. AUGUSTINE to be included in the Series are (in addition to the above)—

TREATISES in the PELAGIAN CONTROVERSY ;

The CONFESSIONS and LETTERS, Vol. II.

The Series will include a LIFE of ST. AUGUSTINE, by ROBERT RAINY, D.D., Professor of Church History, New College, Edinburgh.

It is understood that Subscribers are bound to take at least the books of the first two years. Each Volume is sold separately at (on an average) 10s. 6d.

'For the reproduction of the "City of God" in an admirable English garb we are greatly indebted to the well-directed enterprise and energy of Messrs. Clark, and to the accuracy and scholarship of those who have undertaken the laborious task of translation.' —*Christian Observer.*

'The present translation reads smoothly and pleasantly, and we have every reason to be satisfied both with the erudition and the fair and sound judgment displayed by the translators and the editor.'—*John Bull.*

FOREIGN THEOLOGICAL LIBRARY.

ANNUAL SUBSCRIPTION:

One Guinea (payable in advance) for Four Volumes, Demy 8vo.
When not paid in advance, the Retail Bookseller is entitled to charge 24s.

N.B.—Any *two* Years in this Series can be had at Subscription Price. *A single Year's Books* (except in the case of the current Year) *cannot be supplied separately*. Non-subscribers, price 10s. 6d. each volume, with exceptions marked.

1 8 6 4 —Lange on the Acts of the Apostles. Two Volumes.
        Keil and Delitzsch on the Pentateuch. Vols. I. and II.

1 8 6 5 —Keil and Delitzsch on the Pentatench. Vol. III.
        Hengstenberg on the Gospel of John. Two Volumes.
        Keil and Delitzsch on Joshua, Judges, and Ruth. One Volume.

1 8 6 6 —Keil and Delitzsch on Samuel. One Volume.
        Keil and Delitzsch on Job. Two Volumes.
        Martensen's System of Christian Doctrine. One Volume.

1 8 6 7 —Delitzsch on Isaiah. Vol. I.
        Delitzsch on Biblical Psychology. 12s.
        Delitzsch on Isaiah. Vol. II.
        Auberlen on Divine Revelation. One Volume.

1 8 6 8 —Keil's Commentary on the Minor Prophets. Two Volumes.
        Delitzsch's Commentary on Epistle to the Hebrews. Vol. I.
        Harless' System of Christian Ethics. One Volume.

1 8 6 9 —Hengstenberg on Ezekiel. One Volume.
        Stier on the Words of the Apostles. One Volume.
        Keil's Introduction to the Old Testament. Vol. I.
        Bleek's Introduction to the New Testament. Vol. I.

1 8 7 0 —Keil's Introduction to the Old Testament. Vol. II.
        Bleek's Introduction to the New Testament. Vol. II.
        Schmid's New Testament Theology. One Volume.
        Delitzsch's Commentary on Epistle to the Hebrews. Vol. II.

1 8 7 1 —Delitzsch's Commentary on the Psalms. Three Volumes.
        Hengstenberg's History of the Kingdom of God under the Old Testament. Vol. I.

1 8 7 2 —Keil's Commentary on the Books of Kings. One Volume.
        Keil's Commentary on the Book of Daniel. One Volume.
        Keil's Commentary on the Books of Chronicles. One Volume.
        Hengstenberg's History of the Kingdom of God under the Old Testament. Vol. II.

1 8 7 3 —Keil's Commentary on Ezra, Nehemiah, and Esther. One Volume.
        Winer's Collection of the Confessions of Christendom. One Volume.
        Keil's Commentary on Jeremiah. Vol. I.
        Martensen on Christian Ethics.

1 8 7 4 —Christlieb's Modern Doubt and Christian Belief. One Vol. } First
        Keil's Commentary on Jeremiah. Vol. II. *Completion.* } issue.

MESSRS. CLARK allow a SELECTION of TWENTY VOLUMES (*or more at the same ratio*) from the various Series previous to the Volumes issued in 1871 (*see next page*),

At the Subscription Price of Five Guineas.

They trust that this will still more largely extend the usefulness of the FOREIGN THEOLOGICAL LIBRARY, which has so long been recognised as holding an important place in modern Theological literature.

T. and T. Clark's Publications.

CLARK'S FOREIGN THEOLOGICAL LIBRARY—*Continued.*

The following are the works from which a Selection may be made (non-subscription prices within brackets):—

Dr. Hengstenberg.—Commentary on the Psalms. By E. W. HENGSTENBERG, D.D., Professor of Theology in Berlin. In Three Vols. 8vo. (33s.)

Dr. Gieseler.—Compendium of Ecclesiastical History. By J. C. L. GIESELER, D.D., Professor of Theology in Göttingen. Five Vols. 8vo. (£2, 12s. 6d.)

Dr. Olshausen.—Biblical Commentary on the Gospels and Acts, adapted especially for Preachers and Students. By HERMANN OLSHAUSEN, D.D., Professor of Theology in the University of Erlangen. In Four Vols. 8vo. (£2, 2s.)

Biblical Commentary on the Romans, adapted especially for Preachers and Students. By HERMANN OLSHAUSEN, D.D. In One Vol. 8vo. (10s. 6d.)

Biblical Commentary on St. Paul's First and Second Epistles to the Corinthians. By HERMANN OLSHAUSEN, D.D. In One Vol. 8vo. (9s.)

Biblical Commentary on St. Paul's Epistles to the Galatians, Ephesians, Colossians, and Thessalonians. By HERMANN OLSHAUSEN, D.D. One Vol. 8vo. (10s. 6d.)

Biblical Commentary on St. Paul's Epistle to the Philippians, to Titus, and the First to Timothy; in continuation of the Work of Olshausen. By Lic. AUGUST WIESINGER. In One Vol. 8vo. (10s. 6d.)

Biblical Commentary on the Hebrews. By Dr. EBRARD. In continuation of the Work of Olshausen. In One Vol. 8vo. (10s. 6d.)

Dr. Neander.—General History of the Christian Religion and Church. By AUGUSTUS NEANDER, D.D. Translated from the Second and Improved Edition. Nine Vols. 8vo. (£2, 11s. 6d.)
This is the only Edition in a Library size.

Prof. H. A. Ch. Havernick.—General Introduction to the Old Testament. By Professor HAVERNICK. One Vol. 8vo. (10s. 6d.)

Dr. Müller.—The Christian Doctrine of Sin. By Dr. JULIUS MÜLLER. Two Vols. 8vo. (21s.) New Edition.

Dr. Hengstenberg.—Christology of the Old Testament, and a Commentary on the Messianic Predictions. By E. W. HENGSTENBERG, D.D. Four Vols. (£2, 2s.)

Dr. M. Baumgarten.—The Acts of the Apostles; or the History of the Church in the Apostolic Age. By M. BAUMGARTEN, Ph.D., and Professor in the University of Rostock. Three Vols. (£1, 7s.)

Dr. Stier.—The Words of the Lord Jesus. By RUDOLPH STIER, D.D., Chief Pastor and Superintendent of Schkeuditz. In Eight Vols. 8vo. (£4, 4s.)

Dr. Carl Ullmann.—Reformers before the Reformation, principally in Germany and the Netherlands. Two Vols. 8vo. (£1, 1s.)

Professor Kurtz.—History of the Old Covenant; or, Old Testament Dispensation. By Professor KURTZ of Dorpat. In Three Vols. (£1, 11s. 6d.)

Dr. Stier.—The Words of the Risen Saviour, and Commentary on the Epistle of St. James. By RUDOLPH STIER, D.D. One Vol. (10s. 6d.)

Professor Tholuck.—Commentary on the Gospel of St. John. By Professor THOLUCK of Halle. In One Vol. (9s.)

Professor Tholuck.—Commentary on the Sermon on the Mount. By Professor THOLUCK. In One Vol. (10s. 6d.)

Dr. Hengstenberg.—Commentary on the Book of Ecclesiastes. To which are appended: Treatises on the Song of Solomon; on the Book of Job; on the Prophet Isaiah; on the Sacrifices of Holy Scripture; and on the Jews and the Christian Church. By E. W. HENGSTENBERG, D.D. In One Vol. 8vo. (9s.)

Dr. Ebrard.—Commentary on the Epistles of St. John. By Dr. JOHN H. A. EBRARD, Professor of Theology. In One Vol. (10s. 6d.)

Dr. Lange.—Theological and Homiletical Commentary on the Gospel of St. Matthew and Mark. Specially Designed and Adapted for the Use of Ministers and Students. By J. P. LANGE, D.D. Three Vols. (10s. 6d. each.)

T. and T. Clark's Publications.

CLARK'S FOREIGN THEOLOGICAL LIBRARY—*Continued.*

Dr. Dorner.—History of the Development of the Doctrine of the Person of Christ. By Dr. J. A. DORNER, Professor of Theology in the University of Berlin. Five Vols. (£2, 12s. 6d.)

Lange and Dr. J. J. Van Oosterzee.—Theological and Homiletical Commentary on the Gospel of St. Luke. Specially Designed and Adapted for the Use of Ministers and Students. Edited by J. P. LANGE, D.D. Two Vols. (18s.)

Dr. Ebrard.—The Gospel History: A Compendium of Critical Investigations in support of the Historical Character of the Four Gospels. One Vol. (10s. 6d.)

Lange, Lechler, and Gerok.—Theological and Homiletical Commentary on the Acts of the Apostles. Edited by Dr. LANGE. Two Vols. (21s.)

Dr. Hengstenberg.—Commentary on the Gospel of St. John. Two Vols. (21s.)

Professor Keil.—Biblical Commentary on the Pentateuch. Three Vols. (31s. 6d.)

Professor Keil.—Commentary on Joshua, Judges, and Ruth. One Vol. (10s. 6d.)

Professor Delitzsch.—A System of Biblical Psychology. One Vol. (12s.)

Professor Delitzsch.—Commentary on the Prophecies of Isaiah. Two Vols. (21s.)

Professor Keil.—Commentary on the Books of Samuel. One Vol. (10s. 6d.)

Professor Delitzsch.—Commentary on the Book of Job. Two Vols. (21s.)

Bishop Martensen.—Christian Dogmatics. Compendium of the Doctrines of Christianity. One Vol. (10s. 6d.)

Dr. J. P. Lange.—Critical, Doctrinal, and Homiletical Commentary on the Gospel of St. John. Two Vols. (21s.)

Professor Keil.—Commentary on the Minor Prophets. Two Vols. (21s.)

Professor Delitzsch.—Commentary on Epistle to the Hebrews. Two Vols. (21s.)

Dr. Harless.— System of Christian Ethics. One Vol. (10s. 6d.)

Dr. Hengstenberg.—Commentary on Ezekiel. One Vol. (10s. 6d.)

Dr. Stier.—The Words of the Apostles Expounded. One Vol. (10s. 6d.)

Professor Keil.—Introduction to the Old Testament. Two Vols. (21s.)

Professor Bleek.—Introduction to the New Testament. Two Vols. (21s.)

Professor Schmid.—New Testament Theology. One Vol. (10s. 6d.)

And, in connection with the Series—

Alexander's Commentary on Isaiah. Two Volumes. (17s.)

Ritter's (Carl) Comparative Geography of Palestine. Four Volumes. (32s.)

Shedd's History of Christian Doctrine. Two Volumes. (21s.)

Macdonald's Introduction to the Pentateuch. Two Volumes. (21s.)

Ackerman on the Christian Element in Plato. (7s. 6d.)

Robinson's Greek Lexicon of the New Testament. 8vo. (9s.)

Gerlach's Commentary on the Pentateuch. 8vo. (10s. 6d.)

The series, in 124 Volumes (including 1874), price £32, 11s., forms an *Apparatus*, without which it may be truly said *no Theological Library can be complete;* and the Publishers take the liberty of suggesting that no more appropriate gift could be presented to a Clergyman than the Series, in whole or in part.

⁂ *In reference to the above, it must be noted that* NO DUPLICATES *can be included in the Selection of Twenty Volumes; and it will save trouble and correspondence if it be distinctly understood that* NO LESS *number than Twenty can be supplied, unless at non-subscription price.*

Subscribers' Names received by all Retail Booksellers.

LONDON: (*For Works at Non-subscription price only*) HAMILTON, ADAMS, & CO.

www.ingramcontent.com/pod-product-compliance
Lightning Source LLC
Chambersburg PA
CBHW020541300426
44111CB00008B/746